Clinical Applications
of Hypnosis

Also by George Gafner (with Sonja Benson)

Handbook of Hypnotic Inductions
Hypnotic Techniques

A NORTON PROFESSIONAL BOOK

Clinical Applications
of Hypnosis

George Gafner, LCSW

W.W. Norton & Company
New York • London

For information about permission to reproduce selections from this book, write to Permissions, W. W. Norton & Company, Inc., 500 Fifth Avenue, New York, NY 10110

Production Manager: Leeann Graham
Manufacturing by R. R. Donnelley, Harrisonburg

Library of Congress Cataloging-in-Publication Data

Gafner, George, 1947-
Clinical applications of hypnosis / George Gafner.
p. cm.
"A Norton professional book."—T.p. verso.
Includes bibliographical references and index.
ISBN 0-393-70444-0
1. Hypnotism—Therapeutic use. I. Title.

RC495.C492 2004
615.8'512—dc22   2004057566

W. W. Norton & Company, Inc., 500 Fifth Avenue, New York, N.Y. 10110
www.wwnorton.com

W. W. Norton & Company Ltd., Castle House, 75/76 Wells St.,
London W1T 3QT

1   3   5   7   9   0   8   6   4   2

Contents

Foreword

Stephen Lankton

Sometimes the sky is clear and it becomes apparent that remembering is not ours. We remember the supplies we intended to take to work, find our glasses on the top of the "other" dresser just in time, and suddenly lead ourself to open the middle credenza drawer just in time to recall our intention to take that special conversation piece into the office for your 9 a.m. client to see. In these moments, the clouds evaporate. We can see that we are following our shadow. It is not the other way 'round.

Milton Erickson taught me that consciousness is like bubbles on the surface of streams. It is an epiphenomena of mind. He once talked to a small group of us for three days telling us in detail his theory of psychosocial development. One of my favorite parts concerned his son's dating. He told of how one of his sons went on his first date.

> They went to the malt shop. Sitting across the table from each other, looking in each other's eyes, they had a malted milk [pause] and mucous membrane stimulation. Then, they went to the skating rink [pause] for touching and rhythmical physical activity. Then, back to the malt shop for a hamburger and all the relishes [pause] and more mucous membrane stimulation. He came home and told me he went to the malt shop and skating rink [shaking his

head "no"], but I knew what he'd really been doing: They'd been looking at each other, touching, having rhythmical physical activity, and mucous membrane stimulation!

In an almost endless series of such tales, Erickson built an indisputable case that what our conscious mind considers the "real activity" is merely a social convenience. Or perhaps it is the subtext for the story that becomes our life story. But at the psychological level, the unconscious level, it is a different story. In the case of psychosocial development, that other story is in part the increasingly complex association of the building blocks of experience. Each set of blocks becomes the foundation for more sophisticated and complicated building. We call this process *maturing, growth, development*, and so on. The fundamental fabric is experiential and sometimes behavioral. It is linked to social cues. It is more vast than consciousness can grasp. It steers the vessel of our selves. It is the unconscious. Occasionally, the clouds part and we see it clearly.

In one of my recent Phoenix training workshops, one of the attendees was a self-proclaimed devout cognitive behaviorist who used direct hypnosis. He was only attending for the CE credits. He insisted that he used only direct suggestions in his successful practice. When I asked for some examples of his language with specific clients, he began (italics mine): "*While* you sit there I can speak about many things [presupposition and focusing awareness]. I'll ask you to *relax* [statement to focus awareness] and I want you to *continue to relax* [presupposition] *until* your eyes close [presupposition]. Then either *go completely or partially* into trance [bind of comparable alternatives]. Then *you can go* more deeply into trance *as I count* from 100 to 90 [statement to focus awareness and causal linking]." He counts, and then after counting he continues: "I want you *to believe, or imagine, or think, or see, or pretend* that you see a peaceful field [all possible alternatives]." And so it continued. At least 90 percent of his speech was what I teach as *indirect* suggestion. Yet, he believed and steadfastly insisted he was using direct suggestion and only direct suggestion. After all, he was telling the client to listen, relax, close his eyes, go deeper, and so on. It appeared that nothing I could say would change his mind. His cup of knowledge was full and nothing more could be poured into it. He was content defining his speaking as direct—in fact, for him it was as if there was a stigma attached to anything to the contrary.

In helping a person to change, a therapist must engage this process of experience, retrieve resources, associate them, and link them to both social cues and the internal mediation mechanisms I call the *self-image*. One of the most powerful tools for those tasks is indirection—i.e., indirect suggestion, binds, anecdotes, and metaphors.

Indirect suggestions are defined as suggestions that have a degree of ambiguity and allow for increased latitude in the subject's response. By contrast, direct suggestion is a clear request from the hypnotist for a particular response by the subject. Some research studies have compared the use of direct and indirect suggestions as they pertain to "making" subjects move their bodies. Stone and Lundy (1985) investigated the effectiveness of indirect and direct suggestions in eliciting body movements following suggestions. They reported that indirect suggestions were more effective than direct suggestions in eliciting the target behaviors. The double blind studies revealed that both forms of suggestion yielded approximately the same outcome. Neither showed a significant difference over the other for controlling behavior. But it must be remembered, indirection is *not* meant to control subjects. Quite to the contrary, it is meant to be permissive and allow subjects to make the response that are most relevant for them as individuals.

I want take a moment to cite some other research on this topic. Much interest was generated in the 1980s due to the attention received by the students of Erickson who relied strongly on indirection during the last half of his career. Alman and Carney (1980), using audiotaped inductions of direct and indirect suggestions, compared male and female subjects on their responsiveness to posthypnotic suggestions. They reported that indirect suggestions were more successful in producing posthypnotic behavior than were direct suggestions. McConkey (1984) used direct and indirect suggestions with real and simulated hypnotic subjects. He found that although all of the simulating subjects recognized the expectation for a positive hallucination, half of the real subjects responded to the indirect suggestions and half did not. McConkey concluded that "indirection may not be the clinically important notion as much as the creation of a motivational context where the overall suggestion is acceptable, such as making the ideas congruent with the other aims and hopes of a patient" (p. 312).

Van Gorp, Meyer, and Dunbar (1985), in comparing direct and indirect suggestions for analgesia in the reduction of experimentally induced pain, found direct suggestion to be more effective as measured by verbal self-reports and autonomic lability scores. Further research by Matthews, and colleagues (1985), as well as Matthews and Mosher (1988) at the University of Massachusetts, compared the results of inductions via both forms and showed that either direct or indirect yields similarly successful trances. Interestingly, most studies revealed that subjects hearing the indirect forms of suggestion reported experiencing more satisfaction, a greater sense of involvement, and a deeper sense of relevance than those hearing direct suggestion.

At many advanced workshops I have given homework to trainees to use a checklist and record the frequency of the indirect suggestions, binds, anecdotes, metaphors, and direct statements they overhear in conversations at restaurants and hotels in the evening. Again and again it turns out that the "common person on the street" most often uses open-ended suggestions, simple presuppositions statements, and questions or statements that focus awareness in conversational exchange. The ramification of this observation is that normal communication contains much that is hypnotic. This is why normal communication is so influential on human behavior. After all, it is this type communication that is used by every family to raise their children. And as a matter of course in that process of childrearing, children are, in a sense, hypnotized to avoid and adopt certain feelings and behaviors *as well as* to receive certain interpretations about them. In the most benign sense this is what we call *socialization*, but in the most harmful sense one might say children are hypnotized into the acquisition of various pathologies (Berne, 1972, p. 343; Laing, 1967, p. 80). Is some sort of unusual language necessary to accomplish this? The answer is yes and no. Yes, it is the special language, which most influences the unconscious mind. And, no, it is not unusual language but rather language that is found all around us in normal everyday communication. In fact, indirect suggestion may be successfully used with the subject awake as well; its suggestive influence is much greater than that of a direct suggestion. It frequently exerts an effective influence on people who do not yield to direct suggestion, as pointed out by Bekhterev and Strickland (1998).

Influencing the unconscious is a matter of mindfully using the aforementioned types of indirect suggestions as well as some other more carefully tailored suggestions which are not as common in normal communication. These include conscious–unconscious dissociation suggestions, double dissociative conscious–unconscious dissociation suggestions, binds of comparable alternatives, acquisition of opposites, and a handful of others.

This cursory overview of indirect suggestion reveals a number of basic features that are of particular interest: (1) indirect suggestion permits the subject's individuality, previous life experience, and unique potentials to become manifest; (2) the classical psychodynamics of learning with processes like association, contiguity, similarity, contrast, and so on, are all involved on a more or less unconscious level; (3) indirect suggestion tends to bypass conscious criticism and because of this can be more effective than direct suggestion.

George Gafner is a psychotherapist who understands these points. *Clinical Applications of Hypnosis* rests squarely on the premises that our unconscious experience drives behavior and thought, that therapy must engage this process, that a mixture of indirection and direction is ideal for that job, and that the client's experience must be retrieved from where it is growing in its unconscious garden and then associated appropriately for therapy. In these precepts Gafner correctly identifies his approach as Ericksonian.

His chapters systematically lead readers through the basics of seeding and from language forms needed for therapy to various specific aspects of hypnosis using metaphor. Gafner systematically applies each technique to a range of common clinical complaints including anxiety disorders, depression, and irritable bowel syndrome as well as other stress related gastrointestinal problems. His clinical examples and techniques are often further analyzed at a more microscopic level. His previous books were often praised for their many examples of metaphor and Gafner once again relies on this protocol for his presentations. As a result *Clinical Applications of Hypnosis* gives readers a fresh and candid glimpse into his practice and does so in such a manner that it facilitates learning his style.

Readers of his previous works with Sonya Benson already know that Gafner makes a special contribution to therapy. His hypnosis work concentrates on *ego-strengthening* for his clients. By concentrating on ego-strengthening Gafner helps guide his interventions as well as his therapy's course and length. This is a healthy and optimistic sign for the direction of hypnosis. I applaud and support this approach to building consciousness, and I have included this approach in my work as well. For example, I have written at length about the Self-Image Thinking (SIT) protocols I developed in 1979 (Lankton, 1983, pp. 312–344). This affective and experientially-based method of visual self-rehearsal both links retrieved unconscious resources and builds self-reliance, self-mastery, and, of course, ego-strength for previously feared, difficult, or otherwise anxiety ridden personal and social experiences. The SIT protocol can be delivered in metaphor as I have shown (1989), but is almost exclusively used in a straightforward and direct fashion with the client's compliant participation.

Gafner's approach is to conduct ego-strengthening almost entirely with the use of metaphor and indirection. He provides repeated examples of how therapists can design and deliver metaphors with this aim. He takes the position that, when entertaining stories about things that are firm, the mind retrieves firmness. If the story is about flexibility the mind retrieves flexibility. If the story concerns a change of perception, Gafner believes the mind will retrieve a possible perceptual alteration. In this view, I again agree.

According to Heinz Hartmann, a definition of *ego strength* depends upon adaptation, differentiation, synthesis within the ego as well as plasticity, strength of instinctual drive, and tolerance for tension (1964, p. 56). These functions can not be reached or initiated by direct statements or direct suggestion. They are too pervasive and yet too subtle. Only as the unconscious mechanisms that relate to such ego development are stimulated will they be called into ego strengthening operation.

Such change happens with *metaphor*. Change is metaphor; metaphor is change. All essential cultural growth has been catalyzed by metaphor.

Whether the culture is that of a single mind, a family, a nation, or a world, metaphor is the bridge for finding new connections among old views. It is the way of finding a novel path when existing paths have been exhausted. Gafner's ego-strengthening metaphors are true goal-directed metaphors (Lankton & Lankton, 1986, 1989). I believe they are an additional category of goal-directed metaphors. Erickson's work convinces us that cure is a matter of associating experiential needs to the context in which the client requires them. Isomorphic metaphors usually rely upon outlining the client's problem and then illustrating a resolution—all metaphorically, of course. Goal-directed metaphors are quite different. They outline the needed resources and are employed with the understanding that clients, in the context of being in your office for change, will default to associating the retrieved resources to the context of their concern. Gafner's work is fully in keeping with Erickson's notion of cure:

> Direct suggestion is based primarily, if unwittingly, upon the assumption that whatever develops in hypnosis derives from the suggestions given. It implies that the therapist has the miraculous power of effecting therapeutic changes in the patient, and disregards the fact that therapy results from an inner resynthesis of the patient's behavior achieved by the patient himself. It is true that direct suggestion can effect an alteration in the patient's behavior and result in a symptomatic cure, at least temporarily. However, such a "cure" is simply a response to the suggestion and does not entail that reassociation and reorganization of ideas, understandings, and memories so essential for an actual cure. It is this experience of reassociating and reorganizing his own experiential life that eventuates in a cure, not the manifestation of responsive behavior which can, at best, satisfy only the observer. (Erickson & Rossi, 1979, p. 19)

Readers of all levels of expertise will find that Gafner clarifies various theories, reference sources, techniques, clinical examples, and even many common hypnotherapeutic errors. It will help many therapists as Gafner's explanations clear the sky on seeding, suggestion, metaphor, ego strengthening, goal directed metaphor, and the fundamental themes of metaphoric examples. His discussions of breathing and finding your own voice address usually ignored topics. Gafner's inclusion of this topic is but one example of his thoroughness in covering important training topics and doing so with common sense and clarity. *Clinical Applications of Hypnosis* will help therapists come to follow their own shadows with confidence and gain a sense of accountability.

References

Alman , B., & Carney, R. (1980). Consequences of direct and indirect suggestion on success of posthypnotic behavior. *American Journal of Clinical Hypnosis, 23,* 112–118.

Bekhterev, V., & Strickland, L. (1998). *Suggestion and its role in social life.* New Brunswick, NJ: Transaction Publishers.

Berne, E. (1972). *What do you say after you say hello?: The psychology of human destiny.* New York: Grove.

Erickson, M., & Rossi, E. (1979). *Hypnotherapy.* New York: Irvington.

Hartmann, H. (1964). *Ego psychology and the problem of adaptation.* New York: International University Press.

Laing, R. D. (1967). *The politics of experience.* New York: Ballantine.

Lankton, S., & Lankton, C. (1983). *The answer within.* New York: Brunner-Mazel.

Lankton, S., & Lankton, C. (1986). *Enchantment and intervention in family therapy: A training seminar on Ericksonian approaches.* New York: Brunner/Mazel.

Lankton, C., & Lankton, S. (1989). *Tales of enchantment.* New York: Brunner/Mazel.

Matthews, W., & Mosher, D. (1988). Direct and indirect hypnotic suggestion in a laboratory setting. *British Journal of Experimental and Clinical Hypnosis, 5*(2), 63–71.

Matthews, W., Bennett, H., Bean, W., & Gallagher, M. (1985). Indirect versus direct hypnotic suggestions—An initial investigation: A brief communication. *The International Journal of Clinical and Experimental Hypnosis, 33*(3), 219–223.

McConkey, K. (1984). The impact of indirect suggestion. *The International Journal of Clinical and Experimental Hypnosis, 32,* 307–314.

Stone, J.A., & Lundy, R.M. (1985). Behavioral compliance with direct and indirect body movement suggestions. *Journal of Abnormal Psychology, 33*(3), 256–263.

Van Gorp, W. G., Meyer, R.G., & Dunbar, K.D. (1985). The efficacy of direct versus indirect hypnotic induction techniques on reduction of experimental pain. *The International Journal of Clinical and Experimental Hypnosis, 4,* 319–328.

Preface

When I think of someone like the American naturalist John Muir, I naturally think of Milton H. Erickson. Both were optimistic and future-oriented, and both lived and dreamed in the natural world. Their natural world is my inspiration, and I hope you find my stories and anecdotes about this world both meaningful and useful in your practice.

My first book, with Sonja Benson, *Handbook of Hypnotic Inductions* (Gafner and Benson, 2000), dealt specifically with the induction and deepening phases of hypnosis. In the second book, *Hypnotic Techniques* (Gafner and Benson, 2003), Benson and I broadened the scope by addressing not only the myriad applications of hypnosis within formal trancework, but also those many occasions when hypnotic techniques can be applied hypnotic techniques within conventional psychotherapy. In this book, I step back toward the middle of the spectrum and focus on the practice of hypnosis for a range of problems commonly seen in clinical practice.

Many have told me what aspects they appreciated in the first two books, and I have strived to include these in this book. One is the use of hypnotic language, especially the demonstration of how to use it for maximum effect. Another is an ample sprinkling of stories and anecdotes, tools that readers can readily transfer to their own practices. Another is case examples of real clients, some with personality disorders and multiple problems. To be sure, these examples are drawn from such clients, although composites are used and details have been changed to assure confidentiality.

One thing readers have told me repeatedly is that they appreciate what are referred to as "call-outs." This is when, for example, words to seed an idea are placed in bold face in the text, and off to the right, that word, such as *seeding*, or some other principle or technique is defined. Many have emphasized that this is especially instructive and meaningful. Key techniques and principles, both in call-outs and in the text, are defined in the glossary.

Metaphor, story, anecdote, and other unconsciously directed techniques are woven through every chapter. The bread-and-butter applications of hypnosis are anxiety disorders and chronic pain. I covered pain pretty thoroughly in our last book, so this one has very little on the topic. Chapter 1 offers a brief review of the literature on unconscious process, and hopefully puts to rest the idea that most of our behavior is guided by conscious intention. This chapter lays the foundation for the heart and soul of this book, which is unconsciously directed psychotherapy. In every chapter, I strive to provide an empirical basis, whenever possible, for recommended treatment approaches. However, psychotherapy—-and hypnosis—still remains more art than science, and, frankly, I hope it stays that way.

Many people have also told me how much they appreciate my discussion on metaphorical ego-strengthening, which is the cornerstone of my hypnotic treatment. In this one and in the other books, I have suggested that clinical practice move beyond the tired behavioral enhancement of self-efficacy by opening up this vital area with indirect techniques that do indeed produce change, as evidenced by self-report, new behavior, or improvement on a self esteem measure. I firmly believe that ego-strengthening, which Hammond and Hartland and others have advocated for many years, is an idea whose time has arrived. In Chapter 2 I hope to push the clock ahead on this technique, which, possibly more than any other, can bolster the repertoire of the therapist. Perhaps after reading this chapter you will be convinced of the importance of preparing the soil before planting the seed, and that you really might get there faster by slowing down at the beginning and attending to ego-strengthening. Chapter 3 continues the exploration of the unconscious and delves deeper into applications that you can use for "stuck" clients.

Chapter 4 addresses getting started with hypnosis. Chapter 5 covers the therapist's voice, breathing, and other essential considerations. Chapter 6, Treatment in Brief, offers musings, insights, and clinical vignettes from a career of practicing—and teaching—therapy.

Chapter 7 jumps into anxiety disorders, especially PTSD (posttraumatic stress disorder), a diagnosis that is being assigned to a wider swath of the population. The treatment of this disorder is now breaking out of its traditional constraints, and new treatments are addressed in this chapter. Chapter 8 addresses chronic depression, a clinical entity that predominates in many therapeutic practices. But depressed clients do not have to drag us down, as there are new tools you can put in your toolbox! Chapter 9 covers the treatment of gastrointestinal (GI) disorders, especially irritable bowel syndrome. Hypnosis has an especially strong track record with GI problems, and hypnotic treatment of these and other mind-body disorders is the future of hypnosis. The Appendices contain additional stories and anecdotes, along with a couple of my stock inductions and favorite stories from previous books.

Most of all, I hope to provide a readable book that opens up horizons for your practice and gives you new tools for the treatment of everyday clinical problems. If you're new to hypnosis, read on, as I'll tell you how to get started. If you're already a hypnosis practitioner, my only advice to you is the Wildermuth principle: Don't forget to breathe.

Acknowledgments

Thanks and appreciation go to my wife, Judy, for her continuing love and support. To write may be human, but to edit (and market and all the other facets of publishing) is truly divine, and for those things I am deeply appreciative of Anne Hellmann, Michael McGandy, Deborah Malmud, and the staff at Norton Professional Books. I thank the following people for locating resource materials, or reading portions of the manuscript and suggesting invaluable additions and corrections: Jeff Zeig, Sonja Benson, Bob Hall, Eric Jackson, Julie Barkmeier-Kraemer, Diana Lett, Anne G. Scott, Matt Weyer, Lynn Flance, Karen Douglas, Tom Dollar, and Olivia Arrieta.

Clinical Applications
of Hypnosis

Part I

Principles of Unconsciously Directed Psychotherapy

Chapter 1

Unconscious Process

Whether your therapeutic preference is CBT, Gestalt, Erick-sonian, or another modality, you may be surprised to learn that recent psychological research underscores an important finding: that unconscious or automatic process accounts for more of a person's mental functioning than was previously believed.

Erickson Had It Right

Bargh and Chartrand (1999) posed a compelling question, which goes like this: What if you were a psychology professor who does experiments on conscious awareness, and you keep finding that your subtle manipulations of people's judgments and behavior are successful, causing experimental subjects to like or dislike the same person, to feel sad or happy, or to behave rudely or with eternal patience? Furthermore, none of the subjects have a clue as to what caused them to feel or behave the way they did, and when you explain to them that **unconscious process** accounted for causal effects, they refuse to believe you.

One reason is because few of us like to think that what we do is outside of conscious control. Current research adds to the mounting evidence that Milton H. Erickson and Jay Haley had it right all along—that most of a person's everyday life is determined *not* by conscious intention and deliberate choice but by features of the environment that operate outside of conscious awareness and guidance (Bargh & Chartrand, 1999).

The Unconscious Historically

Let's examine the genesis of the unconscious mind in Western thought, and try to understand the underpinnings of current CBT (cognitive-behavioral therapy) theory and technique. When I attended graduate school at the University of Michigan in 1970, few had heard of Milton H. Erickson, and the primary method taught was what was then called "behavior therapy." There was no cognition, just behavior. We were led to believe that behavior modification could cure virtually any psychological problem. At this time, scholars worked intensively to counteract Freudian theory and practice, which still was predominant in training programs for social workers, psychologists, and psychiatrists.

To Freud (1901/1965), human behavior was determined mainly by biological impulses and the unconscious interplay of psychic forces put into motion by those impulses. People were unaware of this intrapsychic struggle and its causal effect on their behavior, although, through psychoanalysis, awareness was possible, along with a subsequent change in maladaptive patterns of behavior. In other words, several years of psychodynamic therapy two or three times a week might cure the neurosis.

Skinner (1938), Watson (1913), and other early behaviorists believed that behavior was outside of conscious control, but placed the source of control not in the psyche, but in external forces. Everyone's behavior was dictated by environmental events working in combination with reinforcement.

In the mid-20th century, humanists (Rogers, 1961) and self theory proponents (Kelly, 1955; Rotter, 1954) posited that inner drives in combination with external events determined behavior, and that a "causal self" mediated between the environment and a person's responses to it. A person's response was clearly an act of conscious choice. Fifty years later, this view continued to dominate theories of motivation and self-regulation. It was the conscious self that governed experience and behavior, and by creating *meaning*, the self was freed from life circumstances and overcame limitations (Orbach, 1995). This conscious self was the only protagonist in the story, and was solely responsible for choices in life. After all, people were rational beings whose *conscious* goals were determined by attitudes, not unconscious instincts. The essence of the self was the striving for self-expression and a deeper understanding of the world. Intentionality lay at the heart of self theory and humanism. Intentionality could be focused on one's self or another, or any aspect of reality, and was the key to a comprehensive and integrated perspective.

Erickson is often given credit for first recognizing the unconscious as a positive entity (Orbach, 1995). However, around the same time (the mid-20th century), Fritz Perls (1969), one of the founders of Gestalt therapy, saw the unconscious as a vast storehouse of unactualized potentials. While Erickson's avenue to this *Via Regia*, or "Royal Road," was hypnosis, Perls arrived there through dream analysis. Let's remember that Perls's and Erickson's generative years—the 1930s, 40s, 50s, 60s, and 70s—were dominated by Freudian thought and practice, such that contrary approaches were regarded as mere heresy. Perls and Erickson traveled parallel paths during this time. Perls encouraged his clients to explore dreams, daydreams, stories, or activities of daily life, on the assumption that details derived from these things revealed the varied facets of the self. Erickson reached the same place, but from the angle of the therapist, who would ask the person in trance to drift and dream, and, with formal hypnosis or without, tell stories and anecdotes, instructing clients that their unconscious was wise and omniscient:

> . . . it is important for a person to know their unconscious is smarter than they are. There is a greater wealth of stored material in the unconscious. We know the unconscious can do things, and it's important to assure your patient that it can. They have to be willing to let their unconscious do things and not depend so much on their conscious mind. This is a great aid to their functioning. (Erickson, in Rossi & Rossi, 1976, p. 9)

The cognitive perspective also accounts for psychological phenomena in terms of deterministic mechanisms, even though there is acknowledgment of higher-order choice, or "executive processes" (Barsalou, 1993; Neisser, 1967). Such theorists saw free will as a homunculus, or "little person in the head," something that could not be accounted for by scientific explanation.

The mainstream of contemporary psychology currently embraces both the fact of conscious or willed causation of mental and behavioral processes *and* the fact of *automatic* or environmentally triggered responses. This view of conscious and nonconscious, or automatic, process is the norm in the study of attention and coding, memory, emotional appraisal, emotional disorders, attitudes and persuasion, and social perception and judgment (Bargh & Ferguson, 2000; Bargh et al., 2001). However, CBT proponents who research the effect of cognitive-behavioral techniques on such problems as anxiety and mood disorders usually make little mention of **automatic process**. Automatic thoughts are a rare exception in a procedure guided by intentionality and conscious choice.

Has "Unconscious Mind" Outlived Its Usefulness?

Over the years, different writers have substituted various terms for the *unconscious*, such as *inner self, inner adviser, creative intelligence, inner voice, imagination,* and even the *deepest part of you.* Stephen Gilligan (2003), in an effort to humanize and broaden the term, suggested we consider poetic terms, like *soul* or *soulfulness.* In line with Gilligan's self-relations therapy, he would see this new construct placed relationally. In other words, unconscious mind is not inside us as individuals, but rather it exists *between and among* people, and it is the job of the therapist to help clients recognize this so they can connect with others.

Gilligan (2003) also wondered if the unconscious is really so intelligent. He asks, if the unconscious is so smart, why did clients do so poorly in life until they began to see Erickson? Gilligan puts this forth as supporting evidence for the relational locus of the unconscious.

To be sure, Gilligan has been one of the most brilliant writers on hypnotic technique for many years, and anyone who is fortunate to

attend one of his workshops witnesses a virtuoso of embedded suggestion and overall technique. His book, *Therapeutic Trances* (1987), is
one of the finest books on hypnosis ever written, and I recommend it
highly whenever I can. However, I liked the old Gilligan better, before
he placed hypnosis in the realm of mindfulness. Many believe that
calling the unconscious "soul" might dilute an eminently useful
construct.

Directing Therapy at the Unconscious

A central premise of this book is that automatic process in
psychotherapy not only must be accounted for, but also is highly desirable in targeting change at *both* conscious and unconscious mental
functioning. Of course, hypnosis is the preeminent boulevard to the
Via Regia, the unconscious, which can be defined as all that lies
outside of conscious awareness. But why limit yourself to hypnosis
when standard talk therapy also lends itself commendably to accessing
unconscious process? Seeding may be a useful place to begin.

Seeding

You are working with a client, Betty, and later in the session you
intend to ask her to *think about* a more productive relationship with
her boyfriend. You might *seed* this target action with idle conversation
at the beginning of the session, first setting up seeding with hypnotic
language:

Betty, recently I was talking with a colleague about the postal service and the delivery of mail, and how some people receive their mail inside, and some must go outside, and someone I knew once had a red reflector on her mailbox, and she always imagined a color different than red. "You spend too much time on self-reflection," a friend told her, but on the friend's car the happy face bumper sticker had peeled away long ago.	apposition of opposites apposition of opposites metaphor seed lead away

So too, with another client, Salvatore, you intend to introduce *slowing down*, and early in the session you mention the slowness with which the business office processes insurance claims; or, you nonverbally seed slow by writing some words very s-l-o-w-l-y on your notepad.

In both of these examples, seeding is carried on outside of conscious awareness, while unconsciously you are tilling the soil so that the target can germinate. Thus, in the first example, *activation* of the seed occurs later in the session:

Betty, when you come back in two weeks I want you to have thought about—*we mean thinking here, not actually* doing *anything*—*what you can do to have a more productive relationship with your boyfriend. Will you do that?*	activate seed commitment

and

Sal, letting go of your ex-wife may be *too tall an order right now, but taking five minutes each day to* slow down *can be of immense help in your situation. Here's a handout that describes a relaxation procedure. Will you begin this* tonight, tomorrow, before the weekend, *all or* at some other time in the near future? . . . very good, Sal. I will look forward to discussing your experience with you next time.*	restraint suggestion covering all alternatives

With both Betty and Sal, in addition to seeding and activating the seed, you can then reinforce it in any variety of ways, directly, by mentioning it again before the session is over, or indirectly with further embedded suggestion.

Does this sound like a lot of work? Isn't it simpler to *just tell them what to do*? Of course it is, but after practicing psychotherapy for a few weeks you quickly learn that people often don't do what they are told to do. If therapy were only a straight-forward transaction, instead of a chess game, we wouldn't need books like this that emphasize indirection in influencing behavior change.

What is Seeding?

Seeding in psychotherapy is akin to priming in social psychology. In research on priming, such tasks as word completion and problem solving improved with seeding, which Zeig (1990, p. 23) defined as "the activation, or change in accessibility, of a concept by an earlier presentation of the same or closely related concept." An example from social psychology elegantly illustrates this process. Groups of research subjects were shown various word pairs prior to selecting a brand of laundry detergent. Those who were shown "ocean-moon" more readily selected Tide (Nisbett & Wilson, 1977).

Jay Haley (1973) first mentioned Erickson's "seeding ideas" in *Uncommon Therapy*, and since then Geary (1994) and Zeig (1990) have further explicated the technique. What's the difference between suggestion and seeding? With seeding there is always follow-up. A third step is recommended in this book: **reinforcement**. In other words, don't just seed and activate the seed, but reinforce it. The technique can be summarized by the acronym SAR: seed, activate, reinforce.

Let's say you have a garden. You don't just throw the unopened seed packet down on last year's dried weeds, walk away, and return later to pluck those juicy tomatoes. No, you have to till the soil first, and take all the other necessary steps to ensure germination and healthy growth, all the way to harvest time. With beetles, blight, drought, rabbits, frost, and everything else faced by the gardener, as well as the psychotherapist, I wish I could say for certain that the odds of treating bulimia in your borderlines were as good as growing Burpee cucumbers. Nevertheless, try it: SAR: seed, activate, reinforce. This is an excellent way to begin indirection, both in hypnosis and standard psychotherapy.

Direction versus Indirection

When we read the work of Albert Ellis, Aaron Beck, and Donald Meichenbaum, we may wonder, "Are they *always* direct?" The answer is, "Yes!" Prominent CBT therapists like them seldom drift into story and anecdote. No buttressing metaphors, few subtleties. "Client, here's what you need to do, and here's why," they say.

When we read the work of Milton H. Erickson, Brent Geary, Joseph Barber, Cloe Madanes, Jefferey Zeig, Stephen Gilligan, Stephen Lankton, and others noted for indirection, we may think that they're never direct. Wrong! Many times they are very direct. Even D. Corydon Hammond (1990), a brilliant innovator in hypnosis for many years, is by and large very direct, emphasizing directive inductions, such as the **arm catalepsy induction**, and highly directive techniques, all within formal hypnosis.

In fact, directiveness dominates all modalities of psychotherapy, as well it should. After all, we adults like to think that we operate almost exclusively in a "left brain," linear world, where we get the bills paid, get the kids off to school, and other vital functions of life are fulfilled. These things dominate our mental processes, and so it follows that psychotherapy should be a similarly straightforward transaction: "Doctor, here's my problem. Now tell me what to do about it." Oftentimes, I tell clients what to do, and I'm not talking about an ambiguous function assignment or paradoxical directive, but straight, unfettered direction:

> *Between now and next time, I want you to make me a list of the five worst situations that aggravate your social anxiety.*
>
> *You need more exercise. I want you to walk around the block every morning, and please keep track of your progress on this card.*
>
> *You are unduly influenced by your mother. Beginning tomorrow morning you need to implement only 90% of what she tells you to do.*
>
> *Hypnosis will not help you. I don't know what can help you. You may just be treatment resistant.*
>
> *Please stop talking now so I can hear from your wife.*
>
> *Therapy is not the answer for you. You need to get a life! Now, here's what I mean by that.*

But, many times, metaphor and analogy are just too hard to resist, as their impact can be very direct.

See this roll of duct tape? We use it for people who might need some help in letting their wives speak.

This doesn't exactly apply to you, but a while back I had another hypomanic client and his wife in here, and I said, "Sir, listening to you is like taking a drink from a fire hose."

More Concrete Metaphors

I keep a saguaro rib in my office, and I use it often. The saguaro is that green titan of a cactus with mighty arms extending upward. They can weigh a couple of tons and often live to 200 years or more. When they die and decay on the desert floor you find these long sticks, or ribs, that once supported the giant. I once was working with a man named Febronio, a rather rigid man who resisted all effort to help him loosen up and let go. In trance he was the recipient of the "Balloons" story (see Appendix 4) and other techniques, but still he clinged to issues from the past. This contributed to significant unhappiness at home with his wife and stepchildren.

I have three copies of Hammond's (1990) *Handbook of Hypnotic Suggestions and Metaphors*, which everyone calls simply "the red book." One of the copies is well worn, and I reached for it one day when I was working with Febronio. I asked him to stand up. He did, and I handed him the book and had him hold it down at his side. "Okay, just drop it now, Febronio," I said, and he did. He looked puzzled, and then I bid him farewell until next time, when we briefly discussed the purpose of dropping the book. I had also previously told him the Saguaro story. A family has a little saguaro growing outside their front door. The saguaro doesn't seem to be growing very fast, and they decide it must need water, so they give it some water. They keep watering it, it starts to droop, and they water it even *more*. "And what do you suppose happened to that saguaro, Febronio?" I had asked. "Obviously, it died," he had answered.

Well, Febronio was impervious to all those indirect, albeit concrete, measures, and even direct measures. One day, he said in Spanish, "My wife said I should just lighten up and get a life!" I remarked, "Well, she's right!" By now I was growing impatient with him and no doubt he with me, and it was then that I reached for my saguaro-cactus rib. I asked him to hold it. "Do you know what this is?" I asked. "Of course,

I was born and raised here," he answered. I then asked him to describe the qualities of that stick, and he said, ". . . hard . . . it's wood . . . ," and other similar descriptors. I kept prodding him and finally got him to admit that the rib was "strong but flexible." Right then, a light bulb went off, he got the point, and in the end he changed.

Of course, you want to employ such metaphors in a timely and respectful manner. The point is that usually most therapists are very direct. Even Erickson and his followers, like those listed earlier, are, when appropriate, *very direct*. But it doesn't appear that way to outsiders, as their reputations are built on subtly influencing change by using **multilevel communication**, **embedded suggestion**, and other indirect techniques.

Why Use Indirection at All?

We may wonder, then, why is indirection gaining a gradually greater foothold in such a direct world? Certainly there is little research to support its use. Is there a lack of empirical support because the indirect approach of adapting technique to the unique needs of the individual does not lend itself to a manualized study? Probably. Is it increasingly popular because telling clients clever stories helps to keep therapists amused? I hope not. Most of all, therapists are employing indirect techniques more often *because they work*, especially when direct techniques *do not*.

Therapists sometimes feel they need to fail at a technique before they employ a new one. However, if you've read Meichenbaum or Beck, or attended their workshops, think about what they tell you to do if CBT techniques fall flat, or if you meet resistance to them? You do *more of the same*, and try harder to convince clients that they need to work *with* you instead of *against* you—and you know how far *that* gets you.

Well-intentioned (and superbly researched) CBT flows from our hallowed medical model, with its tunnel vision and knee-jerk dictate: If it doesn't work, do it again, and do it harder. In medicine, if diabetic patients fail to comply with their medication and nutritional regimens, give them *more* patient education. Maybe they'll get it right the second time. If they continue to be noncompliant and show up a week later in the emergency room with swollen ankles, give them *more* patient education. Heaven forbid that a different approach should be

considered. Noncompliant medical patients are very much like unconsciously resistant clients in psychotherapy and hypnosis: they want to
get better, but something is holding them back. In these cases it is the
job of the practitioner to get in "underneath the radar," and nothing
does that like indirection. A general rule of thumb is: The higher the
reactance, the greater the indication for indirect techniques.

The Case of Lucinda

I'm working with Lucinda, a 45-year-old criminal attorney with recurrent depression. Lucinda can't make up her mind about leaving her
husband. She has had a good deal of both psychotherapy and medication over the past three years, and now she has agreed to six sessions
of hypnosis. She wants to explore her problem, but she and I both
know that she could "explore" until Doomsday. She needs perturbation with a capital *P* and I tell her exactly that: "Lucinda, hypnosis, if
successful, will either free you from the bonds of unconscious
constraints, let your conscious and unconscious minds finally see the
light of day, or a long-overdue conscious-unconscious dialogue will
occur on their day in court." She has read a fair amount on hypnosis
and answers, "You just gave me a suggestion that covers everything." I
applaud her knowledge of my transparent techniques. It's not necessary to tell her that it was really a **bind of comparable alternatives**. The
main thing is that she's interested in proceeding. We're on the same
page: we both recognize there is a need to shake something loose.

Initial Sessions

Lucinda practices meditation and yoga, and has no negative stereotypes about hypnosis, since she has had it before, which suggests that
she may not have issues of control. It is noteworthy that she is metic-
ulous about being on time, hypercritical of people who are tardy, and
she often says things like "on the hour" or "off the clock." I seed trancework with a discussion of our limited time together, and how some
children these days can't tell time if it's not on a digital clock, and in
posttrance discussion, the concept is reinforced. Her timeliness is
utilized in a conversational induction emphasizing **time distortion,
hypnotic language**, and **ideosensory phenomena**:

Lucinda, in trance, time can seem to speed up *or* slow down, *where, in all outward appearance a minute becomes an hour, or an hour seems like a minute.* One	apposition of opposites
woman *a while back said* sooner *rather than* later, *"How can one* quick *second appear to connect to the next second ever so* slowly*?" while another person said to me, "I can lose track of time and it really* doesn't matter," *while still another noted,*	apposition of opposites
	not knowing/not doing
"Time in trance *is most curious and I intend to pay very close attention to the passage of every minute."*. . .	activate seed

She readily closes her eyes and is drifting off into a nice, comfortable trance as I continue:

That big clock on the wall, it has three hands representing different intervals of time, and you have those *hands out there on your lap. I wonder* when *a heaviness*	dissociation
	implication
or lightness, or some other interesting sensation will be experienced by one or both of those hands. I once knew a man *who imagined a dialogue going on between each hand, and the imaginary discussion went back and forth, between one hand here, the other there, as if each was a* sepa-	metaphor
rate *and* disconnected *entity.*	dissociation
Right said, "I can wonder about a mere tingling *developing now," while Left didn't* say anything out loud, *and instead wondered inwardly with a pleasant* amusement, *absorbed in a host of possible* sensations *and* feelings. *The* man, *remarking later on that experience, said,*	ideosensory phenomena
"They both handled *it in their own good*	pun

time," which I thought was dexterous, *if
not* adroit *or* nimble, *or just a* handy *way*   lead away
to put it.

Over two sessions, Lucinda is provided with metaphorical ego-strengthening stories (Gafner & Benson, 2003), and finger signals are established for "yes," "no," and "I don't know/I'm not ready to answer yet." When asked after each story if her unconscious mind can put the metaphor to use, she signals "yes." I am pleased. The soil is being tilled, and it looks like clear sailing ahead.

Continued Sessions

At the third session we decide the time is right to do an unconscious search for Lucinda's "core problem." Following induction and deepening, she is asked:

> *Lucinda, beginning now, let your unconscious mind drift and dream, dream and drift. When you are sufficiently deep to do the work we need to do today, your "yes" finger will twitch and develop a lightness all its own, and move up into the air.*

Her "yes" finger moves.

I then ask for a finger signal when her unconscious gives her "important information regarding your core problem." After a minute she signals again. I ask for a verbal report and she says,

> *"Myself."*

> *"Very good," I answer. "Doing just fine."*

Against my better judgment, I ask her to tell me more. Her eyes remain closed, but her body tenses as she launches into self-criticism. Trance evaporates. So much for unconscious work for the remainder of the session.

The next session we discuss progress, if any, to date. She is employing her anchor, a circle made with her thumb and index finger, on a regular basis, and she says she has stopped drinking. I had not known she'd been drinking heavily for two years. "How do you feel about hypnotic exploration, 'myself' as the core problem, and those kinds of things?" I ask. "I just don't know," she answers. We don't do hypnosis that day. She talks almost nonstop about her self-doubt, how her mother still puts her down, and how her husband is supportive of her throwing out the whiskey. It seems like perturbation is occurring. I praise her for both her conscious and unconscious work, and remind her to keep using her anchor when she needs "to relax, slow down, take stock of things, or at any other time, day or night."

Therapist Reflection

Even though Lucinda is an amiable and forthright client, I'm sensing some tension and worry. I don't know if she's pushing some of my buttons, or if I'm frustrated by the lack of progress. At any rate, on an unconscious level, I am in some sort of struggle. I know from past experience that when I feel this way it's often best not to speak to control issues, such as ask for unconscious acceptance following a story. In times like this I have found it advisable to proceed by telling a story.

"Simple Rooms" and "The Good Spirit"

By now only a very economical induction is required. She sits back and closes her eyes without prompting, and I ask her to think of the hands on the clock, as well as her own hands, and to drift off into a nice, peaceful trance. Her "yes" finger rises when she is sufficiently deep to do today's work, and then I tell her one of my favorite stories for promoting problem solving, which we call "Simple Rooms," and is based on a similar story that Erickson called "Going from Room to Room" (Rosen, 1982). When a client is stuck, it can often perturb very nicely.

SIMPLE ROOMS

One day a person—let's call her Julie—came inside, from out in the cold, and she said her problem was that she was having trouble *getting from here to there*. So, I asked her, "Julie, in your house, how would you get from *one room to another?*" She then recounted all the possible ways she could think of for getting from *one room to another*. She could walk in, or crawl in on her knees; she could somer- sault in; she could walk in backwards; she could enter slowly or quickly; crawl in on her belly; scoot in on her back; or move in with her back against one door jamb, and then the other; or she could go in with big steps, medium steps, or on tiptoe; and she could even go around the house and climb in the back window, and then go from *one room to another.*

Finally, after several minutes, she thought she had exhausted all the possible ways to get *from here to there.* But then, as we discussed it further, it came to light that there were many other possible ways to get from *one room to another.* She could go in on the hour or half hour; she could go in after drinking a quarter glass of diet soda, or a half glass of whole milk; she could go in while listening to the radio; she could enter while thinking of something important one time, followed by having her mind blank another time; or she could have a friend present while she went into that other room. Or, if she crawled in wearing shorts one time, she could wear jeans another time. She could even walk around the block one and a half times first, or she could take a taxi to the airport and fly from Tucson to Phoenix to Chicago and back again, and then *go from one room to another.* We were still coming up with a long, long list of possibilities when we ran out of time, and we both were indeed very, very sleepy.

At any rate, it was evident to me, and especially evident to Julie, that there was an *infinite number of ways to get from one room to another.*

Now, Lucinda, I want to follow that story with another that may or may not have anything to do with your particular problem.

THE GOOD SPIRIT

A few years back, a friend of mine told me about a strange and wonderful place, Begashabito Canyon, on the western end of the Navajo Indian reservation. I was carried along on his journey as he told me about being there with Albert, a Navajo man. "I couldn't tell his age," he said. "It may have been 50, or it may have been 75 years or more."

"I was walking with him in this canyon, and he mentioned looking for the Good Spirit, a rather intriguing concept, I thought at the time.

"'Good Spirit?'" I asked him. "He never really answered my question. Instead, he averted his eyes and began to talk about the light, chasing the ever-changing light of the canyon, and being consumed by the color and movement, the interplay of sunshine off the redstone mesas, the shimmering horizons, and the constantly changing wind, always the wind.

"During the course of the day he continued this banter, soft and absorbing, and only by listening very closely did I pick up his fleeting mention of the Good Spirit. I would have forgotten many of the details had I not hastily scribbled some notes before the sun went down. To be sure, some of the main points escaped my grasp as soon as he uttered them. Nevertheless, I continue to experience unconscious impressions from that day, gentle bursts from deep within, whenever I feel a taunting wind on my face, or when I dream about the red mesas.

"I accompanied Albert that day through the vast canyon, bouncing in his pickup truck on little-used roads. We got out and walked near the boarded up Cow Springs Trading Post. 'I follow the voices,' said Albert. His pace was deceptively quick, and I could hear our voices reverberate off the walls of the dry riverbed. 'I feel like I'm walking in a dream,' I thought to myself. 'You are,' he whispered over his shoulder. Thunder cracked somewhere in the distance, and I realized that this was no place to be if a flash flood was on the way. At that moment he remarked, 'We can get out just up ahead.'

"'When do we encounter the Good Spirit?' I asked. I really didn't expect an answer, but he did respond after several seconds. 'Years ago, a man was lost in here, and a violent storm was brewing. He caught sight of something in the swirling dust up ahead. The man urged his horse forward, and then he found safety.'

'"What was swirling out there? The Good Spirit?' I asked. He turned around and faced me. I was glad to stop and catch my breath. He then continued, 'One time, three Navajo children wandered away from their mother's sheep camp. A search party could not find them. As dawn broke, the children walked serenely into camp. 'The man with the long coat came, and we followed him out,' said the children.'

"'No doubt it was the Good Spirit in another form,' I ventured. Just then, Albert launched into another story. 'A woman was lost in the riverbed one time during a storm. She was led to safety by an animal. Don't ask me if it was a deer or some other animal. The woman remarked that no sooner had she cleared the wash a great wall of water swept by.' The story brought me back to the present, the soft sand beneath my feet, and I thought of how a dry wash like this could transform into a raging torrent in mere seconds.

"I followed Albert out of the wash, and again we were moving specks in the vast red tundra. I saw a cornfield and heard voices, but there was no one in sight. In a few moments we passed some people talking to each other, but their voices were inaudible. 'Was that the Good Spirit?' I asked after we had passed by. If he answered, I did not hear him.

"My legs were heavy when we arrived back at the trading post. The howling wind was muffled once we were in the pickup truck. Albert took his time starting the engine. I sat back and closed my eyes and contemplated my experience in the canyon.

"Back on State Route 98, we glided down the road. There was no other traffic. We drove over a pair of work gloves in the road. They were on fire. We turned around and headed back. We got out and examined the gloves. By then, one glove was gone, and the other was still burning. We stood there for a very long time, and neither one of us commented. We then got back in the truck and continued down the road." (Adapted from a story in *Arizona Highways* by L. W. Banks, 1999)

When Lucinda was realerted, she remarked, "That was not a reasonable story." "Which one?" I asked, thinking how attorneys tend to use the word *reasonable* as often as we use the word *appropriate*. "The story about the rooms. That was a very strange story," she said.

She remembered the first story, but was totally blank on the second one. "I'll see you in three weeks," I said.

The Last Session with Lucinda

Lucinda looked much improved when she returned. The first words out of her mouth were, "I may have a new appreciation for my husband." "Oh, how so?" I asked. "I think I've been too hard on him, and too hard on myself as well," she commented. "Therapy is done, Lucinda," I said. "You did a lot of hard work. I think you deserve a pat on the back. Keep using that anchor, and give me a call if you want to come in again." She was smiling when she left. I asked her to call me in a month. She did, and noted she was doing well. She called me again in six months and said she was still doing well. I asked her to call me if she needed any help in the future, and never heard from her again.

Clinical Comments

In Lucinda's care, some therapists would have encouraged continued therapy, or at least a booster session in a month or so, in order to check on her progress. Continued talk therapy could have centered on consciously integrating the unconscious changes she had made. To me, that wasn't necessary, as, objectively, she appeared stable, her mood was bright, and she knew she could call for another appointment. In many situations I invariably rely on the law of parsimony: Do only what is necessary to achieve the desired effect. Less is more, and cut them loose as soon as you can.

In subsequent chapters, we will examine the research on other aspects of unconscious process, with a special emphasis on its application in therapy. The next chapter on ego-strengthening underscores another feature of the law of parsimony: We may get there faster by going slower at the beginning of treatment, first attending to a person's need to be unconsciously strengthened before directly addressing the presenting problem. With all clinical problems there are myriad hypnotic techniques that can be of assistance. Seldom is hypnosis applied in a vacuum. Instead, hypnosis may be most useful as an adjunct, and it is the response of the client, not the cleverness of the technique, that is the best guide.

Chapter 2

Ego-Strengthening

Clients enter our office, state their problem, and in our eagerness to alleviate suffering we often hasten to implement measures directed at the presenting problem. In this chapter, I argue for ego-strengthening measures *before* intervening in the anxiety, depression, or other problem. By doing so, we may build a firmer foundation for therapy by bolstering receptivity for the interventions that follow.

Direction versus Indirection

In Hartland's (1971) seminal article on hypnotic ego-strengthening, he offers therapists various ways in which they can help clients overcome long-term problems. For the smoker, he commands, "You can do it!" For the obese, "You can lose weight!" In trance, the client is given repeated authoritarian, highly directive suggestions. Nothing indirect or permissive, just unadorned straight suggestion, plain and simple.

For the better part of the last century, and continuing into the present, this is the way hypnotic suggestion has been delivered by many practitioners, and is presumably what clients want and expect from hypnosis. Haley's (1973) *Uncommon Therapy*, in which he introduced Milton Erickson's work to the world, heralded a fork in the road, and since then some practitioners of hypnosis have come to favor indirection over a highly directive approach.

However, many still practice the old way, especially those who rely on hypnotizability tests, or are influenced by popular training texts of the time. One of the most compelling books of its day was W. S. Kroger's (1963) *Clinical and Experimental Hypnosis in Medicine, Dentistry, and Psychology.* In a section on treating alcoholics with hypnosis, he recommends saying to the client in trance, "Each and every time you hold a drink in your hand, you will think of rotten eggs—the horrible, violent, disgusting smell of rotten eggs" (p. 312). Go ahead, try that right after breakfast on your next substance-abusing client!

Those were simpler times, and I'm old enough to remember them. The term *polysubstance abuse* had not been invented nor had *dual diagnosis*. A person was either a heroin addict or an alcoholic. Abusers of methamphetamines, cocaine, and painkillers were fewer in number and lurked off in the shadows somewhere, and you couldn't become dependent (it was believed then) on either cocaine or marijuana. Wealthy clients may have free-associated their drinking problem on the analyst's couch, but people like Kroger practiced in hospitals and clinics by the day's standards. Aversive alcohol dependence treatment of the time also included Antabuse, a now lesser-used medication that causes vomiting when a person drinks alcohol.

Those were authoritarian times in general. Even though pediatrician Dr. Benjamin Spock advocated permissive parenting, and Mister Rogers was beginning to weave his gentle spell on children through TV, the majority saw things in terms of black and white. There were no personal computers and no Internet. There was no globalism or global economy. Major governments thought East versus West, and the Cold War dominated the country's mindset. People on both sides of the Iron Curtain feared nuclear annihilation. There was no threat from terrorists. Things were either right or wrong. In mental health treatment, psychodynamic therapy was giving way to behaviorism, and people's problems were deficits to be eliminated. With the exception of Carl Rogers, permissive, indirect psychotherapy was still on the horizon, and hypnosis was directive. Clients in trance were told—in no uncertain terms—to give up their symptoms.

Many Tools in the Toolbox

Now, I don't mean to sound like I'm denigrating directive psycho-therapy in general, or directive hypnosis in particular. Much to the contrary. Many of us who practice *largely* in the tradition of Milton Erickson remain respectful of directive approaches, as often they are quite effective. *Whatever* techniques you become adept at, your confidence in them communicates to the client, "This therapist *knows* what he or she is doing." In other words, the more comfortable—and practiced—you are with something, the better it will translate to the client.

Certainly, many practitioners *combine* directive techniques with indirect ones, such as, employing a directive induction, like hand levitation or arm catalepsy, *with* a story that allows for clients to apply metaphorical messages to their own particular circumstances. And other times, especially with a client who *wants* and *expects* directive therapy, I will tell them, in trance, ". . . you *will* let go of such-and-such symptom," or ". . . you *can* now begin to move on from that traumatic event."

I advocate time and time again for two things: 1) hypnosis as an *adjunct* and 2) versatility and flexibility in applying therapy to the individual, letting the client's response be the guide rather than the technique. In a few of my cases hypnosis alone is all that is required. But in most instances, standard talk therapy is absolutely necessary, and sometimes the *addition* of hypnosis greatly enhances therapy. The more tools you have available to help the client, the more likely you will be able to help them.

Let's Be Resilient Together

Fast-forward to the present time. **Self-efficacy**, along with its close cousin, **resilience**—the ability to withstand and rebound from disruptions in life challenges (Walsh, 2003)—are hot topics in academic psychology today. Instead of ferreting out what's wrong in people, we look for what's good and try to build on it. Fredrickson and colleagues (2003) tested subjects in early 2001 and again in the weeks following the September 11 terrorist attacks. Their findings suggest that positive emotions, such as amusement, contentment, and hope, buffer resilient people against depression and promote thriving in the aftermath of crisis. Now, how many *resilient* people do you see in your practice? If you're like me, most of those hopeful and contented types find their way to other practitioners' offices. Many of the ones I see are neither resilient nor high in self-esteem.

The Puzzle of Low Self-Regard

With many clients, no matter how much I emphasize their positive attributes or behavior, they continue to view themselves negatively. Their depression, anxiety, and related symptoms often appear intractable. Understandably, these folks get very down on themselves.

Self-esteem, or *self-efficacy*, can be defined as the belief that one's behavior will lead to successful outcomes. This matter of low self-esteem merits more than a passing glance by therapists, as it is something we confront on a daily basis and often serves to thwart our best therapeutic efforts. Let's remember what Albert Bandura (1997) said: Psychotherapists may bestow the greatest benefit by helping clients build self-efficacy, *not* by giving them specific remedies for their problems.

Of course, there are many ways to help people build self-confidence. We may do so by helping them role-play assertive behavior and other social skills, or by encouraging them to change occupations, improve their relationships, slow down their drinking, diminish negative self-talk, learn relaxation skills, or myriad other interventions that broaden one's range of behavior.

Why Ego-Strengthening?

When nonpsychotherapist researchers study self-efficacy, it is usually domain specific. In other words, research on the self-efficacy of *cancer* or *hurricane* survivors employs measures that specifically test coping with *cancer* or the aftermath of a *hurricane*. The self-esteem studied by psychotherapy researchers is more general, and is often called **ego-strength**, which has been defined by Calnan (1977) as the efficacy of dealing with the environment, or the ability to cope with or adjust to difficult environmental demands in general. Lavertue, Kuman, and Pekala (2002) note that it is hardly surprising that ego-strengthening is considered important to the process of psychotherapy.

Various writers have recognized that building confidence in one's ability to cope with or solve problems is also a necessary ingredient in hypnotic interventions. The lack of this ego-strengthening element is seen in various clinical problems, including bulimia (Vanderlinden & Vandereycken, 1994), smoking (Barber, 2001), insomnia, acute and chronic pain (Mjoseth, 1997), anxiety and depression (Stanton, 1979), chronic paranoid schizophrenia (Gafner & Young, 1998), and many other problems. In a study involving chronic abusers of drugs and alcohol, Pekala and colleagues (2004) demonstrated the effectiveness of a self-hypnosis protocol on self-esteem, anger, and impulsivity. Other writers (Mutter, 1999; Hornyak, 1999) similarly addressed ego-strengthening, but refer to it as an "empowerment strategy." In addition, Maggie Phillips (2001), a longtime proponent of indirect techniques in treating the sequelae of trauma, has touted the value of ego-strengthening to enhance the effectiveness of EMDR, a highly directive technique. And, last but not least, Cory Hammond is probably the most noteworthy contemporary advocate of ego-strengthening for many clinical problems. Hammond (1990) offered a useful metaphor in this regard. He likens the client with a psychiatric issue to a debilitated medical patient facing surgery. This patient requires rest and nutrition as a "building up" strategy prior to undergoing the rigors of surgery.

Lavertue, Kumar, and Pekala (2002) noted the following among ego-strengthening's benefits: improved therapeutic alliance, heightened insight, increased thought clarity, improved self-esteem, and shortened length of therapy. Stanton's (1997) research showed that ego-enhancing suggestions can help clients gain control over their lives, and Calnan's (1977) work demonstrated that the technique is effective for improving quality of life. However, the most significant contribution to the literature was added by Lavertue and colleagues (2002). The researchers enrolled 224 subjects and employed six measures in their study that involved two treatment conditions—relaxation and ego-strengthening, as well as a control group. They found that subjects in both relaxation and ego-strengthening improved in self-esteem and depression.

How Does Hypnotic Ego-Strengthening Work?

We can learn about the mechanisms behind ego-strengthening by examining the experimental social psychology literature. In one study (Kawakami, Dovidio, & Dijksterhuis, 2003), the authors investigated whether priming participants with concepts associated with the elderly and skinheads influenced personal attitudes. After subjects were primed with the elderly category, their attitudes became more conservative; and after being primed with the skinhead category, their attitudes became more prejudiced. The authors' work supports a growing body of research that shows that priming social categories not only directly activates such things as personality traits and positive and negative evaluations, but also produces *attitude change* more in line with attitudes associated with the primed group. Their results suggest a transformation rather than a compliance process. Similar research (Hardin & Conley, 2001) demonstrated that women judged them-selves to be more feminine after imagining a conversation with Barbara Bush, who is characterized as more traditional, than after imagining a conversation with Hillary Clinton, who is considered to be more nontraditional.

Similar research was carried out by Strahan, Spencer, and Zanna (2002). They subliminally primed *thirst* and found that subjects who were subliminally primed with thirst were likely to be *persuaded* by an advertisement for Kool-Aid. However, such persuasion occurred only in subjects who were thirsty. A limitation of these studies is that they did not address the *duration* of such attitude change.

So, do these studies lend support for seeding "strong ego" concepts before attempting hypnotic ego-strengthening? I would say yes, but only if clients are motivated to improve ego strength. Eric Jackson (personal communication, 2003), psychology researcher at the University of Arizona, notes that a further implication of these studies is that they support the view that hypnosis cannot *make* people do something they do not want to do, and that adjunctive techniques, such as motivational interviewing, may be useful in increasing clients motivation to change.

Fairy Tales

In Bettelheim's (1977) *The Uses of Enchantment,* he examined the value of fairy tales. He notes that fairy tales not only entertain, but also offer meaning on different levels, thus enlightening children about themselves and fostering personality development. Many of us use fairy tales with adults as well as with children. Many fairy tales, like those of Hans Christian Andersen, and even Aesop's fables, convey fairly *obvious* messages, so that a fair portion of the meaning, especially for an adult, may be processed *consciously.* Just how much *unconscious* processing occurs, we can never know. If the adult who says, "I know what that means!" makes some attitude or behavior changes as a result, quite possibly some unconscious integration occurred. I frequently use a pre- and post-self-efficacy measure to track progress.

So, let's make the jump to something not quite so transparent, like an ego-strengthening story. Here is a story I frequently read to clients early in therapy. It is adapted from a story Lee Wallas (1985) called "The Little Seedling."

THE GREENHOUSE

Once upon a time, in another state, there was this magnificent greenhouse. A boy walked by it every day on his way to school. He always wondered what it might be like to have a job inside that marvelous greenhouse. School would soon be done for the summer, and one day the boy stopped at the greenhouse and asked if he could have a job there. The boy sat on a sack of peat moss as he waited for the boss to interview him. He waited only a few moments, but it seemed like a very, very long time, and then the boss arrived. She was a large woman with very strong arms. "You can have the job," she said, "but only if you work very hard and do a good job. You must pay close attention and not let your mind drift off in here," she instructed.

The boy was delighted to get the job. When he reported to work the next morning it was immediately evident what the boss had meant, as there was a lot inside the greenhouse to notice and appreciate besides the job. The greenhouse was an immense structure, its windows shining in the sun on the outside, and once inside, the boy noticed the rays of the sun slanting through the thousands of panes of glass. Inside it was warm and humid, and you could find all varieties of plants, hanging from up above, down below on shelves, and down farther yet, on the floor, all kinds of plants, in various sizes of pots. Stepping from one aisle to another, he was enveloped by many smells. Some were familiar to him, but most were unrecognizable odors that blended together into one extraordinary, humid scent, something that arrested his attention in a most pleasing way. Time simply stood still inside there in that marvelous reverie, and he forgot about the outside world.

There were long rows of flowers of one color, and then other colors. In whatever direction he looked there was a magnificent profusion of colors. In whichever direction he turned he could see, smell, and almost feel the growth of those remarkable plants, losing track of time while he breathed in his surroundings, absorbing the greenhouse, inwardly amused that his attention could be engaged while time told by his pocket watch, which hung from his belt, could be suspended.

As you can imagine, it takes several people to keep a big greenhouse going, but only one person was in charge of the operation. She was serious and "all-business," but worked right alongside the others, carefully tending to all the plants. His second day on the job, the boy realized that going to work every day was like walking into a magical, sunny kingdom. Each morning he worked with several dozen seedlings, putting them in small pots, and then lining them up so he could observe and take care of them while they grew.

Little did the boy know that on his workbench, weeks or months before, someone else had also been transplanting seedlings, and lining them up in order to care for them and watch them grow. One day, way back then, a little seedling at the back of the row had fallen over and rolled off, tumbling to the floor in back where it was dark and no one could see it. And there it lay for the longest time, lost and forgotten, defeated, lifeless, shrivelled, and brown on top, and down below the surface, it was dry, compact, and hard, down inside the shallow pot.

One day, while sweeping behind the bench, the boy found this little pot. "What is this?" he asked himself. "This little plant doesn't look like any others. What could it be?" He held it up to the light and figured right then that the seedling was dead. But as he examined it more closely he saw a speck of green near the top of the root ball. His imagination took over. "Hmmm, I wonder what I could do with this . . . ," he said.

He went to the boss and said, "Look what I found. Is it okay if I keep this?" The woman replied, "That's no good, just throw it away. I'll get you a better one. Don't waste your time on dead plants." But the boy persisted and got his way. At the end of the day, the boy looked more carefully at the little seedling. As he broke open the cracked pot he found that down below, deep inside, the plant was very much alive. In fact, it had continued to grow in the dryness and dark, and had formed a strong, compact *root system*. And those roots had continued to grow despite the lack of light and water, and eventually the root ball had become too big for the pot, which cracked from the life force within. He examined the very *strong root system* that had developed. Sure enough, down below it was very much alive.

He planted the seedling in rich soil where it had enough water and room to grow, away from the other plants. After a few weeks it began putting out leaves and branches with more leaves, as its *powerful roots* absorbed the moisture and nutrients from down below, and delivered them upward. Yes, the little seedling was definitely growing. The boy continued caring for the little seedling, which soon grew bigger and bigger and needed a larger pot.

The boy left his job at the end of the summer, and years later he thought back on his experience in the greenhouse. He thought about that little seedling, which now was no doubt a big sturdy tree in somebody's yard. He especially thought about how that little seedling had survived, endured, and eventually prospered—all because of its *strong root system.*

After such a story, you may receive any number of responses in the debriefing, ranging from "I know what that means!" to "That was a really *nice* story" to complete amnesia. An ego-strengthening story can be highly therapeutic, as clients unwittingly self-reference metaphors such as trees, animals, and inanimate objects like roads, as in the story "Highway One" (Gafner & Benson, 2003). But an ego-strengthening story is also diagnostic, a behavioral probe to test response. Hypnosis is a process of constantly floating trial "balloons," and the client's *response* is the guide. Most clients like stories, and they invariably appreciate the effort to build up their sense of self-efficacy before directly addressing their presenting problem. In fact, that's how I introduce ego-strengthening, as a "mental building up," or "mental strengthening."

Hypnotic Language and Hypnotic Ego-Strengthening

Today, direct suggestions often take the form of gentle encouragement:

Yes, you can be confident.

I know and you know you can be confident.

In x situation, you may discover a welcome confidence. . . .

So, *can* and *may* are the operative words, rather than the authoritarian *will*. However, let's remember that some clients may want and expect the word *will*, so keep it in your bag of tricks for when you need it. Just as with highly directive inductions, like the arm catalepsy induction (Gafner & Benson, 2000), you never know when you might need such directive words. In our hypnosis training group in Tucson, we expect interns to gain a facility with a wide range of inductions and techniques, both indirect and direct.

Implication is a type of suggestion that lends itself well to ego-strengthening. The operative word in implication is when. Employed with **power words** and other hypnotic language, implication in trance can be especially potent:

I wonder *when you will begin to ex-*   power word
perience a newfound confidence. . . .

You may already be imagining *or*
exploring *inwardly and* wondering   power words
about a future feeling of confidence, and
when *it happens.* . . .   implication

A direct question in trance can be quite instigative:

Your discovering *that confidence, and*   power word
putting it into practice, will it be in a few
moments *or several* hours *from now,*   suggestion covering all
some time today *or* tomorrow, *or* some   possibilities
other time *in the future, when you least*
expect it?

Or, maybe a more indirect suggestion is desired. Let's remember: the higher the reactance, the more indirection is indicated:

I knew a woman *one time who came in*   metaphor
here *from out* there, *and she had many*   apposition of opposites
deep feelings and things on her mind, and   linking word
she also had attended three sessions *of*   truism
hypnosis, and I told her a little story,   power word
though it wasn't the best *story in the*   restraint
world, and on the spot *she launched into*   surprise
her own story about someone else *who*   metaphor
had begun to experience new feelings and
behavior, and I can't remember if she
called it a feeling of conviction, *a*   suggestion covering all
newfound self-assurance, *or if it was*   possibilities
simply a combination *of poise, security,*
and confidence that was readily evident to
herself and others. . . .

Seeding and Hypnotic Ego-Strengthening

A client named Penelope is arriving in a few minutes and I intend to employ seeding in the service of the target, which is the client's lack of self-assurance. I don't yet know which words or concepts I will seed, but as a place to start I get out a dictionary and thesaurus and list several synonyms: *certainty, certitude, sureness, definiteness, self-assurance, self-confidence, decisiveness, poise, convincing, positive.* Okay, now I look up some synonyms for *new: fresh, recent, novel, refreshed, newborn, original, reinvigorated, rejuvenated, innovative.*

So, by combining just a few of these words I have some good material for seeding. And the good part is that I'll have these words to use with tomorrow's client, who has a similar problem.

For example, in pretrance discussion I casually mention the *certainty* of rain today and how when it rained last week everything seemed so *fresh* and clean in my backyard the next morning. Then, in the hypnosis portion of the session I *activate* the seed:

Penelope, I remember quite vividly and distinctly a woman *who was in here just last week, and she asked to experience an*	metaphor
age progression, seeing herself *in the future the way she wanted to be, and I*	suggestion
can't remember if she saw herself, in her mind, on an imaginary video screen, *or she viewed herself in her* mind's eye, *or if she employed* some other *technique, but at the end of the session, she experienced a newfound self-assurance, which was actually quite*	suggestion covering all possibilities
novel *and* refreshing.	activate seed

Now, let's say that Penelope's symptoms are dear to her and that she has some unconscious resistance to expanding her range of behavior. Then, I might want to restrain her a bit by distracting her at the end of the suggestion:

. . . *actually quite* novel *and* refreshing, *though starting any* long novels, *or even nonfiction books about* fresh water *fishing may be too ambitious an undertaking at the present time*	activate seed lead away

After seeding and activating the seed, I want to reinforce it. SAR—seed, activate, and reinforce. The easiest way to reinforce it is to lead a straightforward discussion when the trancework portion of the session has ended—e.g., "So, Penelope, let's go over what we've covered today. . . ."

If Penelope starts to break out of her old patterns, even in a small way, then I've hit the mark. If she doesn't, then maybe I didn't restrain her enough, and next time, at the same point in the hypnotic patter, I would try:

. . . *actually quite* novel *and* refreshing, *though I in no way intend to suggest that you try something similar at this juncture, as you* may not be ready *for such radical changes.* Someone *one time knew when she was ready for something* (_____) *different* (_____) *and it had* nothing to do with the paws on the dog.	activate seed restrain metaphor pause lead away

Remember, it's the *response of the client* that is the guide. Most people don't require restraint. Maybe Penelope requires more role play before she can feel sufficiently confident to try something new. And maybe you're thinking, "Penelope may need to *talk* about it more." Quite true, but at some point verbal processing needs to convert to action. Change for any of us can be difficult to make happen. With clients like Penelope I frequently use videotaped playback of role-play situations. If, for example, I have a man with social phobia, or even just shyness or undeveloped social skills, I'll have a woman student or staff person engage in a role play, videotape it, and then play it back for critique and analysis. There's nothing more instructive for clients than seeing themselves in action.

Too Hot in the Kitchen?

After several sessions of therapy, some clients are ready to make the jump to the next level, where they actually begin to integrate key suggestions and are poised to put them into practice. This creates anxiety and ambivalence, and it's at this point where some clients drop out of therapy, because it's getting too hot in the kitchen. They may not be able to say, "Can we meet every two weeks instead?" or, "How about we take a break from therapy?" Here they are, clients with long-standing problems, the beginnings of new ego strength, and they're feeling pressure from inside themselves as well as outside, where the therapist is praising their gains and prodding them to work through this bump in the road *once a week*, because that's the way therapy is *supposed to be*. At these points in therapy we might consider opening up a window in that hot kitchen and preempting their escape by *asking them* if they want to alter the meeting schedule. Some may opt for it, and once therapy resumes you'll both be glad for it.

Two Types of Hypnotic Ego-Strengthening

Since the late 1980s we have experimented with different ways to effect ego-strengthening within hypnosis. One major way is through story, or anecdote, and examples of these can be found in previous books (Gafner & Benson, 2000; Gafner & Benson, 2003), as well as in the rest of this chapter. In the latter book we also describe another major technique, which was dubbed "short-burst" by Brent Geary, training director at the Erickson Foundation in Phoenix, Arizona, (personal communication, 1999). We typically employ the short-burst in a deepening or within a story. Operationally, it is essentially an interspersed suggestion. However, it differs from the traditional inter-spersal in that it is actually part of a confusion technique. A **non sequitur** precedes the suggestion:

> . . . *Penelope, you may let your experience deepen as I count backward now from ten down to one.* . . .*10,* . . . *9,* . . . *The descent of an opportune mist* . . .*and you can change, Penelope* . . . *8,* . . .

non sequitur suggestion

The Non Sequitur

The non sequitur creates confusion from which the client naturally wishes to escape, while the therapist provides a way out, and in the desired direction. Keep the non sequitur neutral and purposeless. You don't want to be didactic with it; you just need a short, out-of-context phrase that is mere window dressing for *setting up* the suggestion:

They sold trinkets beside the road, or
The shopping carts always seem to stick together, or
There was a silence between the leaves.

Not: *The Papists stormed the palace.*
Never: *Barking dogs may bite.*
But: *Why do dogs bark?*

A question rivets attention. A shorter question leaves much more to the imagination, thus heightening confusion. In constructing a non sequitur we may have a tendency toward **power words** or hypnotic language. After all, don't these *purposeful* things comprise most of what we do in hypnosis? The fact is no, non sequiturs should not include power words. Think instead of when you throw **fluff** into a story. That's not purposeful or didactic, is it? It's simply boring filler material. Well, a non sequitur is like that. With fluff, listeners may be thinking, "Hmmm, why are those details in there? Perhaps this therapist is conveying some meaning I should grasp." It stimulates wonderment and further absorbs their attention.

Not: *He went deep into trance. (Didactic)*
But: *The depth of the old oaken bucket. . . .*
Or: *When is it a pail and when is it a bucket?*

An incomplete sentence may stimulate even more confusion than a short question. Think how trancework up to this point has been fairly orderly. Perhaps you structure it to have four components: induction, deepening, therapy, and a debriefing at the end. You may employ stock phrasing in your patter, as you give suggestions for things like **time distortion** and **amnesia**. *And* you've mostly talked in complete sentences—structured, orderly, predictable, *comfortable*.

Now you've switched gears and are doing something radically different. That's why when I introduce confusion, whether it's a non sequitur or even a nebulous technique, like a story without an ending, I always tell the client at the beginning of the session, "I may say some things today that don't quite make sense. However, that's to get in underneath the radar, to *help* you." In doing hypnosis for 20 years, I've never yet had someone say, "Oh, no, *don't* tell me something that doesn't make sense." It's framed as helpful. A good doctor does not prescribe bad medicine, as Peggy Papp (1983) said. So, with non sequiturs:

Not: *Red apple. (Too short)*
Fair: *She decided what to order at the restaurant.*
Good: *Should he order corn tortillas or flour?*
Better: *What he saw outside the restaurant. . . .*

Don't use aphorisms or koans. The sound of one hand clapping gets no applause from the non sequitur gallery.

Not: *What if they gave a party and nobody came?*
But: *What if nobody came?*

You don't need to make any points about a favorite topic. Avoid controversy. Nothing about drinking, drugs, or religion. The purpose of the non sequitur is to *stimulate*, but not too specifically.

Not: *He was inscrutable, implacable, and intractable.*
But: *Inscrutable and. . . .*

I have stock non sequiturs, but say it's late in the day and I can't remember them. I may just glance around the room and grab one:

. . . and then there was the lamp shade. . . . , or
The thickness of the carpet. . . .

Keep it simple. Remember the law of parsimony: Do only what is necessary to achieve the desired effect. Less is more. You have a target in mind ahead of time, unleash the non sequitur, wait a few seconds to let the confusion build, and follow with the suggestion:

You can *go deep, or*
You can *overcome this problem, or*
Change is just around the corner, or
There is *hope after all.*

Or with indirection:

She knew *she could go deep, or*
He endured and then he prevailed.

Two or three times in a deepening or story is plenty. Of course, employ a subtle voice alteration for the suggestion. For you, is it a whisper? A slightly deeper voice? Maybe delivered very s-l-o-w-l-y? This vocal shift is a direct communication with the unconscious.

Continuing Therapy with Penelope

Penelope responded well to both short-burst and metaphorical ego-strengthening. After six sessions of hypnosis combined with talk therapy and role play, spaced out over three months, she reported that her goals were met. She looked and behaved more assertively and confidently, and was pleasantly surprised by her quick progress. (If only all the others were that easy!)

With Penelope, I employed the following story, which was inspired by an article appearing in *National Geographic*, "Russia's Iron Road" by Fen Montaigne (1998). This story was used as an induction with Penelope. I have also used it as a story in therapy, as it has ego-strengthening suggestions.

THE IRON ROAD

One time Anton Chekhov remarked that the strength of Russia's vast remoteness comes not from its giant trees and its silence, but from the fact that only migrating birds know where it ends. Through this seemingly measureless expanse rides the *Rossiya*, a train of the Trans-Siberian Railroad, and during the next six days it will journey east across eleven time zones, covering 5,700 miles of track, all the way to the Sea of Japan.

I was on the mighty *Rossiya* that night as it slowly pulled out of the station, heading *east*, and at the same time I began to walk *west*, ever so *slowly*, as if in a dream, and it is only with great difficulty that I can now recall that unique experience, a lingering walk through ten train cars, a six-day journey through time.

Someone asked me once how much I slept during those six days, and I really *can't remember*, though I'm sure I must have slept and eaten at intervals. Important things, though, I do remember, and quite vividly, like the conductors on the platform that evening, their grayish blue uniforms, and how they stood out against the *Rossiya's* bright colors, sky blue on the upper half, and dusky red on the bottom. At the time, there was a clear delineation between the top half and the bottom half, but now, in my mind, the sky blue up there just blends into the dusky red down below.

I stopped to rest in the first car, already *exhausted*, though I should have felt the exhilaration of starting out on a journey. There was an acrid scent. Coal smoke, not from the locomotive, but instead from an old-fashioned boiler. Someone was preparing water for tea. I ducked inside an unoccupied compartment and peered out the window. I saw the outskirts of Moscow, a succession of vegetable gardens, and wooden cabins. There was a green-domed church in the moonlight. I thought of the *Orient Express*, and right now, as I remember being on that train, I *drift and dream*, just as I did then.

My body carried itself woodenly past the other compartments of the first car, down the narrow aisle, and although I heard much talking and laughter from *inside* the compartments, I saw no other person, which caused a curious uncertainty inside me, as I reflected back on the green-domed church, and what I had experienced *outside*. It was as though my mind was in one car and my body in another, or as though it was someone else's experience, a fictitious person whom I am now describing.

I couldn't remember which car was mine, and it was very late now as I entered the second car. In the first empty compartment, I threw back the starched sheets of the narrow berth and lay down. Very soon a face appeared above me. It was Valentina, the chief of the train, and her gold-capped teeth gleamed. "I hear you're a reporter," she said. "Let me give you something to report." Her voice *drifted in and out*, and for a peculiar period of time her lips moved and I heard nothing. Then the light dimmed and I could hear her quite clearly, but could not see her at all.

She told me how the Iron Road is the *backbone of the country*, "Our version of a transcontinental highway," she intoned, a disembodied voice reverberating in sync with the click of the rails. "The Iron Road carries freight and people and helped build this country," she said. She was saying something about how Csar Alexander III had decreed that construction begin in 1891. Her hand hung frozen in the air as she spoke, and for an interminable time again *I dreamed and drifted*.

Whether it was day or night I could not discern, as the window shades were pulled *down*, and soon I found myself up, swaying on my feet in car number three. Valentina was nowhere to be seen, but her words still resounded in my ears, something about approaching the Ural Mountains and "the two secret cities." "They can't be found on any Russian map," she intoned.

Shrill laughter from a videotape penetrated my consciousness. I gazed upon berths filled with travelers, animated, conversing, eating, and smoking. How curious that everyone is so awake, I thought, as it was the middle of the night. They seemed to not notice me as I continued on to car number four, the dining car. The red vinyl booths were empty, and the bright lights jolted me awake. The menu of goulash and caviar held no appeal, as I continued on to car number five. My body wandered in a timeless void, and my mind—I do not recall it then.

The smoke from strong tobacco became a dense fog. I bumped into a man with beady eyes. "Have we come to the two secret cities yet?" I asked. He regarded me suspiciously and gestured out the window. There was a white stone obelisk that said we were 1,670 kilometers from Moscow. "You have just crossed from Europe into Asia," said the man. I groped beyond him in the fog. Someone behind me—or was she in front of me?—announced that the city of Novosibirsk lay just ahead. "How far?" I asked. "Much farther for you," whispered a voice. I knew the place to be Siberia's largest city. "But it's not a secret city," said the voice again. How did she know what I was thinking?

I was exhausted and sat down on a passageway jump seat. I made myself small as people streamed by. Remnants of a smoked fish were discarded down by my feet, far below. I closed my eyes as people marched by, oblivious to the shrunken figure in slumber on the jump seat. Whether it was a waking dream I do not know, but I dreamt of the *strong Rossiya* on the Iron Road. Was it daytime or night-time? Which time zone was I in? I was further lulled for timeless moments by the rhythmic sound of wheels on rails.

Ego-Strengthening Anecdotes

An anecdote is simply a *very* short story. **Ego-strengthening** anecdotes build on *response attentiveness, yearning for growth,* or *eagerness to feel better*. In one session with Penelope I used some of the following anecdotes adapted from Arno (1999). Other anecdotes can be found in the Appendices.

WHITEBARK PINE

The famous American naturalist, John Muir, once counted annual growth rings on a whitebark pine. He described one as 426 years old, but only six inches in diameter. Up higher, in the alpine tundra far above the highest trees, Muir encountered another form of whitebark pine. The small tree often grows beside a large rock, which offers some protection from the relentless blizzards that blast the tree with grains of ice and sand.

WESTERN WHITE PINE

Mature Western white pines commonly grow four feet thick and tower 200 feet above the forest floor. White pine lured early lumbermen from northwest New England to Minnesota and beyond. In fact, it was valued by the English monarch for use as masts for the Royal Navy. Some people wonder how this tree thrives in poor, gravelly soils where it competes with other conifers for growing room.

INSPIRATION WOOD

Western white-pine wood is light in weight, but comparatively strong. It has exceptionally straight grain and seldom splits. One woman, with the unlikely name of Inspiration Wood, spent years carving on a block of white pine, fashioning it into a chain comprised of many interlocking links, a project that tired her hands, but not her mind.

BLISTER RUST

In the 1930s, blister rust threatened the white pine. Initially, it was thought that the blister rust life cycle could be interrupted by eradication of its hosts, currant and gooseberry bushes. However, this did not work, as rust spores can be carried by the wind. Crossbreeding produced naturally resistant white pines, which continue to evolve, building up a resistant strain, generation after generation.

PONDEROSA PINE

Ponderosa pine seems to be associated with the unconquered spirit and wide-open spaces of the American West. Many attain ages of 400 to 500 years, and no doubt many witnessed on the Lewis and Clark expedition of 1804–1806 are still standing. One of the largest ponderosa pines grows in Central Oregon. It is nearly nine feet in diameter and stands 161 feet tall.

PONDEROSA SEEDLINGS

Some Ponderosas grow in dry mountain soil. One study revealed ponderosa seedlings only three inches in height, but with tap roots several feet long. Just a few tufts of leaves are supplied moisture by a highly extensive root system.

The Case of Jerry

Not everyone appears to be in need of ego-strengthening. Jerry, a 32-year-old man, presented with a rather interesting problem: low test scores at the university, where he was studying chemistry. He was referred to me in order to rule out anxiety as a reason for the low test scores.

I gave him Beck depression and anxiety inventories, as well as a self-esteem scale. On all of them Jerry scored within normal. Subjectively he felt fine, and objectively he was calm and in a bright mood. He was a clean-cut, smiling, and affable young man who did not smoke or drink, and there was no evidence of personality disorder. His history was remarkable: a head injury, various fractures, and the amputation of his left arm above the elbow, all sequelae of a motor vehicle accident in the first Persian Gulf War.

Not sure how to approach his problem, I began with a course of metaphorical ego-strengthening, which included the following stories and anecdotes.

FOUND AT LAST

Martin Sheridan, who passed away in 2003, always wondered who had saved his life. He was in attendance one night in 1942 at the Coconut Grove nightclub in Boston's theater district when someone struck a match and triggered a 12-minute fire in which nearly 500 people perished. "Someone dragged me out and saved my life, and I always wondered who it was," pondered Sheridan.

After the fire, he went on to work as a war correspondent for the *Boston Globe*. He was the first civilian reporter on a submarine in a war zone, serving 38 days on the maiden patrol of the Bullhead. Shortly after he left the submarine, it was sunk in the Java Sea. On the amphibious transport Fremont in 1944, a young sailor came up to Sheridan and announced that he was the one who rescued him from the Coconut Grove fire.

Sheridan was stunned. There in the Pacific he had suddenly found the man who had saved his life. He eventually lived to the ripe old age of 89 before passing away of natural causes December 31, 2003. Sheridan often thought back on how he had survived, and the circumstances of his savior's rather strange discovery. (Oliver, 2004)

GREAT LAKES LIGHTHOUSES

Like the Mediterranean of ancient times, North America's Great Lakes are heavily traveled. The freighters of these inland seas carry many raw materials and finished products, and are vital to the economies of Canada and the United States (Roberts & Jones, 1996). Because the Great Lakes are notorious for churning waters and perilous storms, strategically placed lighthouses have played a key role for many, many years.

One time I spoke with a woman who had taken a most curious journey visiting each lighthouse on the Great Lakes. "Why in the world did you do that?" I asked. "Because I wanted to find out what makes them strong," she answered. "But what good was that?" I queried. "Maybe no good at all," she responded, before adding, "I have a little story about my journey, and you may not want to listen to it at all." "Go ahead," I said. "Maybe your story is boring or of little import, but I'll pay attention the best I can." With that, she began her story.

"In your pocket you have your keys on a chain, a chain that lasts a year or two before it is lost or broken. Well, think of all the lighthouses as a sparkling constellation that ring the Great Lakes, a chain of navigational lights extending more than 1,200 miles that has lasted 175 years.

"The South Manitou Island Light Tower soars 104 feet into the blue skies above Lake Michigan. Its third-order Fresnel lens can be seen for 18 miles. The lens consists of hand-polished prisms fitted into a metal frame, and the prisms gather light and focus it into a concentrated beam. The South Manitou, like most light stations, requires regular maintenance and restoration by dedicated people.

"The Grand Traverse Lighthouse on Cat Head Point commands an estuary to Grand Traverse Bay. The station's first keeper was Philo Beers, who was also a deputy marshall. He was needed to fend off a self-proclaimed king whose religious raiders regularly tried to plunder the light station. Today Grand Traverse is a museum where visitors are offered a glimpse of late 1880s life in a lighthouse.

"Coast Guardsmen still live in the Point Betsie Lighthouse, where Lake Michigan's angry waters constantly erode the beach. Steel breakwaters and concrete abutments for an apron at the base of the tower, and during a storm you can feel the walls shake from the crashing waves. Last November, I was in Point Betsie during a relentless storm, and it was quite a visceral experience.

"One of the country's most scenic light stations is Big Sable Point, which is encased in steel plates for protection during storms. It was built on shifting sand dunes and of course requires ongoing restoration.

"In Indiana I saw the Michigan City East Pier Lighthouse. During a fierce storm in the 1930s, the keeper took refuge on the mainland. The three-day pounding of the waves destroyed the elevated walkway, which took several months to repair. In the 1920s, the keeper hurried his three daughters inside whenever the Chicago gangster, Al Capone, raced by in his speedboat.

"On the Great Lakes storms strike more suddenly, and with greater fury than storms in the oceans. The Split Rock Lighthouse in Minnesota was built after many ships were lost during a storm in November of 1905. Since there was no road to the cliffs high above Lake Superior, materials had to be shipped in and lifted up by a steam hoist. In 1939 the Fresnel lens was replaced by a 1,000-watt electric bulb that flashed every ten seconds, and which could be seen for 22 miles. Later on, a fog signal was added, and during heavy weather a deafening blast pulsated every 20 seconds. I heard it very clearly from 19 miles away.

"The lighthouse tenders, or boats that brought supplies to light stations, hold a special place in history. These tenders, like the *Hyacinth*, were named after flowers or trees. I spoke to a very old man who vividly remembered Sport, a spotted mongrel dog, who was a shipmate on the *Hyacinth* for 15 years during the twenties and thirties. 'He lived a sailor's life, and when the snow and ice made it impossible to sail during the winter, Sport yearned to be back on the *Hyacinth*,' said the old man."

By now I had drifted off, and at the same time had become rather absorbed in her story. When I realized she had finished, I realerted myself and asked, "Well, what made them strong? Was it the continuing restoration, the original materials, ships like the *Hyacinth*, or something else that I'm missing?"

She said, "I will answer you only generally and indirectly, in that you're on the right track, and that with the passage of time you will encounter the answer both directly and specifically, but not before you're ready."

For a moment I thought about reading up on lighthouses, or perhaps visiting some myself, but just then I was distracted by a profound dryness and thirst, which made some sense given my long immersion in water and ships during the story.

JOEY

The words spilled out—spontaneously and emotionally—of John Cappelleti's mouth in 1979. As he began to deliver his acceptance speech for the most prestigious award in collegiate football, the Heisman Trophy winner unexpectedly digressed from his prepared remarks. Cappelliti swallowed hard, glanced at his younger brother, Joey, in the front row, and exclaimed, "I want Joey to have this trophy. It's more his than mine because he's been such an inspiration to me."

Joey had suffered from leukemia for several years, and he was as surprised as everyone else by his brother's sudden digression. That speech has been made into a movie, *Something for Joey*, and ever since Cappelleti's speech has been emblematic of strength and courage. (Saraceno, 2003)

Aunt Anna, or "Tante Anne," as my mother calls her, was 39 in 1945 when the Russian army claimed their portion of Germany near the end of World War II. She was taken to a prison camp in Siberia where she was kept for two years. The harsh conditions caused her total deafness and other problems. However, she survived that experience, went on to live a productive life, and is still alive today at age 100.

Continuing Therapy with Jerry

Jerry was a good trance subject and responded with markers of deep trance: **ideosensory phenomena** (in his case, tingling in hand and feet), time distortion, **dissociation**, and amnesia. In fact, right from the beginning he demonstrated complete amnesia for all content. I installed an anchor, or circle, on his right hand, and instructed him to practice relaxation at home at least three times a week. After three sessions, his test scores went up. Sessions were then spaced out, and I saw him three more times over the next couple of months. These sessions consisted of talk therapy, **hypnotic ego-strengthening**, and one session of age progression. In his imagined future, he saw himself quite vividly: college completed, employment at an engineering firm, and happily married.

Clinical Comments

I saw Jerry for a total of nine sessions spaced out over six months. He has received an occasional D grade, but his grades have been mostly As and Bs. He was extremely proud of his performance, as was I. A few years later, he stopped by to say he had graduated. "I'll call if I need any help in grad school," he said. That was the last I saw of Jerry. I'll always thank him for showing me that even "psychologically normal" people may benefit from ego-strengthening.

How do we ever know if a client's improvement is a result of our treatment rather than a consequence of something else? Even in strictly controlled studies we never really *know* for sure. Would Jerry's grades have improved had I provided progressive muscle relaxation or CBT instead of hypnotic ego-strengthening? Maybe.

I believe the main factors were his *wanting* and asking for hypnosis, as well as his readiness. He had experienced a good deal of worry and stress over poor grades, and he was *ready* for a change. In many ways he was the ideal hypnosis client, as he evinced many hypnotic phenomena (especially amnesia), which I believe was key to his unconscious incorporation of the stories.

Chapter 3

Further Perturbations of the Unconscious

Clients who improve—or don't improve—can be seen through the lens of perturbation. In the case of Jerry (at the end of the last chapter), consciously—and unconsciously—he was stuck, and badly in need of perturbation. You may be thinking, "Hmmm, to perturb is to agitate or stir up. I don't want to upset my clients and make them worse." Well, you don't have to. If the client has money you can see him or her supportively for years. Your goal then is adjustment, not change; and both therapist and client can remain comfortable.

However if you can see a client for only a limited number of sessions, I suggest to you that perturbation is your best friend. Perturbation need not be complicated. In Jerry's case, metaphorical ego-strengthening gave him the nudge, or perturbation, he needed. With many clients ego-strengthening builds up, or boosts, so that you have both perturbed and done something therapeutic. However ego-strengthening can also serve as a behavioral probe. Let's say the first couple of exploratory sessions had elicited his wish for a magic bullet (e.g., "Just *make* me get better grades, I don't want to have to *do* anything."). Good, I want to find that out early. Or if an unresolved issue from his accident had surfaced, that's great because I need to find that out. For a more detailed discussion on techniques that perturb, see *Hypnotic Techniques* (Gafner & Benson, 2003).

In discussing volition, or the conscious control of action, Baars (1997) recalled the words of William James, who wrote about waking up one frigid morning in a room without a fire, and thinking, "I must get up." However, he continues to lie in bed, somehow unwilling to leave its warmth and comfort, in order to begin the duties of a busy day. At some point, though, a lapse of consciousness occurs, and the internal struggle of warmth versus cold, which had paralyzed him, ceases. The original idea, "I must get up," overtakes his *inhibitory struggle*, and he rises from his bed.

To Baars (1997), the James anecdote encapsulated phenomenological contrasts and demonstrates the experience of two physically identical actions, and how, as long as a conscious inner debate occurred about the pros and cons of rising, action would be inhibited.

Simple Rooms

I ask you now to think back on the "Simple Rooms" story in Chapter 1. It is used with a client who is "stuck," or, in other words, is experiencing a similar inhibitory struggle. The person in the story recalls all the possible ways to get from one room to another. Perhaps it gave you a feeling of uncertainty, or sense of disquiet when you read it? Or, maybe the story raised further questions. Certainly your impression was not "What a nice story," as it was not intended to be pleasant or enjoyable in any way. It is essentially devoid of hypnotic language. Why? Because its purpose is singular: to assist the person in ceasing an inhibitory struggle. In other words, it is designed to **perturb**.

So often in therapy the goal is not to correct a deficit, or to teach a new skill, but to help the person get out of a rut. In other words, to perturb them. "Simple Rooms" is the best story I know for perturbing someone who is stuck. I have relied on this story for many years, and it serves as one of my stock stories, like "Balloons" or "Greenhouse."

Incubation

You tell "Simple Rooms" to your client in trance, and depending on the degree of amnesia experienced, the realerted client may show a variety of responses, ranging from remembering nothing to "That was a very strange story." Most clients, when asked what they recall, say something like, "All I remember is something about rooms." In all my years of using this story, I have yet to hear a client say, "I recognize your undisguised attempt to perturb me."

The greater the depth of trance, and the more the client experiences hypnotic phenomena, like amnesia and time distortion, the more likely the suggestion will "take." A good response, then, would be a change in attitude or behavior—not immediately, but over the next couple of weeks. This duration is equivalent to response time after the delivery of a **paradoxical directive** in talk therapy.

This process is akin to putting a problem "on the back burner," or when, instead of choosing to make up your mind about something, you say, "I'll sleep on it." Psychologists call this process *incubation*. Now, lest we think we can make silk from a sow's ear, it is important that two prerequisites be in place for successful **unconscious problem solving** to occur. According to Blackmore (2004), these are: 1) the client must do the hard work of struggling with a problem and acquiring the necessary skills, and 2) you must leave the problem and engage in something else, as any conscious effort will prove counter-productive.

Just How Clever Is the Unconscious?

Erickson was fond of saying to people, "You are wise, but your unconscious is a lot wiser." If our clients are bright and articulate and we want to seed such a suggestion before beginning trancework, saying something like that might be highly therapeutic. But if your client is antisocial with an IQ of 85, I might not want to embrace any part of his mind, unconscious or otherwise. Since Erickson's death in 1980, some well-intentioned therapists have misconstrued the above quote and used it to rationalize the willy nilly-bombardment of the unconscious with all manner of suggestions, trusting completely in the client's omniscient unconscious to direct them in the service of therapeutic change. Such a practice is what Hammond (1990) called when-I-wish-upon-a-star therapy. Now, if you practice that way, you may not hurt anybody; however, there's a better way to go about it, and hopefully this chapter will give you some guidance.

What Science Tells Us

The fact that we engage in unconscious learning and perception is well established, something universally agreed upon by experimental psychologists. But what about unconscious problem solving? Claxton (1997) stated unequivocally that "intelligence increases when you think less," and he recommends that we build into our day regular periods of rest to nurture automatic problem solving. However, Kihlstrom (1996) was equally adamant when he wrote, "Your unconscious is stupider than you are." Greenwald (1992) also cautioned us about the limitations of the unconscious, and if you are convinced by his work you will throw "Simple Rooms" into the fire and go back to your tried-and-true CBT techniques. But don't start the fire just yet.

Paul Lewicki (1992) conducted various experiments on a variant of unconscious problem solving called the *nonconscious acquisition of information*. Subjects in these experiments ranged from university professors to preschool children. He concluded that "as compared with consciously controlled cognition, the nonconscious information acquisition processes are not only much faster, but are also structurally more sophisticated" (Lewicki et al., 1992).

Claxton (1997) noted that we may attain much better results with many of our tasks if we perform them *without the interference of the conscious mind*. He offers the example of the child who solves the Rubik's Cube through inattentive maneuvering, while the adult struggles in conscious frustration. For further reading on the fascinating field of consciousness, I recommend *Consciousness: An Introduction* by Susan Blackmore (2004).

What Can Therapists Do?

If you are an intuitive or creative person, let those talents serve you in therapy. If a Eureka insight surfaces while your client is talking, share it with him—right then! If you have a hunch that color crayons and paper should be employed in the day's session, go for it! And if any of this book convinces you to gear your practice toward that big bull's-eye called the unconscious . . . hey, I won't restrain you from doing so.

If you're reluctant, I respect that. I know plenty of very respectable clinical psychologists, as well as psychiatrists, social workers, and others, who do most of their therapy out of a manual, and whose idea of exotic unconscious process is the automatic thought.

Start with a story or anecdote. It's low cost, noninvasive, and potentially *very* beneficial. At the end of your CBT or medication check, you can add an anecdote:

Someone else *I see—she also has*	metaphor
depression *and is just about* your age—	
she, too, was stable on her meds and *one*	matching
time she reported that she had taken up a	linking
new activity, *which in her case was*	
walking. . . .	suggestion

You can't help but get in underneath the radar when you mention *someone else.* Contrast that with the commanding directive, "You need to get more exercise, and I want you to go for a walk every day." For sure, some clients will respond to authoritarian mandates. In my practice, when I come on strong, many of them will do the exact opposite. Whatever your approach, direct or otherwise, if it's important, *repeat it.* Repetition of key suggestions is vital in hypnosis, just as it is in conventional psychotherapy.

The word *and* is perhaps the most important word in psychotherapy because it *links* to where you want to *lead.* I use it often, and I usually pause half a second before delivering the suggestion. Within hypnosis, I'll pause longer, plus I'll say the same thing in different ways to reinforce it.

People in our workshops who get turned on to metaphorical approaches often progress from anecdote to story, perhaps an ego-strengthening story, and go on to using both techniques in formal hypnosis. At this point they see the need for a bigger toolbox, one that can accommodate the myriad possibilities for intervention. We have a story within a story, a story without an ending, and alternating stories (Gafner & Benson, 2003), to name a few, and all of them may produce unconscious perturbation. However, in this chapter we are concentrating on two things, **instigative anecdote** and **instigative story**, such as "The Turtle," which I first heard years ago from Brent Geary, and is composed here in this form by Sonja Benson.

THE TURTLE

In our experience, we have all known many kinds of animals, and perhaps even as children we wondered about what animal we might like to be. I'm not sure how this story started, but it may have had its origin in the mind of Milton H. Erickson, a famous psychiatrist in Phoenix who was clearly a very independent thinker and who thought about the idea of acceptance. Dr. Erickson suffered with polio early on, and the effects were with him throughout his life. Since then, people have imagined many things about his life. Some have thought that all this has to do with recognition of something, while others have wondered if it has to do with simple endorsement of what is, while others have entertained the notion that approval of current circumstances may have more to do with acknowledgement of the status quo. At any rate, words are just words, and stories are mere stories, all of which may or may not have any significance to anyone's situation.

Just the same, we need to know that turtles—yes, turtles—didn't always have a shell. At one time, long, long ago, the turtle was just another soft-bodied animal that lived in a different kind of house. One day, all the animals in the animal kingdom decided to throw a feast for the gods to thank them for the good fortune they had received. All the animals came to the feast to celebrate—all but the turtle, who chose to stay at home.

It was a grand party and there was a host of exotic and tantalizing food at the banquet table. About an hour into the event, the gods, who were very appreciative, announced that they would grant each animal a special wish. All the animals were very happy when they left.

On the way home, one animal stopped by the turtle's house and asked him why he didn't attend the party. The turtle, who never minced words, stated that he never attended parties and that he simply liked to stay at home. However, when the turtle learned that the gods had granted one special wish to all the other animals, the turtle hurried as best he could over to the banquet hall and asked the gods if he, too, could be granted one special wish.

The turtle said, "Please grant me speed because I am such a slow-moving animal." The gods then asked him why he didn't attend the party and the turtle answered, "Because I like to be at home."

The gods then gave the turtle a hard shell on his back so he could always be at home wherever he was. And that's how the turtle got his shell.

Why Are Some Hypnotic Stories So Vague?

With many of these stories, the meaning is vague, or open to various interpretations. Generally, the *less* specific, didactic, and directive a story or anecdote, the *more* likely it is to perturb. Let's say you're interviewing a client, asking him point-blank questions to elicit needed information, and he just offers vague answers. You try harder, and he waxes even more vague. So, taking a different approach, you *join* with him at an unconscious level and say, "Yes, it's becoming more clear to me now, like when you can finally see that penny at the bottom of a mud puddle, or when you can make out a familiar figure in a dense fog." And, reflexively, he suddenly coughs up the straight forward answer you were seeking. The formula would be *vagueness + vagueness = clarity*. Try it some time, it's uncanny how it can work.

I always explain what I'm doing—e.g., "Okay, today in trance I'll be telling you a story. This is directed at your unconscious mind to help free you from (the problem), and people customarily respond in various ways, and sometimes not at all." If I'm going to be asking unconsciously directed questions, that, too, is explained ahead of time. You don't want to spring any surprises on your client. The worst thing you can do is an age regression or some other technique without first getting their okay.

Instigative stories and anecdotes communicate, on an unconscious level, *respect* for and *acceptance* of the person your client is, with all his blind spots. It's like giving him a blank slate to write on, and he can write something or nothing, it's up to him. I have found that when offered such freedom many people will opt for change. It's akin to that oh-so-liberating suggestion, *not knowing/not doing*: "Nothing to know, nothing to do, no one to please, don't even have to think; and all you have to do is breathe, and you don't even have to listen to the words. . . ."

We have used "The Turtle" to promote acceptance of one's life decisions or problems, to be "at home" with one's self, or to stimulate wonderment or unconscious search. As such, its meaning, or meta-message, may be more obvious than many of our other stories. Contrast "The Turtle" with this story.

PHANTOM FLOWER

The story was told to her often as she was growing up, and after much telling and retelling, she may now remember only mere fragments, though important elements remain etched in her mind. After she was born, her mother exclaimed, "Look at her belly button! She has both an innie and an outtie." "By Jove, she does indeed," said the old doctor. "In all my years I've never seen one exactly like that."

At first they called her Outtie, then Innie, and said silly things like, "You'll drive an Audi when you grow up," or, "You'll be part of the in-crowd." But a compromise was reached and the name Ina ended up on her birth certificate. "Ina rhymes with China," said her father, and she went through life known as Ina Outlander, a name people tended not to forget.

Now, Ina was a dreamer, as well as an explorer, and though memory was not her strong suit, she showed up for work each day as a tour guide at Inland State Preserve in south Florida. It was mid-morning and Ina was leading some orchid seekers through swampy shadows. It was a dim, gray-green world in the preserve. Shafts of sunlight penetrated the canopy. "This water looks like weak tea," said a man on the tour. "What you will see today depends on the angle of the light and openness of the canopy," Ina said absentmindedly.

"Where are we now?" asked a woman. "I think I'm lost," said another. Ina responded: "We've come farther than you think, and we're now deep within this 5-by-20-mile channel. Over the centuries, organic material has collected here, and now it's like a big valley filled with sponge." The group sloshed up and down in their hip boots in the semi-darkness, keeping an eye out for things they knew inhabited the preserve: pygmy rattlesnakes, alligators, manatees, Everglades mink, panthers, and black bears.

"To answer your question, sir, I'm lost too, but we always find our way out," said Ina. You never want to come in here alone, or at night. Let's move on, we have orchids to find!" she exclaimed. Ina was keenly aware of orchid poachers, and that's why she always used indirect routes. "No way any of them will ever find their way back there," she liked to tell her boss.

Before setting out she had told the group that Inland Preserve has more orchid species than any place in the U.S. Among all the species was the legendary ghost orchid. "When will we see our first ghost orchid?" asked a man. "We'll spot one soon," said Ina over her shoulder. "They are as rare as they are elusive," she added. "How many miles have we come?" asked a woman as she caught her breath. "I recalled before, but not presently," answered Ina.

They plunged deeper into the preserve. "Precisely how many orchid species live in here?" asked a man. "I remembered a few moments ago, but not presently. Faster now!" said the guide. The group trudged on with renewed determination. Soon, Ina stopped abruptly and pointed down to her right. They followed her hand, and then she made half a turn and gestured down near her feet. "Behold, the ghost orchid." There it was, leafless with bright spindly petals on slender spikes, the flower that appears to float in the air. No one spoke. The shadows lengthened and the whir of night insects was beginning. Ina spoke in a mere whisper. "It blooms sometimes in June, some years in July, and this year in August. It's pollinated by the sphinx moth, which I've never seen."

They gazed at the phantom flower for what seemed to be several minutes. Ina's words penetrated the sounds of approaching night. "Who will remember this spot?" she asked. No one answered, and soon they were on their way out of Inland Preserve.

More on Metaphor

This last story is not didactic, at least on a conscious level, and it's not exactly *hypnotic*, as words like *explore* and *discover* aren't italicized. Instead, it is intended to absorb attention in the story, and after that the meaning is left up to the listener. She can respond however she wishes. When I read an article (Mclintock, 2003) on a Florida preserve where orchids grow, I thought, "Wow, I can make an instigative story out of this."

Employing these and similar stories and anecdotes in trance is my number-one way to instigate or provoke—to *perturb*— a client who is stuck. I see so many clients who find themselves in a rut. They don't know whether or not to stay in a relationship, they can't let go or forgive, and they have so many other problems. They have had CBT and medication. They have been supported by friends and family, and nothing has changed. Is theirs a *conscious* problem? Of course not. They are *stuck*, the problem resides in the unconscious, and our job is to perturb it.

Siegelman (1990) reminded us of the importance of listening for a client's metaphor, as often it represents the need to articulate a pressing inner experience, and clients may not be able to express it any other way. However, not all metaphors flow from meaningful affect. Some clients, especially older ones, rely on "dead metaphors" that, instead of facilitating understanding or new information, serve to keep them stuck. Koetting and Lane (2001) advised us to listen for such well-worn, cliché metaphors—e.g., "argument is war," or "I'll never get to first base with my father," as such metaphors may herald resistance in therapy. They advise countering them with similar language—e.g., "Let's discuss how you can step up to the plate with your father."

I remember working with a client, Misty, who was gradually taking on new behavior and expanding her role. She said she felt like a butterfly emerging from the cocoon. I then matched her experience with an elaborate story about Monarch butterflies, their *strength and endurance*, how those wispy little things migrated from Mexico City up to Canada and back again. I thought I had a great story until she reminded me that several *generations* of Monarchs are required to make that trip, not just one. I made the same mistake when, with an agrarian refugee from Guatemala, I used the iceberg to represent the unconscious. He had no idea what in the heck an iceberg was.

Research on Metaphor

We must look to the communication literature for most studies on metaphor. In an exhaustive meta-analysis of the persuasive effects of metaphor, Sopory and Dillard (2002) concluded that:

1. Metaphorical messages are more persuasive than literal messages. So, when Josef Stalin said you have to break some eggs in order to make an omelet, we got the point. He didn't have to spell out how he killed millions of his countrymen. Or, when I scold my interns for running over 50 minutes, and buttress it with a metaphor like, "Mussolini made the trains run on time," they ask, "Who was Mussolini?"
2. The sooner the metaphor is introduced, the more persuasive it is. This would seem to support our practice of asking a couple early in the session how the *wall* is that they've constructed to regulate intimacy, and then returning to it near the end: "Well, I wonder if we've loosened any bricks in that wall today?" Also, perhaps it supports seeding. For example, I mention *freedom* and *loosening up* before trancework, relate the "Balloons" story during hypnosis, and at the end of the session reinforce *letting go* with discussion and conscious integration.
3. The more *novel* the metaphor, the more persuasive it is. So, this would mean that my tired and hackneyed metaphors about roads and plants are less likely to have an impact than more novel ones. Well, my burden is heavy, what can I say?
4. Extended metaphors are less persuasive than nonextended ones. Now, this definitely flies in the face of clinical practice, especially my own. Think of Erickson's long metaphors about learning to walk, and write the alphabet, and other developmental markers, as a way to teach them how to respond in trance. Sonja Benson's

favorite induction is "The Road" (Gafner & Benson, 2000), which embeds various suggestions for trance, all within an *extended metaphor* about driving down a road.

Glucksberg's (2003) research showed that we understand metaphorical meanings as quickly and automatically as we understand literal meanings, and aside from metaphor, Frey and Eagly (1993) demonstrated that *vividness* can undermine the persuasiveness of a message. This certainly supports the practice of permissive practitioners of hypnosis, where we let the client fill in the blanks. So, instead of saying, "I want you to imagine yourself in a small wooden boat on a crystalline lake on a warm, sunny day," you say, "You can imagine yourself in a very comfortable place, and I don't know if that's inside or outside, if it's daytime or nighttime, . . ." So, throw that *Roget's Thesaurus* in the fire; you don't need it.

Angus and Korman (2002) concluded a study of tape-recorded therapy sessions, noting that metaphoric expression in verbal discourse is so prevalent and automatic it essentially becomes invisible. They also concluded that changes clients undergo in therapy will be evinced as metaphor, and that the co-creation of elaborated metaphor themes by client and therapist is a marker of good therapeutic outcome.

Clients and Their Metaphors

Working together with your client on a metaphor can be rewarding in a number of ways. For one thing, it encourages active participation in treatment, and, selfishly for us, it breaks up the tedium of therapy. Discussing and reworking and transforming a metaphor—e.g., the *weight* of depression on my mind, is one thing. There is a whole lot else you can do with metaphor in hypnosis and out, such as altering the outcome or some aspect of a recurrent nightmare; mutual storytelling; and the amplifying the metaphor technique (Gafner & Benson, 2003), to name a few.

Bill O'Hanlon has elucidated pattern interruption better than anyone else in the field, and this is very germane to client metaphor. In a *Brief Guide to Brief Therapy* (Cade & O'Hanlon, 1993), the authors list 15 various ways therapists can help alter a pattern, or, in this case, a metaphor: alter the duration; change the frequency; alter the time, day, week, location, intensity, etc. When you change even a small aspect of a client's metaphor, get ready for change! Practitioners call this list "O'Hanlon's list," and I use it as a handout for clients in my anger management group. As we discuss altering one small aspect of their anger instead of "controlling it," I can see the wheels turning in their heads, as it is a whole new way of seeing things, and, as such, instills hope.

Chrissie and Her Stepfather

Bert, age 34, attends the initial session of family therapy with his step-daughter, Chrissie, age 14. They are stark contrasts to each other. Bert, a software engineer, is neat, dressed in shirt and tie, while Chrissie is dressed in the Goth style of the day—black clothes, black-dyed hair, garish makeup, looking harsh and defiant. I see them together briefly, and Bert offers a brief synopsis: Chrissie has poor grades and has been ditching school. She came home drunk one night, and she is rude and disrespectful. I ask Chrissie to comment, and she shoots me a hostile, just-drop-dead look.

Chrissie then is asked to go to the waiting room while I get more history from Bert. He has been the stepfather of Chrissie for nine years. Chrissie's mother, age 39, refused to attend, telling her husband, "You do something for a change. I have to work." Despite his preppy appearance, Bert is an environmental activist. He says Chrissie formerly liked the outdoors, "but now she just likes her friends. She hates everything. I don't know how much more of this I can stand," he adds.

I then see Chrissie alone. I offer her some pretzels and candy from a dish, and try to engage her on friends, music, anything, but she just stares at me. Finally she hisses, "Save your breath, asshole!" I think, "I *do not* need this." More profanity follows. I take a deep breath and regard this especially toxic teen. (My forte is not teenagers, and it is the summer when I have no interns to take the case.) As she seemed less hostile with Bert present, I ask him to return.

I say, "Bert, all of this is stressful for everybody, and relaxation can be helpful, just as *exploration* can be useful. I want you to go along with me as we do some hypnotic *exploration*. You up for that, Bert? Good, just sit back and I'll read you this little story, and, Chrissie, you can lean forward and observe, sit back and relax, or just let your mind wander." I don't yet know what I'll do with the case. At least I can observe them while I read a story.

EXPLORING THE CANYONS

As a child, Bert, you may remember exploring, in a closet, in a back yard, perhaps in a real forest or in a woodland of your imagination. *Explorations*, of course, occur later on in life, a deep pondering of this, a diligent search into that, recognizing that some *explorations* continue for many years.

John Wesley Powell's 1869 expedition through the canyons of the Green and Colorado Rivers was the last great exploration of the continental United States (Powell, 1987). But unlike expeditions elsewhere, Powell's had no imperial purpose. He was not out to clarify boundaries on a map, or to shut out rivals, or to plant crosses or flags. Powell's expedition had a sole and pure purpose: to *explore* territory within a 300-mile canyon. Powell and his companions had no idea that this "canyon" was really a chain of canyons a thousand miles long.

This exploration had no official funding or sanction, unlike that of Lewis and Clark. In fact, Powell, who had lost one arm in the Civil War, funded much of it himself. His party included restless mountain men, drifters, and seekers of adventure and gold. Powell told them, "Our purpose is to *discover*. We will observe, map, and comprehend. Then we will *find out* and we will *know*." The expedition came to be known as the Powell Survey.

Bert's eyes are now closed and he has drifted off very nicely. Chrissie continues to fidget. I decide to stop the story right there. I tell Bert I'm about to count from one up to five, and then he can open his eyes. Now Chrissie is fidgeting even more, and finally she bursts out, "This is *total* bullshit." But Bert is unfazed, and as he starts to speak I expect him to report on an image or sensation or idea. However, with his eyes still closed he launches into his own story, which went something like this:

Bert Speaks, Chrissie Listens

> *I remember it quite vividly . . . it was the middle of March, 1989, and we set out on a mission of extreme importance. There were six of us, five alive and one not, and we began down the road. . . .*

Bert pauses for maybe a minute. Chrissie's mouth is agape and her body cataleptic. My rather short story has ended, but I collect myself and ad lib a continuation:

> *Powell's journey is now well known and forms an important part of American history. However, as we know with many stories, the map is not the territory. . . .*

Chrissie spews out more hostile words: "Just what's *that* supposed to mean?!" It's good to know she's finally paying attention. I continue, borrowing some material from another story.

> *A previously unpublished account of the expedition was found in 1950 among the papers of Dr. Hull Clark of Saint Somnambulus College in Canada. Included in his account were long-lost wood engravings of the Powell survey, which were recently authenticated by Lankton and Erickson, Inc. These wood engravings clearly delineate the labyrinth of canyons, Indian tribes, and flora and fauna. . . .*

Now, Chrissie jumps in again. "This is total horse shit!" she exclaims. I look at my watch. We're out of time. "Can we continue this next week?" I ask lamely. Chrissie is about to object, when her stepdad opens his eyes and says, "Yes!" Soon Bert is trailing his daughter down the hall. I wonder what I've gotten myself into. And I'm late for my next appointment.

Keep Them Coming with a Good Reframe
If you see couples and families in your practice, you know the mere fact of an appointment can provoke a crisis. People don't look forward

to facing their unhappiness, and often they cancel or just don't show up. A primary goal of the therapist, then, is simply to keep them coming until they can see some benefit from therapy. Being competent and dependable, and helping them feel like they are in good hands, can help, as can well-targeted reframes, as well as stories and anecdotes.

According to Shoham-Salomon and Rosenthal (1987), of all the techniques and interventions we have at our disposal, the *most healing measure is the reframe*. We can wrap a positive connotation around virtually any behavior, issue, or problem, and in so doing neutralize negative affect and show understanding. Call to mind predominant values shared by people, such as caring, honor, strength, love, protectiveness, duty, and so on, then apply a reframe that "fits." I confess that I was distracted and thrown-off that first session with Chrissie and her stepdad, and forgot to apply a reframe. However, had I done so, I would have zeroed in first on Bert, as he *cared* dearly for his family and showed *strength* and *resolve*. Together, Bert and Chrissie could have been told that the family had obvious **resilience** and *flexibility* in difficult times.

Chrissie is harder. Would I be missing the mark if I said she *cares* about her family beneath her harsh exterior? Maybe. You never know until you try. If you don't connect you'll know immediately, because they'll signal this nonverbally. Could I comment to her that she *cares* deeply about her clothes and makeup to look the way she does? Maybe she'd see that as banal or insipid. Or, that she has *courage* to venture into this arena of family therapy? I know that if I had to sit in a room with her and her friends I'd need more than a good reframe to want to go back again!

Bert Continues His Story
There is less negativity the next time Bert and Chrissie return. I start out with them together, and Bert reports that Chrissie has been attending class most days, and has been home at night. "Do we want to continue where we left off last time?" I ask. "Yes," says Bert, as he cranks up the footrest on the recliner. Chrissie has a bored look on her face. I begin my hypnotic patter with a conversational induction. I finish the "Three Lessons" story (Appendix 4) and wait to see if Bert will chime in. He does:

His name was Ed. Oh, how we loved Ed . . . and we were out there in the desert, four of us and Ed's body . . . searching for the place he would spend all eternity. . . .

Chrissie exhales deeply and says, "Here we go again with Edward Abbey. He made me read all his books."

We buried him there . . . poured whiskey on him like he wanted . . . the most beautiful place in the world . . . and only a few of us know where it is. . . .

He went on with something about walking through Glen Canyon before they flooded it to make a lake and recreation area. I now was getting a strong sense of melodrama from them both.

I **realerted** Bert, who now had tears in his eyes. We were almost out of time again. I encouraged continued progress and we made an appointment for three weeks. "Bert, tell your wife she's invited next time," I said.

There is a lot of lore in the southwest about environmentalist and writer, Edward Abbey, who *did* die in 1989, and who authored books like the *Monkeywrench Gang* and *Desert Solitaire*. In the Department of Veterans Affairs you occasionally see people who are legends in their own mind—e.g., "I was a Navy seal but because of our secret ops the records were destroyed." Bert's and Chrissie's case was in the early 1990s, so Bert would have been about 15 when Glen Canyon was flooded in the early 1970s, and 33 when Abbey was secretly buried. Nevertheless, I didn't believe him for a minute. My impression was that he told his story to impress his daughter.

The next time, he came with his wife. Sally was ten years his senior. Both noted that Chrissie had "really shaped up a lot." They denied a marital problem, which I would have bet on. No more therapy was wanted or needed. Bert's story had cured his daughter. (Ever since, I've wished I had queried Sally about her husband's story even though it was immaterial to therapy.)

Letting Go of Bruxism

Cynthia, age 40, divorced and with no children, had taken various medications for bruxism, and had tried dental appliances. She had headaches during the day and she tossed and turned at night. She was bright, articulate, and accomplished; however, she was very tense, ruminative, and over-controlling. I knew immediately my job was to help her to let go. This required using the confusional **mystifying induction** (see Appendix 5) to get her to respond. The mystifying induction is one I reach for to counteract unconscious resistance, or if the client is having difficulty going into trance. After that, I told her some **instigative anecdotes.** (Additional instigative anecdotes are listed in the Appendices.)

THOMAS EDISON

Many inventors had to overcome skepticism and cynicism. Thomas Edison was told that the phonograph had little commercial value, and that the telephone would never replace the telegraph. In the time of silent movies, Harry Warner of Warner Brothers once remarked, "Who the hell wants to hear actors talk?" In 1977, the president of Digital Equipment Corporation stated, "There is no reason anyone would want a computer in their home." (Chowder, 2003)

COPY MACHINE

In 1938, Chester Carlson got tired of making copies with carbon paper, and came up with a method to make copies automatically. The IBM company first scoffed at his bulky machine, but he persisted, and the rest is history. (Chowder, 2003)

RED-CROWNED CRANE

Red-crowned cranes in Japan might have become extinct in the bleak winter of 1952 had farmers not saved them with gifts of grain. (Ackerman, 2003)

LOST IN PLAIN SIGHT

Recently, in a major antiquities museum in Egypt, the director stumbled on some bundles stored away on a shelf near a busy work area. It was a magnificent archeological discovery! Later, contemplating his find, he thought, "They were actually *lost in plain sight.*" (Hawass, 2003)

BREADSACK

It was John Muir's habit to let his breadsack roll downhill before him, thus producing the crumbs he enjoyed with tea for his frugal meals. (Teale, 1982)

I had set up finger signals with Cynthia, and after delivering them, I asked for unconscious acceptance of the metaphors. She responded affirmatively, a very good prognostic indicator, and over the next three sessions I gave her these three stories. She let her yes finger lift when I asked for unconscious acceptance of them.

MADISON'S LOSS

When Madison was a young girl, she was always losing things. Her parents would tease her, saying that she'd lose her head if it wasn't attached. Since Madison was particularly worried about *losing* her most favorite things, she learned to *hold tightly* to those things most dear to her. She remembered thinking all the time as a child, "I don't want to lose my head." Now, as an adult, just thinking about losing things made her heart jump and her hands sweaty. At moments when she'd least expect it, a familiar voice came into her mind: "*Madison, just let go and enjoy life.*" She found this voice very comforting indeed.

She thought a trip to the beach would be good. While there, her son, Jordan, wanted to take a bucket of sand home with him. Jordan held that handful of sand tightly in his little clenched fists. Jordan didn't let go of the sand until they were halfway home, but she just figured that sand on the front seat of the car was a small price to pay for a fine day at the beach.

The next day, Jordan wanted to fly his kite, and even though the wind was strong, he learned, through trial and error, that he could indeed *control* the kite with *a firm hand*, but only if he held it *loosely*. (Sonja Benson, personal communication, 2003)

TOOTHPASTE

There are many things that we do day in and day out, often with little variation of any kind. For example, many people go to bed each night at approximately the same time, and then they become accustomed to getting up at about the same time in the morning. Occasionally these things can become rather monotonous and boring, or else these routines become so automatic that we don't even pay any attention to them. We do certain things before bed, and we do certain things after getting up, much of it really not very noteworthy.

Now I heard about this woman—Dorothy, was her name—and she came to Arizona from Iowa. The way I remember it, Dorothy was getting ready for bed, and she took a deep breath before the bathroom mirror, and realized how tired she was, and then she began to brush her teeth. She began to think about what she had to do the next day, and one of those things was planting a five-gallon-size tree she had purchased. It was a pine tree, the kind that thrives in hot, dry climates.

Now, as she continued to brush her teeth, with very slow, light, deliberate, and circular motions, she began to wonder about just how to plant that tree in the morning. It's interesting how people can more or less think of two things at the same time, and this is what Dorothy did, all in the matter of two minutes, although it seemed like many minutes had really passed.

She thought about brushing her teeth, and how she really didn't need to do it the same way every evening. She remembered television ads for toothpaste, how they put paste on all the bristles, but she only put a little dab in the corner, had done it that way for years. As for the tree, she was used to just banging it on the ground before pulling it out of its container. It usually came out just fine, the firm root ball intact, ready to stick into the hole in the ground. She wondered if this was one of those trees in a pot that had no taproot. If so, she would need to work the soil around the tree in every direction in order to encourage lateral growth. Certainly, numerous roots growing out were better than one root plunging deep. More nutrients could be taken in from the soil as these lateral roots anchored the tree to the earth in all directions. I've always wondered how deep a central taproot can penetrate anyway, given the rock-hard layers beneath the desert surface. At any rate, the backyard soil was pretty soft beneath Bob's woodpile over in Indian Hills.

But if she tried dabbing the toothpaste on a different part of the bristles, that would represent quite a departure for her, and so would just yanking the tree out of its container without hitting it on the ground first. After all, intact root ball or clean teeth, they were kind of the same thing anyway.

She continued the slow circular motions, not even seeing herself in the mirror, and she entertained other ways to get that tree out of its container. At the same time, she thought of curved toothbrushes, children's toothbrushes, and even those rather odd-looking ones, but weren't they for cleaning dentures?

A small shovel would slide smoothly in between the soil and the container, but a big shovel might do the job faster, if she was in a hurry, and whenever she purchased a toothbrush she had a choice among soft bristles, medium bristles, or hard bristles, which reminded her of the question, "Do you want to go into light trance, moderate trance, or deep trance?" What she selected was what she got, and it was always curious how a person could imagine and wonder about trees and brushes at more or less the same time.

GRINDING CORN

Someone was telling me something one time, and during that time, time seemed motionless, as if it, too, was just waiting. During that time, I thought about trance, and it came to me that you don't need to have a translator to have a "trance-later," as silly as that might sound.

He told me a story, true or not, I don't know, or if I knew at one time, I have simply forgotten all but the salient details. The story had to do with an Indian tribe in what is now known as the Joshua Tree National Monument, in California's great Mojave Desert. The *Brux-not-asazi* tribe lived in that area for many years before disappearing without a trace in the early part of the last century.

They simply called her Girl, an Indian girl of 11 or 12, who worked industriously grinding corn with the women of the tribe. Her daily output was quite remarkable in that she regularly ground enough corn for several families. The women marveled at Girl's strength and perseverance, and believed that she no doubt possessed a special gift in addition to her obviously powerful hands, arms, and back.

However, there was a problem with this remarkable girl. It turned out that she not only ground corn during the day, but she insisted on also grinding corn well into the night. Grinding corn was in her daydreams and night dreams as well, and she typically slept but two hours a night.

In the eyes of the others, Girl's activity upset the natural order of things, and one evening her mother instructed her to report to the medicine woman's house for special counsel. Once inside, the girl fell into a deep, deep sleep. In her dream, a barely audible voice whispered,

"J-u-s-t g-r-i-n-d c-o-r-n

d-u-r-i-n-g t-h-e d-a-y."

She drifted and dreamed for what seemed like many hours, and then the whisper returned:

"J-u-s-t g-r-i-n-d c-o-r-n

d-u-r-i-n-g t-h-e d-a-y."

Girl's mind was in a fog when she awoke in the morning. However, her body felt profoundly relaxed, as if she had experienced an immeasurably deep and satisfying sleep, which, of course, she had.

Cynthia finally let go. Sure, she was still very responsible, but she was much less tense during the day. And at night she no longer needed her bruxism. Thinking back on that case, I believe that had I delivered the "Grinding Corn" story earlier in therapy it would not have been accepted by her unconscious. However, after tilling the soil first with the mystifying induction, then with instigating anecdotes, and finally with stories, she was ready to accept it.

Tummy Ache for More than Half a Century

It started routinely with a computer alert, indicating a consultation request, and was among ten other consults for relational problems and anxiety management. This request indicated that an 84-year-old man had been having abdominal pain for 56 years, and he suspected "psychological reasons as the cause." Furthermore, when the psychiatric nurse asked him if he had ever tried hypnosis, he eagerly remarked, "Let's do it."

At the time, I suspected it would be a difficult case, so I asked Eric B. Jackson, a psychology extern, to assist me. During the first session, we got to know Gus, a retired insurance salesman, who lived with his wife of 68 years. Life had changed for Gus a few months back when he had suffered a mild stroke, which had left him with depression and mild cognitive defects.

He strode into the office with confidence, sat down, and launched into his story. Life had generally been good to him until recently. As a result of the stroke he was having difficulty balancing his checkbook. Also, his abdominal pain was worse, something that had been thoroughly evaluated by doctors over the years. "It's all in my head. I know it is," he stated. He noted that this symptom began after his discharge from the army after World War II. He had experienced some gastrointestinal problems due to poor nutrition during his stint as a cryptographer in Germany, and while hospitalized, the army doctor had pointed to his stomach and pronounced, *"You'll always have a pain right there."*

We asked him if he believed in the unconscious mind, and he answered, "You bet I believe in the subconscious." He added that he also believed in "the power of hypnosis," though he had never been treated professionally with the technique. In the second session, we used a sound machine on "ocean waves" mode, along with an audio amplifier because of to his moderate hearing loss. Eric employed a conversational induction and a counting-down deepening. He was distracted during the procedure, moving his legs and often shifting in the recliner. During debriefing, he claimed that he had difficulty hearing us, even though the audio amplifier had always been reliable and extremely sensitive with other hearing-impaired clients. He stated, "I don't think this is going to work," and appeared very discouraged. "I don't want to waste your time," he added. He reported that his abdominal pain was a 5 on a 0–10 scale, the same score as when we began the session. We patiently listened to his concerns and encouraged him to return the following week.

Since we sensed some unconscious resistance, we offered strong **restraint** the next session. We told him that hypnosis wasn't for everybody, "and perhaps your subconscious mind isn't ready to approach this problem." He recoiled from this restraint with, "I'm as ready as I'll ever be." In keeping with a restraining posture, we reluctantly agreed to proceed with hypnosis the following session, adding, "The jury is still out on whether the time is right." We told him that we had failed to elicit a **naturalistic trance state**, when one becomes absorbed in something pleasant, like getting lost in a good book, or listening to music. He answered that he achieved such a state when he listened to, or even thought about, the music of the Big-Bands-Era Harry James. "Well," we told him, "hypnosis here is just like that, only, with a guide—two guides in your case—a person may drift off even deeper."

We began the following session by asking his pain score, which he noted was a six. We put away the audio amplifier and sat close, one therapist on either side of him, and employed the mystifying induction (Appendix 5) and the "Balloons" story (Appendix 4). Debriefing yielded total amnesia, time distortion, and a pain score of "one or zero." "We're starting to get somewhere, Gus," we told him.

At the next session he reported that his pain had remained at "about one" in the interim. We again used the mystifying induction, and this time elicited unconscious ideomotor finger signals, asking him to designate responses for "no," "yes," and "I don't know, or I'm not ready to answer yet," all on his preferred right hand. Once these were set up, we asked him, "Gus, we want to ask a question of your subconscious mind. Are you ready to let go of this problem? Taking as much time as you need, you may answer with one of your fingers." After several seconds the index finger on Gus's *left* hand twitched. Upon realerting, he was asked his pain score, and he said, "It's a one or a zero. I don't think it'll be a problem anymore."

And it wasn't a problem anymore. He was seen two more times, and his pain score was the same. He asked for an audiotape to help him sleep, and we made him one. Three years later, Gus called and asked for a new tape because he couldn't "hear that one anymore." I made him a new one, which he now says "works just fine." His belly pain remains "one or zero."

The Greek Chorus

The Greek chorus, one of the most eminently useful techniques in psychotherapy, can also be used in hypnosis. This technique, which strengthens the hand of the lone therapist, employs an imaginary "supervision group" or collection of colleagues who offer divergent input on the case. This is a potently instigative technique. I reach for this technique often when a case is bogged down and going nowhere fast.

The Case of Madge: The Greek Chorus Applied Directly

Madge, age 85, was the caregiver of her husband of 60 years. She never loved him; in fact, she hated the old man, she said. But when she married him after World War I, she said, "I gave my vows and I'm not a women's libber," she proclaimed in her reedy voice. Her husband, Spud, sat at home in his tray chair (this was in the 1980s when older adults were commonly confined to these contraptions, which looked like big high chairs for children), banging his tin cup, demanding more prune juice. Madge gained comfort from glancing fondly at two photos on top of the refrigerator: one of beloved president FDR, and the other of Spud, a fresh-faced lad in his World War I doughboy uniform. They had no children and few friends. Life was closing in on Madge, and she couldn't stand it anymore.

We talked about the pros and cons of placing Spud in a nursing home. She remained ambivalent, wringing her hands over an extremely tough problem. We talked for a couple of sessions, and then we tried hypnosis for the goal of stress management. She responded well to induction and deepening and the "Three Lessons" story (see Appendix 4). The second session went like this:

> . . . now, Madge, I want to speak to the deepest part of you, way down in your subconscious self [subconscious was her term]. there was a woman I saw one time, and she also went deep into hypnosis, and I told her a little story about when I was trying to make up my mind about selling my car, a '53 Chevy—I remember it well because you could start it without a key—and I didn't know what to do, so I got some advice from five friends, yes, all five of them. The first one said, "Run an ad in the paper and just sell the darn thing." The second friend said, "Take it down by the border, leave the key in it, and just walk away. In no time it'll be down in Mexico, and you report it stolen." The third friend said, "No, keep that car and cherish it until it gives up the ghost. After all, it's been a fine, loyal, and devoted automobile all these years." [This suggestion produced a marked eye flutter.] The fourth one said, "See what the kids think. One of them might have room in their garage for an old Chevy." And the fifth friend said, "Advice is cheap. I'm not going to tell you what to do because one day soon you'll either fish or cut bait." [This produced a wan smile on her lips.]

I saw Madge again after one month. She had a spring in her step and looked as though the world had been lifted off her shoulders. "Well, he died," she remarked. "Oh, I'm so sorry," I replied. "When was the funeral?" I had not seen a funeral notice in the local paper. "He's just dead, leave it at that," she answered. Immediately I thought, "Oh, my gosh, she's killed him!" But she said, "Don't worry, there was no foul play. Just consider him dead, plain and simple."

I never saw Madge again. Several months later, I *did* see Spud in the obituaries. Had he gone to live elsewhere in the meantime, or had she just pronounced him dead in her mind? I never found out. All I know is that the Greek chorus had somehow perturbed her, and that she had evidently incorporated something from it to help herself.

The Case of Darren: The Greek Chorus Applied More Indirectly
Darren, age 26, was declared 100% disabled by the Department of Veterans Affairs for lupus, a condition that was first diagnosed while he was in the army. The condition waxed and waned, and when I first saw him he was essentially symptom free. His army career had been cut short and his wife had divorced him. Now, he had a fiancée who was strongly encouraging him to return to the workforce. However, he said, "Other vets are telling me I'm crazy to risk $2,000 a month tax free by trying to work." "The green poultice"—or issue of secondary gain. I knew that I had just put on my hip boots and waded out into cold water.

We hashed the issue out verbally for a few sessions. Then, I suggested hypnosis. In an exploratory session, I seeded *decide* and *making up one's mind*, and two weeks later I got a little help from my Greek friends:

> . . . that's the way, Darren, and when you're sufficiently deep in order to do your unconscious work today, let me know by nodding your head . . . good . . . and we know about yours and his and theirs and ours, and if it's yours, you say, "It's mine," don't you? I know I do if it's mine, and a person came to me once with an interesting problem. He'd lost $75,000 in Las Vegas, and had to sell his Internet business, which was called *Your Mine*. I forget just what he sold on the Internet, but it was doing real well when he was forced to unload it because of his gambling debts. "I sure miss my *Your Mine*," he lamented.
>
> Now, this guy was fortunate in that he had a variety of ways besides gambling to recoup his money, and he was indecisive about which direction he should take, so he assembled seven friends and asked them for advice . . . okay, now, Darren, take two deep breaths and let yourself sink even deeper and deeper, very good. . . .

The first friend shook his head and said, "I don't know what to tell you. You just have to make up Your Mine." "You mean *get it back?" he asked the friend. "Yes, make it up, get it back" answered the friend. The second friend said, "You need to go to the shopping mall and have people fill out a questionnaire to help you decide." The third friend said, "Tech stocks or mutual funds." The fourth one said, "Work hard. Be a clerk in a convenience store if you have to." The fifth friend was adamant: "I agree with Joe, who said that you* just have to make up Your Mine." *The sixth friend said, "You will make your fortune on Ebay." And as for the seventh friend, I really can't remember his words, but I do recall that he said them emphatically.'"*

Darren cancelled his next appointment and left a message on the phone. "I'm going back to school," he announced.

The Case of Melissa: The Greek Chorus Applied Even More Indirectly
Melissa missed her family in St. Paul, Minnesota. Her fiancé had just accepted a job in that city and he expected her to accompany him there. However, she had nearly two years to go in a doctoral program in Tucson, Arizona, and could not transfer elsewhere. She loved the Southwest and had originally moved there for her rheumatoid arthritis. "I hurt every minute I'm back home," she lamented. In fact, her body ached already just thinking about it.

We talked, and talked some more. She discussed the issue with her family and her minister, as well as with her fiancé. She prayed and meditated. Her body continued to ache, and now her grades were starting to suffer. We began hypnosis. After a couple of sessions of ego-strengthening, I tried an exploratory **age progression**. She responded well up until the point when she was asked to imagine herself in the future. She failed to signal when she could see herself "in the future, any time in the future when you can see yourself the way you want to be. . . ." Then she said, "Just nothing, nothing at all." She was realerted and praised for her strong effort. In an attempt to generate a meaningful response, I gave her an **ambiguous function assignment**. I asked her to "drive to Gates Pass in the early morning hours, park, take exactly 20 steps down the path, stop, look down to your left, and the first rock you see, right then something will come to you that can help you with this problem." She returned next week and said, "I'm totally worthless—that's what came to me."

I suggested that we give therapy a rest for a few weeks, and in the meantime, I consulted a colleague. She asked me, "Is this client really impervious to perturbation?" It got me thinking. To be so unperturbable is akin to being "treatment resistant," isn't it? No way, that's not Melissa. I slept on it. A week later, while I was driving to work, Bach's *Choral Fantasy* came on the radio, and just then I realized that I had forgotten all about the Greek chorus.

Melissa returned to therapy and she was hurting more than ever, both in body and mind. She was maxed out on oral pain medications as well as gold shots. I knew she responded well to direct suggestions for pain management, and so I led her through an imagery exercise where she immersed herself in a warm bathtub. I offered her the **not knowing/not doing** suggestion, saying it in different ways, and then I was quiet for several minutes. A *Bells of Arcosanti* CD played softly in the background. She fell asleep briefly. I asked for a head nod to show she was still with me, and she nodded.

> . . . *Melissa, beginning now, I want you to count backward, in your mind, very slowly to yourself, like 100 . . . 99 . . . , occupying your conscious mind with your counting, while I tell you a little story for your unconscious mind, which need not even pay attention if it doesn't want to. One time I saw a man—his name was Ollie—who was originally from Wisconsin, and he had lived in Tucson a number of years, and he was having considerable difficulty making up his mind about something. So, he assembled four of his friends so that he could seek their advice and counsel about his important decision. The first friend said, "Ollie, you need to . . . ." That's right, the friend spoke, and his lips moved, but the words were absolutely inaudible, which left Ollie feeling as though he was grasping a handful of air, a rather disconcerting experience.*
>
> *The second friend spoke in a loud and commanding voice, but as he started to speak his voice trailed into silence, which*

left Ollie scratching his head, perplexed and dumbfounded. Ollie later recalled, "This reminds me of a very bizarre dream," and maybe it really was a dream, I never found out for sure.

The third friend had a very bushy mustache and beard, and it was impossible to see his lips move, and it didn't help that the man stuttered and got stuck on his words and never really did get past the first two words.

And right now, Melissa, I want you to take two more deep, comfortable breaths and let yourself drift off even more . . . that's the way. . . ." And that brings me to the fourth and final friend. He did not speak at all, but Ollie gazed deeply into his eyes for the longest time . . . and as if reading the friend's mind, Ollie discovered the answer to his dilemma.

And now, Melissa, I'm going to count from one up to five, and by the time I say five you can reawaken as a body but not necessarily as a mind . . . five, four, three, two, and one!"

Melissa had the punch-drunk appearance of someone who is realerted with confusional suggestions. She had no recollection of the session's contents, and once I thought she was okay to drive, I bid her farewell and asked her to call me in a week. She left a message two days later. "I'm staying here. If he still loves me in two years, maybe I'll join him up there," she said. I called her, congratulated her on her decision, and offered some supportive sessions. "No, I'm fine. I've got a lot of studying to do," she said. I never saw her again.

Clinical Comments

There are many ways to perturb. You can do it by making an unconscious search, by asking questions like, "Does this symptom serve any purpose?" or, "By having this problem, are you punishing yourself for something?" In other words, you are plumbing the depths for an unconscious hidden agenda. This approach may or may not produce valuable data.

You can tell a story or anecdote, or use techniques like a story within a story, or a story without an ending. I like the latter technique, telling the client, for example, a story about someone searching for something. I stop near the end, and then launch into an unconscious search for a solution. Remember to set up finger signals ahead of time. A similar technique is to tell a story, or offer a long, boring induction, and suggest, for example, "Something will come to you that will help you with this problem when you are waiting at the stoplight at 22nd Street," or "*when* you see a flash of light." You then give suggestions for amnesia. This way *unconscious* processing proceeds with no *conscious* awareness and, importantly, you are tying the suggestion to an event that you know will occur. With this, your client must be able to achieve a deep trance in which amnesia occurs. Don't expect a solution to be generated right away. I usually schedule them back in two weeks because, if an answer surfaces, it usually does so between a week and two weeks later. The case of Melissa was unusual in that unconscious processing occurred within only a few days.

Many clients experience some amnesia in the normal course of trance. Here, you need to offer suggestions to foster even more amnesia. You can give a direct suggestion like, "Beginning now you can just forget anything I said here today." That is inelegant but works with many. I usually prefer indirection, such as, "I went to sleep last night and had a dream, and when I woke up I could remember very little of that dream." Confusion, like the realerting above, may produce amnesia. Distraction also causes amnesia. Erickson was known to realert clients abruptly and hustle them to the waiting room, or realert them and launch into a shaggy dog story.

Mainly, you want to remember those rooms. There really are innumerable ways to get from one room to another.

Part II

General Techniques for the Practitioner

Chapter 4

Getting Started with Hypnosis

If you're already practicing hypnosis you probably can recite material from memory or otherwise generate different inductions appropriate to children, adults, groups, or particular clinical situations. Therapists new to hypnosis most often begin by reading a script. At the start of his career Milton Erickson spent a great deal of time writing out and refining inductions as he committed them to memory. I read many inductions, stories, and anecdotes, as it's way too much for me to remember. As I'm reading, I look up frequently to monitor the client's response.

If you think you cannot remember the important elements that drive hypnosis—like **hypnotic language** and key suggestions—then by all means continue with your script. Gradually wean yourself from it. With a script or without, the more you practice, the more your confidence will grow, and this comfort and facility allows your clients to trust and let go.

Using Prepared Scripts: "The Rainbow Garden"

In Tucson, Arizona, people in the hypnosis training program are doing residencies in psychiatry or internships in psychology and other disciplines. We provide them with various books and scripts they can read as they begin practicing inductions and deepenings, first in the experiential training group and then with clients. However, we also encourage them to devise their own material and seek out other resources they may need. Still, I was surprised when one intern exclaimed, "Look at the great induction I found on the Net!"

She was working with a 9-year-old girl with school phobia, and after examining many possibilities, she had settled on a highly directive guided-imagery exercise called "The Rainbow Garden," a story she had located on Hypnosis.com. I checked the site out myself and found that it catalogs hundreds of scripts for virtually any problem. You don't have to register or pay. You just click on what you need and print it out for yourself or a friend. You may be wondering, is this like Turbo Tax, which is taking all that business away from accountants? Will clients no longer need a licensed mental health professional for hypnosis? Of course not. Those with requisite training know that applying hypnosis, like any assessment or intervention, is a small part of the treatment picture.

Directive versus Permissive Language

What are the differences between *directive* and *permissive* language in hypnosis? A highly **directive suggestion** is authoritarian, whereas a *permissive suggestion* offers some direction, but attends to the ongoing process in a general way that is more respectful. I will transcribe some portions of the Rainbow Garden exercise (www.Hypnosis.com, October 23, 2003). I will use the same image, but at intervals switch to using permissive, rather than directive language. Italics are mine.

In this exercise you will *practice deep self-communication. You* will *use relaxation and imagery to stimulate your imagination. By increasing your self-awareness, you* will *heal, balance, and center yourself.*   authoritarian language

In the following exercise, you may *begin to notice a number of interesting things. You* may *begin by finding a comfortable position in the chair, that's the way, and then you can take three deep, comfortable breaths.* . . .   permissive language

Today you may *discover how relaxation, along with your imagination, can help you communicate with the deepest part of you, and in doing so, relaxing your body, and stimulating your mind, we can only wonder about the possibilities. . . .*

With any script, you must both read *and* observe the client's ongoing behavior. However, when you download a script off the Internet, you just read it, the person responds, and then they are cured. If you read a script *and* you've had training in hypnosis, you know that you need to **pace**, or comment on, the ongoing behavior. If the client shifts nervously in the chair, suddenly opens her eyes, starts to talk, shows **abreaction**, or any of the countless responses clients have to hypnosis, the trained practitioner knows how to adjust her language to address the client's particular reaction.

Directive language is more economical. It is short and sweet and to the point. Remember: After the first session or two, once the person responds favorably to hypnosis, you will then need *fewer* words to induce trance. For many of my clients, I simply say, "Okay, sit back and get comfortable and I'll be quiet while you let your experience deepen. When you're sufficiently deep for today's work, let me know by nodding your head." As an example, let's continue with more of "The Rainbow Garden."

Use *the power of your mind to stimulate your imagination and increase your self-awareness. You* will *travel through the* authoritarian language *Rainbow Garden awakening many levels of human experience and come to know yourself in completeness.*

Some people respond well to *you will,* and some also enjoy new age jargon and imagery that provide all the details. Their imagination doesn't have to expend energy filling in the blanks. Contrast the above paragraph with the following, which begins to incorporate more subtle shifts in the hypnotic language.

An imaginary journey, through a place called the Rainbow Garden, may stimulate your conscious mind, or your unconscious mind, or both, or some other vital part of you, I can't not even begin to ponder or imagine the possibilities. One	suggestion covering all possibilities double negative
person one time, she explored . . . *and eventually* discovered *new knowledge about herself, or* was it *wisdom she gleaned?*	power words metaphor power words direct question

Hypnotic Language

Hypnotic language encompasses suggestions, like the **suggestion covering all possibilities**, and *power words*, like *imagine, story, notice,* and *appreciate*—words that are thought to stimulate a sense of wonderment. Hypnotic language and a permissive approach do not allow for *commanding* a person to do something. Instead, they invite people "in," and begin to absorb their attention. This is where effective hypnosis begins.

In "The Rainbow Garden," the listener is led to a "beautiful rainbow," and there at the end of the rainbow is a "beautiful pouch." Everything is just luminescent and gorgeous in the Rainbow Garden. Then, it gets even better.

> *Pick up this pouch and look inside and see there are many magical seeds. Magical seeds that you can scatter. Reach into your pouch and scatter the seeds . . . see a profusion of red blooming flowers . . . bright red poppies . . . smell the rich odor of red roses. . . .*

If I wanted to stay with a nature image at this point in the story, I might lead the person through a forest on a sunny day, maybe a rainforest in Washington, a pine forest in Georgia, and offer *permissive* suggestions.

> *. . . and you notice the trees, the sky above . . . and are those leaves or pine needles crunching beneath your feet? And the scent, is it fresh, earthy, or some other pleasant or interesting odor?*

What If the Client *Hates* Forests?

Unless you've been informed by the client that an image is suitable, you are taking your chances when you use highly-structured, one-size-fits-all images, such as a green forest, a crystalline lake, descending down a staircase, finding a "safe place" in a house, or any other such image. I've known many clients whose previous hypnosis included such approaches. One man told me how "the hypnotist" read him what was intended to be a pleasant induction about going out in a rowboat on a calm lake. "I had my eyes open the whole time and I came close to being sick," said the man, "and he didn't even see how I was reacting." It turned out that the man's daughter had drowned in such a lake.

That's why you have to constantly monitor the *ongoing response* of the client. In the end, that's all that really matters in hypnosis. I usually induce trance, introduce more hypnotic language along with **hypnotic phenomena**, and allow the client to fill in the details.

We can all imagine *many things, just as we can remember many things, pleasant, enjoyable experiences that are* absorbing, *or* engrossing, *or that simply* fixate attention *or invite* immersion *of interest, and I don't know if it was on the* outside *or* inside, *if it was* night *or* day, *or if you were* alone *or* with others, *and perhaps such a pleasant experience has already surfaced from your unconscious mind.* . . .

suggestion covering all possibilities

apposition of opposites

One person *I knew, he said, "Listening to music my mind drifts and dreams," and* another *remarked, "When I'm lost in a movie or a good book, my conscious mind attends to the story, while the back part of my mind dreams and drifts."*

metaphor

metaphor

When *that's there, a pleasant image, Linetta, taking as much time as you need, let me know by nodding your head.* . . .

implication

Communicating in Trance

With all the prompting, it is rare that the client will not have generated an image long before I asked for a head nod. But that's okay. Clients are usually way ahead of us. When we do **age regression**, and ask them to go back in time to a particular incident, they usually get back there *right away*, while we go on talking needlessly. The main thing is "the dance," where you and your client maintain an ongoing communication in trance. That way you avoid *presuming* whether they've generated a healing image, or experienced a tingling in their right hand, or any number of target responses.

Finally Leaving the Rainbow Garden

In the end, the Rainbow Garden (combined with some family therapy) was a tremendous success. The girl soon returned to school. Problem resolved, case closed. This is a good example of why I seldom stand in the way of an intern if she has a plan. If any of the trainees have something they *like* and have confidence in, this will translate as positive expectancy to the clients, and chances are they will improve.

The First Session

Let's remember that many clients new to hypnosis don't know what's expected of them, and that you're actually training them how to respond. Normally I don't do hypnosis the first session, but use the time to take a history, and do baseline measures, of anxiety, depression, or self-efficacy, etc., and see if they have any negative stereotypes about hypnosis that need to be dispelled.

If the client *wants* a directive procedure so that he *knows* when he is "put under," that's fine; however, if he has cervical pain, I know that I don't want to do an arm catalepsy induction. I want to elicit a **naturalistic trance state**; for example, helping him to "lose track of time" by imagining himself engaged in a pleasant activity, like driving a car, or listening to music. I let him know that hypnosis is much like that, except that he'll have a guide who will help him go deeper. This begins to address control issues. If I pick up on *any* **issue of control**, no matter how small, I make a careful note of this.

One of the main things I want to find out during the first session is whether the client views hypnosis as a "magic bullet" that will, for example, "make me not hungry anymore," or "make me forget" about something from the past. With these clients I weed out hypnosis right from the start. I usually recommend therapy other than hypnosis for them.

In the second session I start with a conversational induction, something like the alternative to the "Rainbow Garden," then do a counting-down deepening, and offer the "Three Lessons" story, whose meta-message is that people have resources within themselves to solve their problems.

Another way to start is employing Erickson's and Rossi's (1976) four-step procedure. Let's say you're beginning therapy with Bill, who needs help managing anxiety. You've taken down his history and you know that he is *proud* of his accomplishments to date, and he has mentioned his physical *strength* despite his difficulty managing anxiety. Furthermore, Bill has noted that he has a naturalistic trance experience when he becomes *absorbed* in driving his car. Keeping these factors in mind, you implement Erickson's and Rossi's four-step procedure: **absorbing the attention**, recognizing the current experience, associating suggestion to the current experience, and *utilizing* the client's values, orientations, and goals.

Beginning now, I'd like you to select a spot on the wall, or anywhere in the room, and when you've chosen a spot, let me know by nodding your head . . . and most certainly, Bill, you've had many obstacles thrown in your way, *and despite these roadblocks you've* endured *and* maintained, *and you'll* continue to notice *these difficulties as you* begin to overcome *them.*

1. absorb attention

2. recognize current experience

3. associate suggestion to current experience

And you can imagine the feeling of strength *and* confidence *as you find long-awaited pleasure in that* accomplishment.

4. utilize values

Now, let's do the same four-step process, but more indirectly.

Bill, I had another man in here one time and I explained to him how we customarily begin the trance process. I

metaphor

asked him to look around the room like this [therapist's eyes move up and down, left to right], *and to find a spot on the floor or ceiling, or on a wall, any place*	modeling
at all, and once he had selected a spot, he nodded his head [Bill finds a spot on the wall behind the therapist, and nods his head.] *And I said to him,* "That's the	1. absorb attention
way," *and then we proceeded.*	pacing
In your case, Bill, it seems that so far in life you've traveled *a truly arduous road,*	2. recognize current experience
and that road might be no less difficult in the future, as potholes will occur and maybe even a landslide will block the	
road. Nevertheless, I know the driver can begin to successfully *negotiate any obstacle that may occur.*	3. associate suggestion to current experience
People *standing beside the road, watching that driver go by, they may*	metaphor
notice a refreshing look of confidence on his face, and they can only imagine *how he will fare several miles ahead, as he*	power words
discovers *long-awaited pleasure in his* accomplishments, *and maybe even a renewed* strength *and energy.*	utilize values

An Advantage of Indirection

Much hypnosis practiced today is just the opposite of the above; in other words, it is highly directive. As I discussed in Chapter 2, it is helpful to know directive approaches so that you have them ready for the people who ask for them. However, if we sense resistance or ambivalence, a more indirect route may be more disarming. Furthermore, if all you've learned to date is directive approaches, it's good practice for you to try something different! (See discussion of direction versus indirection in Chapter 2.)

You may be thinking, "This sure is an economical way to induce trance." You bet it is, and the reason it works is because you know something about Bill. You've listened closely to his words, and you know where he's coming from and what he wants out of life. Let's say, however, that you've misinterpreted what he's told you, and you miss the mark. Then, he won't respond, and you'll know this immediately because his eyes will waver from the spot, and he'll probably shift uncomfortably in his chair. If this happens, it's okay, because next time you can try an approach that is less economical and a bit more indirect, but which also continues to pace and lead the client's responses.

Bill, I'd like you to select a spot in the room, anywhere at all, where your eyes can settle, and when you've chosen that spot, let me know by nodding your head . . . that's the way . . . and I know and you know that any person who looks at any one spot for any length of time, his attention becomes absorbed *in that spot . . . and sometimes that spot can become* hazy, *or* fuzzy, *and sometimes kind of a* tunnel vision *can develop, and sometimes a person's eyes* feel heavy *and then they might have a tendency to blink . . . [Bill's eyes blink],* that's the way *and those eyes can close any time they want [Bill's eyes close]* . . . that's good . . . *and now, Bill, you can begin to* notice feelings and sensations *in your body. In your case, I don't know if that will be a tingling or numbness in one hand or the other, or maybe a heaviness or lightness, coolness or warmth, or some other interesting sensation somewhere in your body. . . .*

1. absorb attention

2. further absorb attention

3. suggestion

4. pacing
5. leading
6. pacing

7. suggestion covering all possibilities

Connecting Corridors

Let's take a look at how a story can both induce trance and address a therapeutic target, which in this case is increasing the person's lateral thinking.

Benjamin and Louise were deep a discussion that had gone on for some time, so long in fact that neither could have guessed precisely how long *they had been there.* "Lost time *pleasantly spent,"* said Benjamin. *Just then Louise abruptly changed the subject.* "Benjamin, you hear the word corridor, yes, corridor, and *maybe you think of a hallway in school, a gallery or passageway,* inside *or outside."*

"Precisely that, but in more general terms," *he answered before continuing.* "For sure, encouraging the advancement of connections or passageways on the inside, laterally, up and down, *and in every* conceivable direction *is a very good* thing. "You know, then, where I was going with this," said Louise." Forget *all that talk about inside and consider for a moment the much larger outside, in the natural world, that is where scientists are already discovering the benefits of creating* mental/fundamental *corridors that connect isolated wildlife habitats."*

"Ah, the natural world *and* connec-tions. Broken *chains,* broken *promises come to mind. Please tell me more, and I'll* listen *closely* without allowing *my intu-ition or imagination to* stray beyond *the immediacy of the words,"* said Benjamin. *He sat back just then, closed his eyes, and* feigned *(or so it seemed to Louise) a profound and compelling contemplation.*

"Benjamin, *you know and I know of Florida's remote Pinhook Swamp, with its fast-growing slash pine and spiky palmetto weeds, regimented and crowded together*

time distortion

repetition

suggestion

suggestion covering all possibilities

restraint

misspeak

suggestion
lead away

restraint

distraction

due to years of logging and draining, devoid of natural corridors *of 150 years before. But imagine the same area restored with longleaf pine and fire-resistant grasses, no more toxic runoff from fires, a natural waterway restored.*

"A biologist said, 'Soon you'll be able to drop a minnow in the swamp 60 miles up north, and it will swim all the way down here, and keep on going.'*"*

"It's called connectivity," *whispered Benjamin.*

"Quiet, I talk and you listen, or just let the words drift mostly out and once in a while in," answered Louise, as she continued. "They acquire private land to make protected wildlife corridors. *In the Osceola National Forest they create a vital travel route for the Florida black bear, not to mention the flatwoods salamander and everything else in the ecosystem.*

"They even do this in cities, like Macon, Georgia, where they're building a 35-mile-long riverbank greenway that will go through the city and connect *wildlife refuges on either side."*

"Yes, connectivity," *uttered Benjamin, but she ignored him this time, glancing down now at her left hand which had fallen asleep.*

"Hemmed in wildlife populations can't migrate or replenish themselves in time of trouble, like drought or fire. . . ."

"The idea of corridors *is intuitively appealing and definitely intriguing," inserted Benjamin.*

suggestion

suggestion

suggestion

suggestions

"For you to think—not to say," added
Louise. *"Great Interior Park is* not on   restraint
your map, *Benjamin,   restraint and in
there are immense swaths of* connectivity,   suggestion
for grizzlies, wolverines, and linkage zones   suggestion
for lynxes, larynxes for voice foxes, *and*   lead away
other things you can conveniently forget   amnesia
beginning now."

"I'm back inside where I never left,"
answered Benjamin, *"and you can only
guess what I* may unintentionally   confusion
remember *from today's experience."*
(Snyder Sachs, 2002)

Three Components of a Hypnosis Session

For the purposes of this book, I divide hypnosis into three parts: 1) the induction phase, in which trance is induced, 2) a deepening phase, in which trance is deepened, and 3) the therapy component. I have often found that, for training purposes, therapists understand the process better if it is divided in this way. However, many practitioners of hypnosis make no such distinctions, and will, for example, have no formal deepening, and others will blend all three components into one long procedure that may include a story or ask for client response along the way.

Of course, the deepening could be many things, a counting-down from 10 to 1, a "period of silence during which you can let your experience deepen all by itself," or even a story, "and while you listen to this story you can imagine, just imagine, without any conscious effort, your experience deepening. . . ." Having a formal deepening affords you an opportunity to intersperse added suggestions, as well as to further observe client response while you prepare for the therapy portion. (For in-depth reading on both induction and deepening, please see *Handbook of Hypnotic Inductions* (Gafner & Benson, 2000).)

While both induction and deepening can be highly therapeutic in and of themselves, their primary function is to set up therapy, which can be many, many things. Considering what was accomplished last session, and the agenda that was set with the client for the current session, this component could consist of story, story within a story, story without an ending, or another application dealing with story; exploration around a specific topic or issue; *age regression* to a certain time or incident, perhaps preparatory to an *abreaction* and **reframing** procedure; **age progression** to an unspecified time in the future to retrieve imaginal mastery or competence; automatic writing or drawing; **ego-strengthening**; problem solving; and other approaches, to name a few. Many of these are outlined in our last book, *Hypnotic Techniques* (Gafner & Benson, 2003), and many of them are covered in the present volume (see Glossary). With all of these techniques, I strive to emphasize ongoing communication with the client, usually in the form of **ideomotor finger signals**, hypnosis as an adjunct to standard psychotherapy, and that we need to let the *client's response*, rather than the cleverness of the technique, be our guide.

Books to Read

The things that drive hypnosis are hypnotic language and hypnotic phenomena, such as **amnesia, time distortion**, and **dissociation**, to name a few. As you mention these things in an induction, deepening, or story, it is likely that the client will experience them. These phenomena are covered again in Part 3, in relation to particular disorders.

The definitive book on hypnotic phenomena is John and Janet Edgette's (1995) *The Handbook of Hypnotic Phenomena in Psychotherapy*. I wish this book had been available when I was starting out. Now, I consult it often. I have three copies of D. C. Hammond's (1990) *Handbook of Hypnotic Suggestions and Metaphors*, as interns and staff frequently consult this invaluable tome, which people fondly refer to as "the red book."

One of the most eloquent voices in the field for many years has been Michael Yapko. His *Trancework* (2003), already considered a classic, may be the best overall primer on clinical hypnosis. His *Treating Depression with Hypnosis: Integrating Cognitive-Behavioral and Strategic Approaches* (2001) is an absolute must for practitioners who treat mood disorders. An excellent feature of Yapko's work is to demonstrate how science can inform the artistry of hypnosis.

I believe that many of the truly excellent books on hypnosis were written in the 1980s. One such reference book is *Hypnosis: Questions and Answers* by Bernie Zilbergeld, M. Gerald Edelstien and Daniel Araoz (1986). Another is *Therapeutic Trances* by Stephen Gilligan (1987). Stephen and Carol Lankton have written many superb books, and a particularly profound and useful one is *The Answer Within: A Clinical Framework of Ericksonian Hypnotherapy* (1983).

The Letters of Milton H. Erickson by Jeff Zeig and Brent Geary (2000) is one of my favorites. For other texts by Zeig, see the References at the end of the book. And last but not least, let's not forget the works of Ernest Rossi and Dr. Erickson, also listed in the References.

I regularly read three hypnosis journals: *The American Journal of Clinical Hypnosis*, a publication of the American Society of Clinical Hypnosis; *Contemporary Hypnosis*, the journal of the British Society of Experimental and Clinical Hypnosis; and the *International Journal of Clinical and Experimental Hypnosis*, a publication of the Society for Clinical and Experimental Hypnosis and the International Society of Hypnosis. Another fine journal that I see less frequently is the *Australian Journal of Clinical and Experimental Hypnosis*. Newsletters can also keep you abreast of current events in the field. Two that I subscribe to are the newsletters of the Milton H. Erickson Foundation in Phoenix, Arizona, and the newsletter of the International Society of Hypnosis.

Chapter 5

The Therapist's Voice

In trance the client may communicate verbally or nonverbally, but the therapist communicates only with her voice. Hypnotic language and key suggestions drive hypnosis, but that vehicle goes nowhere without a good voice.

Developing Your Hypnotic Voice

In the hypnosis training program in Tucson, Arizona, one of the first things interns grapple with is their voice. Bob Hall, health psychologist, and I remind them, ". . . you have your *conversational* voice (sounding casual, with broad affect, and no great attention to enunciation), . . . your *therapeutic* voice (serious, even, narrower range of affect), . . . and then you have your *h-y-p-n-o-t-i-c* voice (in a hoarse whisper for effect)."

Often this is the first time interns examine how they come across to clients in general, and with something so specific like one's voice, the training starts to get very personal. Sure, they know they have to dress appropriately, not chew gum during therapy, and minimize the use of colloquialisms, like "You really rocked in trance today" or "That was awesome," when talking to clients many years their senior. Some young interns might speak in "Valley Girl," with inflection at the end of each sentence, or strangle words in their throat instead of enunciating at the front of the mouth. Also, many people need a reminder that if they rest their chin on their hand, hold their hand next to their cheek, or have a hand anywhere near their mouth, it *obstructs their voice*.

Generally, a hypnotic voice will have less pitch and volume, and will be melodic and smooth. Few people are born with a rich, clear, inviting hypnotic voice. Most of us have had to develop our voice through much practice. Some interns may imitate their trainers, which is fine; nevertheless, I remind them that the trainers have had many years of practice, and that before the end of the year, in addition to mastering various inductions, deepenings, and techniques, they "must find *your own voice*." I encourage practicing modulating their voice while driving, in the shower, in front of a family member or pet, or with a tape recorder. It's also important to practice in everyday conversation and standard psychotherapy, perhaps lowering your voice an octave, slowing down at the start of a sentence and speeding up near the end, pausing longer than normal before answering someone's question, experimenting with inflection, and *massaging* a key suggestion. The possibilities are endless.

"But I Just Can't Find My Hypnotic Voice."

Sometimes this straight talk about finding your own voice isn't enough. In those times I reach for the following story, which offers assistance by way of metaphor (Gafner & Benson, 2003). Of course, this story also has applications in therapy.

FINDING YOUR OWN VOICE

Samuel Edgar loved life. He especially loved going to work every day as an announcer at KVZX Radio. He was very comfortable at work, confident that he did an excellent job.

At KVZX, Samuel played music and interviewed people on the air. It was called "Hour with Edgar," although it lasted an hour and a half. Every day there was a different topic that listeners called in about: foreign policy, teen pregnancy, the next solar eclipse—something different every day. Samuel talked and people listened. They listened in cars, at work, and while jogging. Hour with Edgar enjoyed the highest rating in the city. Samuel Edgar was famous, a celebrity. Everybody knew his voice, although virtually no one knew his face. In the supermarket one day a woman recognized his voice as he spoke to the cashier. "It's amazing! You sound just like you do on the radio," she exclaimed. One time he was even offered his own TV show, but he turned it down. He couldn't be happier doing just what he was doing, his "Hour with Edgar" on the radio.

Samuel's voice was strong, resonant, and commanding. He was keenly aware that he didn't look the way he sounded, but it didn't matter that Samuel was skinny, pale-faced with acne scars, that he had a pronounced overbite, and was stoop-shouldered. Ever since he had fine-tuned his voice back in radio school, he had come to notice every aspect of his voice. He reveled in his ability to find just the right inflection, or how he could draw out a vowel, his precision in matching the call-in situation. "It's a gift," said his boss. "It's intuition and timing," said the production assistant. "No, it's just practice," answered Samuel modestly. At any rate, he had a deep appreciation for his voice. And, privately, Samuel actually found the sound of his own voice quite stimulating. Nearly intoxicating, in fact, and sometimes he would begin to speak to himself and just drift off . . .

One day at work, Samuel's throat became very dry. He drank a quart of water and a bottle of juice, but his throat remained dry as a bone. After the show he said, "I don't think it went very well today." The technician just smiled politely. When he awoke the next morning Samuel's throat was drier than ever—and scratchy. His customary singing in the shower yielded only a painful croak. "I sound like a sick frog," he thought. After breakfast, he essentially had no voice, just a squawky whisper. At work, a substitute filled in. "Come back when you're ready," said his boss.

Samuel consulted a specialist, who told him, "We need to do some tests." A week later, the doctor said, "We still don't know. We have to do some more tests." Samuel was devastated. He fingered his throat where his voice used to be and tears welled up in his eyes. KVZX told listeners that Samuel Edgar was "out sick" and "Hour with Edgar" was replaced by music and news. The doctor sent him for more x-rays and blood tests, and more specialists were called in. His case was even presented at the university.

"What do I have, Doc?" he pleaded. "We still don't know. I'm very sorry," replied the doctor. Then one day the doctor called him. "Come in today at 2:00. We have some very good news." In the office, the doctor regarded him seriously. With a wan smile she said, "You have *essential voice loss.*" "But what's that? What's the treatment?" he pleaded.

Samuel never understood the diagnosis or the treatment, which began immediately. He was given pills and throat sprays and speech therapy for two hours every day. After three weeks he was no better and he was more aggravated than ever. The doctor tried to be reassuring: "Samuel, these treatments will help. The body eventually heals itself, you'll see." She even told Samuel a story about a little boy who skinned his knee. "A scab formed and as the skin healed, the scab fell off, and today you can barely see the scar," she told him. But the story just infuriated Samuel. "I don't want stories, I don't want hackneyed metaphors. I just want my voice back!" he yelled in a loud whisper.

Three more weeks passed with no improvement. Samuel complained. He wrote angry letters to the doctor and left croaky messages with her answering service. "I want a second opinion!" he demanded. "We've already had fifteen second opinions," answered the doctor patiently. At the next visit, the doctor grasped his shoulder, gazed into his sad eyes, and said seriously, "You've got to relax, calm down. This will take time. You've got to cool off, let your body heal. This is absolutely essential. After all, you have *essential voice loss.*"

Samuel redoubled his efforts to follow what they had taught him about relaxing his mind and his body. Every once in a while his fingers would wander up to his throat.

Maybe it was starting to feel different in there. One day the speech therapist praised him for responding so well. "It's coming back," she said. "Yes!" said Samuel. For the first time in months he was encouraged.

One day the speech therapist announced, "Okay, we're there. It's time for you to select your voice." "What do you mean?" asked Samuel. "Your voice has essentially improved as much as it can on its own. It is now time to select a voice implant. There are a lot to choose from, but the decision is up to you." Samuel was perplexed. The therapist added, "*You'll discover this in your own way.* One client one time said that in selecting her voice she learned a lot about herself, things she might not have discovered in any other way."

Samuel was given a packet of compact discs to listen to at home. On each disc were 57 essential voices, each with dozens of variations, with names like Effortless Voice and Calm Voice. He soon realized that all the potential combinations afforded him an *infinite number of voices*. Samuel could sound exactly like he did before, with the ability to modify or modulate his voice according to the situation. Or he could have a completely different voice, one that would be totally unrecognizable to the radio audience. The flexibility and versatility of it all was nearly overwhelming. After narrowing down the possibilities, he said, "I'll sleep on it."

The next day he met with the doctor and speech therapist and Samuel still had not made a selection. "I've decided to keep listening and noticing, just to see what comes up," reported Samuel. "That's fine," they told him. "We know that when you're ready you will make a choice."

Like a Radio Announcer

When your client is sitting back, with eyes closed, you are somewhat like a radio announcer whose sole currency is his voice. At that point, your new perm, nice skirt, sensible shoes, engaging smile, or state license on the wall count for nothing. All you've got is your voice.

Often we hear interns say, "But I just *don't like* the sound of my voice." They also say they don't like the way they look on videotape, but I tell them, "That's tough. I need to see your work, and video-taping is how we do it." Some people just don't have a very hypnotic voice. It's squeaky, hoarse, grating, nasal, or otherwise unpleasant to listen to, and then I will tell them, "Your voice needs some work." Ever see a film starring Marilyn Monroe with her high-pitched voice? Well, we had an intern once who sounded just like Marilyn Monroe. Of course, she was painfully aware of it more than anyone else. But by modulating her breathing and voice over several months, she developed a fairly decent hypnotic voice. So, even if you don't have a great voice, there's still hope for you.

Sonja Benson and I were conducting a training once, and we asked the trainees how adding hypnosis to their repertoires had augmented their psychotherapy practice. We received some of the usual responses, like "It gave me more tools to help people," etc. Then, a woman said, "It has helped me in two major ways: For the first time, I pay attention to nonverbals, and I *notice the importance of my voice.*"

Now, in the rest of this discussion, let's focus on things you can do to help your hypnotic voice.

We Can Learn Much from Actors

Patsy Rodenburg, director of the voice department at Britain's Royal National Theater, and voice coach for actors like Ralph Fiennes and Nicole Kidman, has written several books, including *The Actor Speaks* (2000). I draw on this book for much of the following discussion. Her approach is geared toward actors, but it applies equally to practitioners of hypnosis.

The Vocal Process

BODY. Watch a dog bark, a bird sing, or a baby cry. In each instance, the whole body is involved in generating sound. Voice makes use of the entire body, from head to toe. Posture, the angle of your head, and the drop of your shoulders all contribute to the quality of your voice. Actors often speak (or sing) *standing up*, which allows them to literally put their whole body into the effort. As a hypnosis practitioner, you are usually *sitting down*, which allows you to employ only about half of your body. We need to make full use of that half.

BREATH. When I was a young child, my mother would catch me daydreaming with my mouth open, and disturb my fantasy with, "Are you catching flies?" During hypnosis you can never drift off too much, as you must attend to the ongoing process of your client. However, you *can* simultaneously notice your own breath as well as your client's breath. With practice, you will be able to monitor the client's subtle cues *and* at the same time monitor your own voice.

Generally, people breathe through the mouth if they are under stress or when their thoughts are shorter or fragmented. The nasal breath is often a longer breath, sometimes connected to longer thoughts. Your client's long, nasal inspiration—and exhalation—may signal unconscious work. Make a mental note of what you were saying at the time.

Breath is your strong ally because *breath powers the voice.* Breath enters the body, the lungs fill, the rib cage expands, the abdominal muscles open, and as you expel air, a column of air is created that supports the voice as it produces sound. I often reflect on this column as an aid when I'm doing therapy.

Tension Is Not Your Ally

If you carry a lot of tension in your upper body, then it will show in your voice. Tension will *not* help your voice. Breathe in deeply through your nose, and as you slowly exhale, make a hum. Notice tension anywhere? If you answer, "In my throat," think of how much tension is in your throat when you're doing hypnosis.

Vocal sounds are produced when the air from the lungs passes through the larynx, or "voice box," and from there through the pharynx, mouth, and nose. The jaw, mouth, lips, tongue, and soft palate all contribute to turning breath into sound and words, which is what hypnosis is all about.

Some Tension Is Normal

Some degree of tension is normal and helps keep us alert. Unnecessary tension may send a mixed message to your client, who may think, "This therapist is talking about relaxing but with tension in her voice. Something's not right here. . . ." If your voice shows a push or a strain, it may push clients away instead of inviting them in.

Of course, with practice you become more comfortable and confident; however, any tension must be reigned in for your voice to be liberated. Take another deep nasal breath, and hum as you exhale. Is there tension in your shoulders? Is your spine too rigid or slumped? Is your jaw loose, or is it clenched tight?

Film versus Theater

The movie actor works in short spurts, usually doing one scene before resting and going on to another. This is like conventional psychotherapy, where a lot of time is spent listening, punctuated by periods of talking. The theater actor, however, is often "on" for an extended period of time, just like the hypnosis practitioner, whose induction, deepening, and therapy component may last for 30 minutes or more. This can be hard work, and if you have four or five hypnosis clients in a day, you must pace your voice as well as your overall energy level. I *always* have a cup of tea or water handy so I can quench a dry throat or silence the annoying cough that can develop at inopportune times.

Exercises to Help Your Voice

Rodenburg (2000) recommended the following exercises for actors. These exercises can also be done between clients on a busy day.

ARMS. With feet apart, stretch your arms out to the sides and let them drop. With arms at your sides, lift the shoulders up and then let them fall. Circle your shoulders clockwise.

Standing straight, hold your hands behind your back. Gently lift your arms away from your back and then release them. Allow your shoulders to drop to their natural position.

SPINE. Stand with your feet close together and undulate the spine very slowly. You may actually notice the tension in your spine for the first time. Ideally, your spine should be more like a coiled spring than a rigid pole. The more you keep your spine active and warm, the more you will stay in contact with your whole body.

BACK OF RIB CAGE AND UPPER CHEST. Hug yourself with arms crisscrossed, reaching gently for the shoulder blades. Keep the shoulders released. Now, bend the knees gradually, and still hugging yourself, bend over from the waist. Breathe in deeply. Feel the back open. Take several long breaths. Let the arms drop down and slowly come up.

NECK AND HEAD. Let your head drop forward so your chin touches your chest. Massage the back of your neck. Lift your head and then gently rotate it in a circle.

JAW. Scrunch up your face and release. Massage the face and jaw hinges. Make a big smile. With the jaw open, stick out your tongue and flatten it against your chin.

THE PUSH. Push against a wall as though you need to push it down. Look at the wall, not at the ground. As you push, release the shoulders and breathe. Now you will feel the lower breath. You are in touch with your real physical and vocal power.

THE LIFT. Lift a light chair over your head as though you intend to throw it. With the chair above you, release the shoulders and breathe. Again, feel the power.

Being Centered

Your center is the place or position of complete physical balance with a minimum of tension, where your breath and voice can work at their most free and efficient levels. If you're leading a group relaxation exercise, say, as part of a lecture, it is usually easier to feel centered because you're standing up and have the use of your whole body to power your breath.

But if you're like me, 99 percent of your hypnosis will be done sitting down. Now, being centered may mean having both feet on the ground, spine straight, shoulders loose, head balanced, and jaw unclenched. Some of you may feel more comfortable with your legs crossed. This will impede your breath to some extent; however, if crossed legs serves as your anchor, go for it. Your comfort communicates comfort to the client.

Clinical Comments

The Erickson Foundation in Phoenix, Arizona, has an excellent audiotape called "The Personal Growth and Development of the Therapist" (Zeig, 1990). In it, one of the main things that Jeff Zeig addresses is the therapist's voice, and he leads the listener through a variety of exercises that help the development of this voice.

I encourage you to find an image or metaphor for the breath that helps you in therapy. I use the image of a balloon rising, as well as imagining the aforementioned "column of breath" to help center myself. Erickson often gave suggestions such as, "My voice will go with you" or, "Maybe my voice will take the form of the voice of a trusted friend, which can go with you." Your voice is a potent ally in therapy. Practice it, develop it. And, as I mentioned in the Introduction, perhaps most important is to remember the Wildermuth principle: *Don't forget to breathe.*

Chapter 6

Treatment in Brief

Let me share with you some musings, learnings, impressions, and odd occurrences from doing hypnosis for many years.

No Feeling

I was seeing an elderly couple who had been married for 60 years. The husband was mildly demented and oblivious, and she was the unhappy one. "Can't you just hypnotize him?" she asked.

No other measures to date had affected the wife, so I said, "Let's give it a try," thinking that I might reach her as a by-product of her husband's therapy.

I did a long procedure, and he promptly fell asleep. Near the end, the wife asked, "Am I supposed to *feel* something?" Undaunted, I asked her to be patient and close her eyes while I continued. After about five minutes, she opened her eyes and asked, "Are we having fun yet?" I was crushed.

Therapeutic Reactance

Haven't we learned that reactance is always a counterproductive phenomenon? Not so (Arnow et al., 2003). The study hypothesized that reactance would negatively influence treatment outcome in 347 chronically depressed clients, who were treated at nine different sites with either the medication Nefazodone, the cognitive-behavioral analysis system of psychotherapy (CBASP), or combination therapy. Reactance *positively* predicted the outcome in CBASP on two of four scales, and these effects were independent of the therapeutic alliance, which also positively predicted the outcome. So maybe the wife in the preceding anecdote got something out of hypnosis afterall.

Discharging Negativity

It may look like negativity, but it could also be doubt, anxiety, ambivalence, or any number of things that we see in the client. However, for simplicity's sake, let's just call it negativity. One method for discharging negativity is to have the client change chairs. Oftentimes he leaves his negativity in the first chair. I also will ask questions to which the client must answer no. "It's not hot out today, is it?" "No." Answering no to questions like this can neutralize negativity.

I was working with a woman once named Dee who was "wound" pretty tight. She could not let go and experience trance, plus I got the sense that she was fighting me on some other level. Dee was very proud of her independence and how "I don't need a man in my life." In trance, I told her a story about a woman who practiced "honest domesticity," who was "acquiescent and malleable," practiced "self-abnegation," and found comfort in being a "lesser vessel."

Dee showed marked eye flutter during this story and was angry when realerted. "What a terrible story!" she remarked. However, she loosened up after that, and went on to accomplish her goal in therapy.

Such a resistance-discharging approach, like one using humor, must be employed judiciously. Indeed, sometimes it backfires, but most often it doesn't. With any technique, I let the client's response be the guide, and if something has even a *chance* of moving therapy along, I usually try it. Whenever I have a client who doesn't respond well to conversational or directive inductions, I get out the candle. There's nothing like attention focused on a candle flame.

Why Clients Terminate Hypnosis Early

Of the thousands of clients I have treated with hypnosis, and cases I have supervised, several have dropped out of treatment after the first session. In each of these cases I believe that either their notion of a "magic bullet" was dispelled (which is okay), or that I did not sufficiently attend to **control issues** (which is not okay). With all clients, it is of the utmost importance that we help them feel in control of the process. We can do so metaphorically, e.g., "You're always in the driver's seat," or by inducing trance, realerting after a minute or two, and then inducing trance again. Where loss of control is palpable, I bring them in and out several times before proceeding. An additional benefit of this is that people tend to go deeper when re-induced.

The Sounds of Hypnosis

I've always dreamed that one day I'd have a totally sound-proof office, impervious to ambulance sirens, outside conversations, or a load of oxygen tanks clanking down the hall. At my Department of Veterans Affairs office, I place a white-noise generator outside the door, but it does little to mask the sundry intrusions of the busy corridor. During a session with a client named Arnulfo, oxygen tanks rattled by, but he didn't hear them.

During the next session with Arnulfo, two women stopped and talked right outside the door. I remember their words, as I was very annoyed by their disrespect. Part of the conversation consisted of something like "You gave up on that *big form*," and a minute later she repeated, "I can't believe you just let go of that *big form*." Arnulfo never stirred, and was not *consciously* aware of the discussion.

The salient clinical issue with Arnulfo was that during the first Persian Gulf War a friend of his had been killed by a *"bag farm,"* the large synthetic bladders in which fuel is stored, and he was tormented by guilt over his death. Debriefing yielded amnesia for anything I or the women outside the door had said.

He returned in three weeks and told me he had had a dream in which the the Virgin of Guadalupe had told him to "give up my bag farm." Suddenly, he was better. No more therapy was needed. An errant conversation in which the words "big form" happened to be used had evidently accomplished more than I had in three months of hard work! For me, this case embodies the mystery and wonder of unconscious work, as we never know just what someone's unconscious will select to use in its own unique way.

Since then, I've wondered about having someone stage a "strategic" discussion outside the door when I'm mired down in a difficult case. That would certainly broaden the definition of the covert therapist!

"Some Amnesia"

After discussing with Brenda hypnotic phenomena people typically experience in trance, she exclaimed, "I want some of that amnesia!" Brenda, age 25, had crippling obsessive compulsive disorder (OCD), was on several medications, and her skin was a mess from constant picking. Her mother, who was getting on in years, worried about who would look after her in the future. Brenda's goal in therapy was unrealistic—"to be the editor of Glamour magazine, and maybe a model, too." She was given eight sessions of ego-strengthening hypnosis and achieved time distortion, dissociation, and other markers of deep trance, but not amnesia. She remembered nearly every word I said.

"When am I going to get some of that amnesia?" she asked. I reinforced what she had accomplished, but had to admit to her that amnesia might still be a ways off. Dejected, she dropped out of therapy. I had planned to do the **confusional inductions** next but they were now moot.

"I'm Just Not Using My Tools."

Silas, an articulate and high-functioning man, was a helicopter pilot in Vietnam until he was shot down one day. A lengthy hospitalization followed, along with numerous surgeries over the ensuing years. Twelve sessions of ego-strengthening and other interventions helped, "but only for a week after the session," he said. He understood the use of an **anchor** and the need for regular practice; however, he often remarked, "I'm just not using my tools,."

One session I employed the **amplifying the metaphor** technique (Gafner & Benson, 2003). This technique, which is both directive and permissive, involves **imaginal exposure**. He selected "the blue skies over Nha-trang" as a symbol to represent the problem, and stroking his cat on his lap as a symbol for the absence of the problem. Both symbols were then magnified, and the second one was tied to his anchor, which was a circle he made with thumb and index finger on his left hand.

After hypnosis, Silas was exhausted. I praised him for his arduous unconscious work. He returned in a month and announced his decision to return to Vietnam with a veterans tour that was bringing medical supplies to the Vietnamese. This was a major step for Silas. I considered him successfully perturbed.

He returned from his trip with observations and reframes similar to those that have been reported by others who have made the trip. The bomb craters were filled in. The jungle had grown back. "Where I was shot down, there's a school there now . . . I didn't remember that hill being there. . . ," were some of the things he reported. Life goes on, and Silas could finally move on too.

Accepting Gifts from Clients

When a therapist sees a client for a long time, he gets to know the client and the client gets to know him. My therapy sessions with Gina were progressing well. Her social phobia was improving, and I believed that therapy could terminate soon. Just then, I found a gift-wrapped bottle of Tangueray gin in my mailbox. As she was very inquisitive and I had not been careful with self-disclosure, she had found out something about me.

When I suggested termination, she balked. She and I both knew that the relationship had changed. I saw her a few more times after that, and then she went on her way.

How often do we get in trouble because of a departure from standard practice? Let me count the ways! Giving or receiving a gift is certainly one such departure. But aren't clients just like us, in that they enjoy expressing gratitude or appreciation? With some gifts—and I don't receive very many—I say, "Thank you, but I must give it to the volunteers," though not a bottle of alcohol.

Many believe that there is no gift, no matter how nominal, that doesn't have strings attached. A psychologist in Buffalo, New York, told me once, "I have a very firm rule about gifts: I won't accept it unless I can retire on it." (And he is still working.)

Frost Bite

Anna Mae, age 45, reclusive, eccentric, and diagnosed with psychotic depression, always wears her sunglasses. My goal for her was to help her do something—anything—with other people, and her goal was stress management. She responded well to the first session of hypnosis. Too well, in fact. In that session I offered the "Three Lessons" story, in which ". . . the young girl is going through the woods to the house of the wise woman, and passing by an icy cold stream, she thrusts one hand into that cold, cold water. That hand stung at first, but in no time it became very numb. . . ."

Later that day she saw her primary care physician and asked her, "What is that red mark on my hand?" The doctor answered, "Why, that's frost bite, I'd know it anywhere." Anna Mae called me with this finding and said, "I don't know about this hypnosis . . . only the forces of evil have controlled my mind in the past. . . ."

No further hypnosis has been used and I still see her supportively every two months.

Eyes on a Roll

Anselmo, age 53, a Yaqui Indian, stated his problem quite clearly: "I can't remember anything before age 12, and I want to find out what went on." "Sorry, we don't retrieve lost memories here," I told him. We settled on anxiety management as our goal.

I saw him six times spread over four months. He responded with very deep—with no **intrusive phenomena**—to standard inductions and deepenings, as well as stories whose meta-message was "letting go." He used his anchor at work and during practice relaxation at home.

One thing Anselmo did—which I had never seen before—was he very slowly rolled his eyes up into his head, paused for a second, and slowly rolled them down again, with no accompanying eye flutter. Slow, methodical, pronounced, and, I thought, very *conscious*, perhaps a self-deepening measure. In fact, it was so even and regular that I thought, "Is he putting me on?" In the end, I learned to ignore it. The main thing was that he otherwise responded well to hypnosis and his "anxiety management" goal was met.

Things that Go Bump in Trance

Clients emit a lot of sounds during hypnosis, things that may be distracting to the therapist: a wheezy breath, a rumbling smoker's cough, the snick-snick sound of the oxygen concentrator. Some the therapist can ignore, some she can't. Fortunately, most people are thoughtful enough to turn off their cell phones.

Things like eye flutter, the oxygen cannula falling from the nose of a client with lung disease, and snoring are fairly common. But other reflexes might be more annoying, like the sniffling nose that does not abate. One time I was working on a guided age regression and said, ". . . and you may not remember what you had for breakfast one year ago today, but you can remember. . . ," and just then I heard a gurgling sound in the client's stomach, and you guessed it, flatulence followed. The person was totally unaware, deep in trance, and I just moved on the best I could. Matching or pacing ongoing behavior didn't even cross my mind (where was my power of negative hallucination when I needed it?).

I've been deep into a story and heard a "beep-beep" coming from the client's pocket. With eyes closed, he pulled out his pill box, popped a pill into his mouth, swallowed it down, and settled back again as though nothing had happened. Once, in trance, a woman's hearing aid suddenly went "shriek!". She woke up and casually remarked, "Needs a new battery," and then settled back into her seat. I don't think she heard a word I said.

An intern was working with an obese woman once. As he was suggesting that she could drop off into a nice, comfortable trance, she had a seizure and fell to the floor. This half traumatized the intern, but the client wasn't fazed. She remarked, "Happens all the time," and climbed back into the chair and closed her eyes. Needless to say, after that session no more hypnosis was done with that client.

When I was working with a woman who had a dramatic presentation, I remember quite vividly that midway through the procedure a big tear rolled down from her right eye. Shortly afterward her nose began to drip. I became amusedly absorbed in this, without being too distracted. All of a sudden, a stream of tears gushed down her right cheek while the drip from her nose grew stronger. All of this moisture found a confluence on her chin, which soon overflowed onto her blouse. She remained in deep trance, and I found myself hurrying through the procedure, trying to ignore the growing stain.

After she was realerted, she snatched a handful of kleenex, dried her eyes, and blew her nose. She reported a "great experience," and only while she was walking out the door did she notice the wet spot on her blouse. "That must be from me," she said with embarrassment.

"A" for Effort

I encourage interns to compose original stories for their clients. Some of the names of the characters they have created for their stories, though not totally original, certainly had zest: Cole Newcastle, Electra Fann, Sonny Disposition, and Beladonna Sweet. I remember one story designed for a client whose main interest was hiking in the mountains. The protagonist, Carmen Get-It, was encouraged to *discover* something on a "mental switchback," and I believe she really did discover something about herself before therapy was completed.

In the mountains near Tucson, Arizona, is a place called Quitobaquito. An intern selected Quitobaquito as an **embedded suggestion** for quitting smoking! The client continued to smoke, however, as he wasn't yet ready to give up his habit.

Sincerity

I had an intern once who was a walking textbook on both theory and practice. He could reel out a reframe that made your jaw drop. He composed wonderful stories. His sense of timing and intuition were true gifts. However, despite all of these wonderful qualities most of his clients *simply did not return*. Why? Because he came across as insincere, they reported. He did not convey that he *cared* about his clients and it was painfully obvious to everyone.

Not Knowing/Not Doing

The technique of **not knowing/not doing** is one of the most effective in hypnosis, in my opinion. There is no other technique that is so permissive and liberating, and frees the client to respond in her own way. An example of this is: "Gina, here today, there's absolutely nothing at all that you need to do, or know, or think about or feel, and certainly nothing to change. In fact, you don't even have to listen to the words, which may tend to drift in and drift out."

Misspeak

Seldom written about, **misspeak** is an invaluable indirect technique. The first part, which sounds like a slip of the tongue but is really the suggestion, is quickly followed by the "real" words. These "real" words serve to lead the conscious away from any analysis. For example, ". . . it's the *shame*/same burden others carry, and casting that off is usually a good thing," or "she discovered, to her delight, some resources in the dark *allies*/alleys of her mind." However, this might be too much of a mouthful: ". . . you may find yourself *sipping tastefully*/sitting peacefully among the dangers." As with many techniques, using misspeak once or twice during a session is enough, heeding the **law of parsimony**.

Repetition

If it's an important suggestion, repeat it, but not too much. Well-crafted repetition helps people to remember a suggestion. In 2003, Senator Ted Kennedy used repetition in a speech about the Medicare bill: "It's a *good* deal for the drug companies, it's a *good* deal for the HMOs, and it's a *bad* deal for senior citizens."

Persistent Delusion

This may rank as the most distasteful example of utilization ever. Jasper, age 25, was stable on risperdal and other medications; however, he continued to harbor a very corrosive delusion about Jews. He perseverated on Jews in the Third Reich, Jews and Communism, and Jews in the media. He said that the Inquisitions in Europe were a "digestive enzyme" for Jews.

He was referred for anxiety management, and selected "train mode" on the background sound machine because, you guessed it, it reminded him of trains going to the concentration camps. I encouraged him to become absorbed in his repellent image and he responded with very deep trance. He received straight A's in graduate school next semester and he was eager for more hypnosis when—darn!—he moved to another state.

Unintended Consequences

You just never know. I used a very tame **bind of comparable alternatives** ("Do you want to go into mild trance, medium trance, or deep trance?") with a Middle Eastern woman. She reacted with intense eye flutter, followed by spontaneous realerting. Debriefing yielded no *conscious* awareness of anything upsetting. Thereafter, I avoided that technique and she responded well.

Weeks later, during a discussion about her family, I found the smoking gun. In the 1980s, her uncle had been a prisoner in Saddam Hussein's Iraq. He was eventually released and fled the country. However, during his imprisonment and torture, he was asked, "Do you want your left arm amputated at the wrist, or at the elbow?" He answered, "Wrist." They amputated his *right* arm at the shoulder.

Not in the History Books

In the early 1990s I saw a man in his seventies who came to the V.A. for the first time. He had been plagued by PTSD (posttraumatic stress disorder) symptoms ever since World War II. He had been started on Trazodone, which helped, but he wanted to learn "some relaxation techniques" to help him sleep. According to him, he had been a paratrooper at Normandy after the allied landing in 1944. His job was to "shoot any of the colored truck drivers who were yellow." He claimed that he shot and killed some thirty of these African-American truck drivers, who were in fact fellow soldiers who were abandoning their trucks when coming under fire.

Our one session of hypnosis was interrupted due to the man's intrusive thoughts. He just couldn't get these memories out of his head. Before he left, he said, "I've lived all my life seeing their faces in my nightmares, and I guess I can stand it a few more years until I die." He passed away a few years later, and medication was the only treatment he ever accepted.

Like a Recipe

A good hypnotic story contains components that the therapist assembles from varied ingredients. She assembles these ingredients, along with her experience, composing stories with perhaps a kernel of an idea or two. Intuition guides the recipe's directions.

An intern once asked me, "What exactly goes into a good story?" I answered first with a question, which was, "Have you ever enjoyed a dish at a restaurant and asked the waiter for the recipe? Later he returns with a list of ingredients. For example, if the dish was Persian rice, he says, 'Basmati rice, lemon, salt, honey, slivered almonds, and turmeric.' No directions, just the ingredients." A good hypnotic story is like a list of ingredients with which the client makes the "dish" he is craving and which will cure his problem.

Sleepwalker

An intern was once working with a sleepwalker. During trance, he gave the client the posthypnotic suggestion that he would awaken from sleepwalking *whenever his feet touched the floor.* The suggestion worked and the client woke up every time he touched his feet to the floor when he began to sleepwalk.

Toe Scrunch

An intern, was working with a man who experienced anxiety in his job as a receptionist at a clinic. "I can't use that anchor (circle with index finger and thumb)," he said, "because everyone would see it." So, the intern assigned a different anchor that was "invisible":, scrunching up his toes inside his shoe. "It works like a charm," said the client.

Warts

Hypnosis has a strong track record with dermatologic conditions, so I had reasonably high hopes for helping Augie. He was a 39-year-old man from an Indian tribe in New Mexico, and had AIDS in remission. He had developed condyloma, or warts, all over his hands and arms. His doctor had cut them, frozen them, given him medication, and still the warts returned.

Augie said he believed strongly in the unconscious mind, and he also mentioned the word *time*, and talked about issues of time. The unconscious and time were fed back to him by psychologist Bob Hall and me in a "two-operator" approach, which involves ego-strengthening stories while having the client generate a healing image. After two sessions the warts started to clear. In the third session we made him an audiotape. I never saw him again, but checked with him by phone a year later, when he said, "Whenever a wart pops out, I just pop in the tape, and it goes away."

The Relationship

Partially in response to the identification of empirically supported or evidence-based treatments by the American Psychiatric Association and the American Psychological Associations, John Norcross, from the University of Scranton in Pennsylvania, convened a task force to gather information on empirically supported *therapy* relationships. Among the elements of this relationship they found to be demonstrably effective were **therapeutic alliance**, **empathy**, and **collaboration**. None of this comes as a surprise to those of us who practice hypnosis, where these elements are greatly enhanced over standard talk therapy.

As policy makers make decisions about which therapies to fund, some people like Norcross remind us that studies of such scientifically sound treatments usually ignore three essential elements of therapy: the person of the therapist, the therapy relationship, and the client's nondiagnostic characteristics.

Let's Never Forget Repressed Memories

In the 1970s and 1980s some well-intentioned therapists used hypnosis with clients to cocreate images of abuse from "repressed" memories. This resulted in harm to supposed perpetrators and further tarnished hypnosis' name.

Many clients believe that if they remember something in hypnosis it really happened and, accordingly, they need to be reminded that such recollection *may* be valid but it also *may* be fantasy, distortion, or confabulation. In court such memory is recognized only with corroboration. Current research (Jackson, Payne, Nadel, & Jacobs, 2004) underscores the notion that memories formed under stress cannot be relied upon.

This discussion is not intended to minimize clients' real trauma—whether factually recalled, repressed, or suppressed. You will see clients whose goal is to recover "repressed" memories, and you need to at least proceed with caution. I won't do it, plain and simple. Recovering "repressed" memories is often a hidden agenda that interferes with the course of therapy.

You also may see clients whose goal is to discover past lives, or wish to explore their abduction by extra-terrestrials. These people go to someone who practices *hypnosis*, not meditation, progressive muscle relaxation, or stress inoculation training. That's the paradoxical power and mystery of hypnosis. To the general public the word *hypnosis* may evoke thoughts of awe, wonder, and potency. We like this because it makes our job easier. But to maybe an equal number of people the word *hypnosis* may equate to mind control, channeling, past lives, magic, or the devil. The word has always had some baggage, and maybe always will.

Part III

Treatment Approaches to Common Clinical Problems

Chapter 7
Anxiety and Trauma

The bread-and-butter applications of hypnosis are anxiety disorders and chronic pain. Practitioners may choose from a panoply of techniques for chronic pain (Gafner & Benson, 2003), and numerous techniques that can be applied to anxiety and trauma. Hypnosis is ideally applied within a trusting relationship in which therapist and client work together toward a goal. Occasionally hypnosis may be applied alone, but most often its potency—and efficacy—is as an adjunct.

Hypnosis as Adjunct
In their oft-quoted meta-analysis, Kirsch, Montgomery, and Sapirstein (1995) made the strongest case yet for the addition of hypnosis to cognitive-behavioral therapy. They examined 18 studies in which CBT was compared with the same therapy supplemented by hypnosis. These studies involved chronic pain, insomnia, obesity, phobia, and other disorders. The results demonstrated that the addition of hypnosis *substantially enhanced treatment outcome.*

The literature is replete with other studies and case reports that laud hypnosis—and hypnotic techniques—as an adjunct to traditional therapy. To name a few, Cochrane (1989) used both direct and indirect suggestions in the treatment of generalized anxiety disorder

(GAD); Lumsden (1999) combined hypnosis and CBT in the treatment of posttraumatic stress disorder (PTSD); Singh and Banerjee (2002) combined hypnosis and rational emotive behavior therapy (REBT) to treat panic disorder; Krepps (2002) combined CBT and Ericksonian utilization in the treatment of claustrophobia; and Gordon and Gruzelier (2003) incorporated hypnosis and neurolinguistic programming (NLP) in the treatment of the anxiety and pain of a ballet dancer. Furthermore, if we wished to peruse the plethora of studies and reports that combine a conventional therapy like REBT or CBT with a modality that goes by a name *other than* hypnosis ("guided imagery," "meditation," "stress management," etc.), then we would be further convinced of the value of adding an unconsciously directed technique to conventional therapy. Just about every new client I see has previously had something like CBT. Many will announce during the first session, "I don't want more CBT," or "Don't ask me the miracle question." For sure, many have benefited immensely from it, and we don't have to be told of the solid empirical evidence of CBT; nevertheless, let's face it: manualized or "solution-focused" approaches alone are rote, lack heart and soul, and often fail to address problems at their core, which is the unconscious.

The Stress Management Program

Opposite is a handout we give to clients who are referred for hypnosis.

The handout seems to answer many clients' questions right from the start. Importantly, with it we can weed out those seeking a ready-made solution, or a "magic bullet," and those whose goal is to recover lost memories. In the first session, the therapist takes a history, does baseline scales for anxiety, depression, and self-esteem, and covers things like negative stereotypes about hypnosis and control issues. The second session begins with a conversational induction, counting-down deepening, and "Three Lessons" (see Appendix 4). Clients are asked to communicate in trance with a head nod at first, then finger signals are established in a later session. In the second session, the therapist offers an ego-strengthening story, and in the third session "Balloons" (see Appendix 4). The vast majority will have responded well up until this point. For them, we audiotape the fourth session and instruct them to listen to the tape at least three times a week. Then, they are done.

Stress Management Program
Family Therapy Training Program
Southern Arizona V.A. Health Care System
Tucson, AZ

What is it?
This is a program in which the client is taught self-hypnosis, commonly for the management of anxiety (stress), chronic pain, or for ego-strengthening ("self-esteem" building).

How is this done?
The process, which normally requires 4 to 5 sessions, is individualized to the client, who customarily sits in a comfortable chair, and the therapist employs an induction, or relaxing words, designed to facilitate entering trance. Metaphors, stories, or other devices are used to get in "underneath the radar." As such, the process is directed at both the conscious and the unconscious minds. The process is interactive in that during the session the patient will be asked to respond with a head nod or finger signal, for example, "When you begin to notice a heaviness in your hand, let me know by nodding your head."

Is it necessary to close your eyes?
People may close their eyes if they wish. If not, they can look instead at something in the room, for example, a spot on the wall.

What is hypnosis?
Most people already experience hypnosis, for example, when their mind is occupied by a pleasant activity, such as listening to music, or driving down the road, when they lose track of time. According to the American Psychological Association, hypnosis is defined as "a procedure wherein changes in perceptions, sensations, thoughts, feelings, or behavior is suggested." Hypnosis has much in common with other techniques, such as guided imagery, meditation, and progressive muscle relaxation.

Continued on next page

Continued from previous page

Who is likely to benefit?
Most people who are interested in experiencing trance will benefit. People who may not benefit are those who seek a "magic bullet" for their problem.

Will it make my anxiety (or pain) go away?
Learning this procedure often helps people manage their symptoms. Many do experience a significant degree of relief; however, it is necessary to practice the application of self-hypnosis on a regular basis. Usually we provide the client with an individualized audiotape to assist in practice.

How is change measured?
Our therapists commonly rely on anxiety or self-efficacy scales, or on a subjective measure, such as the client's self-report of progress.

What if I want to retrieve lost memories?
Using hypnosis for lost or repressed memories is not practiced in this clinic. The Stress Management Program only addresses issues in the here-and-now.

Who are the therapists?
Interns are experienced with this procedure and receive ongoing training and supervision. Staff are Bob Hall, Ph.D., and George Gafner, L.C.S.W.

How many sessions are required?
People usually learn the procedure in three or four sessions. They then may return to their regular practitioner for ongoing care.

There is no need to get into any other issues. These are primarily clients with GAD, chronic pain, or anxiety secondary to a psychotic or mood disorder. Some will call in the ensuing months or years for a booster session, or because they've lost their tape, and then they're seen again for a session or two. For those with OCD or a phobia, we often need to see them for additional sessions, *as well as* combine hypnosis with CBT.

The Instigative Anecdote

For those with OCD or a phobia, and for those with a marked unconscious resistance, we often reach for a very handy tool, the **instigative anecdote**. Following are a few examples:

ZIEGFIELD FOLLIES

Doris Eaton Travis, age 99, one of four living dancers from the Ziegfeld Follies, has outlived most of her children. She had a successful career with a chain of dance studios, graduated from college 11 years ago, and continues to be vital and vigorous, with regular appearances on TV. She says that even today, "If I'm struggling with some problem, I'll just turn on the music and dance." (Kinetz, 2004)

NATURE PHOTOGRAPHER

A seasoned nature photographer and her apprentice found themselves in Monument Valley on the Navajo reservation in Arizona. The apprentice gazed upon the reddish expanse and asked, "Isn't it wonderful to be so absorbed in your subject?" The photographer answered, "Always use a tripod and cable release so you can move out from behind the camera and relate to your subject, with no machine in between." (Cheek, 1991)

CYCLOTRON

Physicist Ernest Lawrence experienced a moment of discovery in 1929. He was reading an article in a German journal about a new way of speeding particles to high energies by repeated applications of low voltage through vacuum tubes. As Lawrence's German was weak, his attention was drawn to a diagram, which showed the vacuum tubes arranged in a *straight line*. While absorbed in that diagram he had an *epiphany*, suddenly recognizing that if the tubes were placed in *a circle* instead of a straight line, there might be no limit to the energies obtained. This idea of a "proton merry-go-round" resulted in the cyclotron, or atom smasher. (Herken, 2002)

SPREAD OF OAK TREES

Botanists have wondered how, since the last ice age, oak trees spread at the same rate as trees whose seeds are carried by the wind. They finally realized it was due to Blue Jays.

ROLE OF BIRDS

Birds are playing an especially important role in the dispersion of seeds in rain forests, helping spread the seeds of vital trees across manmade gaps in the forests.

Such anecdotes are employed as the therapy component of the trancework session. The therapist typically asks for unconscious acceptance of the anecdote. Finger signals for "Yes," "No," and "I don't know/I'm not ready to answer yet" are established. The therapist then says, "I want to ask a question of your unconscious mind. That little story about the birds that I just told you, is that something your unconscious mind can put to use? Taking as much time as you need, you may answer with one of your fingers. . . ." If the client answers yes, that's good. The therapist has a green light to proceed, and this usually means that he has broken through any unconscious resistance. He can then go on in a subsequent session to an intervention that more directly addresses the presenting problem, such as an age progression ("I would like your unconscious mind to drift and dream, to any time in the future, when you can see yourself the way you want to be. . ."), the amplifying the metaphor technique, a **desensitization** exercise involving **hierarchy** and **imaginal exposure**, or conventional CBT outside of trancework. Once the therapist has broken through resistance the client may only require ego-strengthening and an audiotape.

The important thing is that the resistance (and this is almost always *unconscious*) be identified, and then problem-solved. I always tell clients what we are about to do in a session. This way we are both on the same page, and they can consciously integrate changes.

Sometimes in lieu of an instigative anecdote I'll use an instigative story. Examples of such stories, as well as additional anecdotes, can be found in the Appendices.

Now, let's turn our attention to the intriguing topic of PTSD.

Golden Wedding Bands

The diagnosis and treatment of posttraumatic stress disorder (PTSD) came into its own in the 1980s when the *Diagnostic and Statistical Manual* (*DSM-IV*) first operationalized the disorder. This development lit up psychiatric nosology like a strobe light and helped establish PTSD in the public nomenclature. Since then, many previously undiagnosed people have come forward in search of help, and treatment techniques and research grants have flourished. Behavior therapy, though respectable and well established, had begun to languish by 1980. Thanks to Albert Ellis and others, *cognition* was added to behavior, and what came to be known as cognitive-behavioral therapy, or CBT, emerged on the scene around the same time as the *DSM-IV*. It was a marriage made in heaven—or so it seemed.

Married Many Years

Let's consider for a moment an even more crippling psychiatric condition, a psychotic disorder such as schizophrenia. For this problem, adjunctive therapies, like family therapy, may be of assistance, but the first-line treatment for psychotic disorder is medication. If the person refuses to take medication, all therapeutic efforts are directed at one thing: getting the person to take the medication so symptoms can be controlled.

So, too, with PTSD. Though many argue persuasively for eye movement desensitization and reprocessing (EMDR), the gold standard for the treatment of PTSD is cognitive-behavioral therapy, with many clients receiving immense benefit from adjunctive medication. In CBT, the central purpose is to *expose* the trauma, activating the fear response so that the person becomes habituated to it, and accordingly symptoms are reduced. If the person is reluctant to reopen an old wound, the therapist keeps picking at the scab anyway. After all, research has amply demonstrated that this is what you have to do to help the person to feel better. The wide body of literature includes randomized clinical trials for war veterans (Keane, 1989) and rape-induced PTSD (Foa, Rothbaum, & Riggs, 1991), to name a few.

Such treatment often emphasizes behavior over cognition (or feeling) and may include any variety of systematic desensitization, flooding, prolonged exposure, and implosive therapy (Barlow, 1988; Levis, 1980; Rachman, 1980). **Habituation** is effected as the person experiences the stressor over and over again, and eventually is able to tolerate its noxious effects, and consequently there is a diminution of anger, depression, panic, and related symptoms. A *reframing* or cognitive restructuring often accompanies the habituation—e.g., "I don't blame myself for it anymore."

Controlled studies may involve individual and group therapy, along with a version of the following method: Clients describe their trauma into a tape recorder and then listen to the tape a prescribed number of times a day throughout the study. CBT is responsible for providing trauma survivors with tremendous relief. We may wonder, then, why even use other techniques, such as hypnosis?

Off to the Marriage Counselor

Ask a therapist in a rape crisis center or a Veterans Affairs mental health clinic when the last time was a person with chronic (holding the pattern for longer than three months) PTSD was willing to "open up that old wound." Most of them will answer, "Almost never." So, you wonder, what magic did those CBT investigators use? Certainly their remunerated subjects aren't like most therapy clients —the ones who no-show, people with medical problems and personality disorders, drinkers and pot smokers. No, people like that are summarily excluded from clinical trials (Yapko, 2001).

But the criticism doesn't stop there. CBT for the treatment of PTSD has some serious drawbacks. Pitman and colleagues (1991) found that exposure techniques may exacerbate alcohol consumption, depression, and panic attacks, and Allen and Bloom (1994) pointed out that exposure therapy was contraindicated in clients with marked psychological dysfunction, personality disorder, suicidality, impulsivity, substance abuse, and resistance. A study by Litz and Blake (1990) found that therapists who specialized in CBT used exposure techniques in little more than half of their cases.

However, in a famous consensus of experts, Foa, Davidson, and Frances (1999) found that anxiety management, cognitive therapy, and exposure therapy were rated as highly effective, whereas hypnosis was rated low, along with EMDR and psychodynamic therapy. In fact, CBT so dominates research grants and the literature that methods such as hypnosis may be automatically dismissed by many practitioners.

At the Divorce Recovery Group

So, clients are reluctant to reopen old wounds? I am reminded of how homeopathy and osteopathic medicine began in part as a reaction to the treatment of psychotic disorders in the 1800s. The gold-standard therapies in those days included dehydration, anemia, bleeding, purgatives, cupping, and leeches. Such treatments left the patient so weak and depleted that delusions, hallucinations, and acting out were reduced. The fact that often the person was left sick or dying was beside the point. Psychosurgery, such as prefrontal lobotomy, only added to the depletion. Some would argue that current neuroleptic medication for psychotic disorders, though highly effective, also carries serious risk for some clients. For example, neuroleptics such as olanzapine were prescribed with confidence for many years until in 2003 the Federal Drug Administration issued a warning that this medication carried a considerable diabetes risk.

Back to the Altar

Am I saying that CBT should not be employed in the treatment of PTSD? Of course not. Am I saying that we should consider other approaches *in addition* to CBT? You bet. If you accept unabreacted emotion as a possible definition of PTSD, then it is necessary to aim—sooner or later—for exposing what heretofore has not benefited from the light of day. Given that few clients readily embrace exposure early on, you have to be creative. In the story "Simple Rooms," how many ways are there "to get from here to there"? *Innumerable* ways. We know that people treat PTSD with any combination of medication, EMDR, narrative therapy, Gestalt therapy, psychodrama, group therapy, psychoeducation, a number of bodywork therapies, meditation, CBT, hypnosis, and spiritual counseling, to name a few. Most of these methods will address *exposure*, and some get there rapidly, others slowly; some harshly, others gently.

I saw a woman one time who was adamant: "I don't want to talk about it, end of discussion. I'm going to yoga and I address it privately in my journal, and I don't care to do anything else right now." I said, "Fabulous!" and wished her good fortune on her journey of healing. Another person was less forthcoming. He had filed a PTSD claim with the V.A., and hemmed and hawed during a discussion of treatment options. Finally, he declined all treatment. What *unstated* aspect of the problem might have been operating in his case? The *color* had changed right before my eyes. The room turned green, but not green like shamrocks in Ireland, green like the *green poultice*, or what therapists call **secondary gain**, something that may very well come into play in PTSD treatment. If you are treating a client for PTSD as a result of an automobile accident and he has filed a lawsuit, don't expect him to get better. You probably wouldn't either if you reacted to the accident in the same way. If you're seeing green in a session, save yourself and the client a whole lot of trouble by having a frank discussion and letting him know that occasional supportive psychotherapy or something like yoga, instead of active treatment, would be more appropriate at this time.

Get There Faster by Going Slower

Hypnosis should seldom be used by itself, but instead as an *adjunctive* therapy. Again, it is not a magic bullet or cookie cutter, and should be employed along with standard talk therapy or another therapy. Also, as discussed in Chapter 2, within hypnosis it is often desirable to implement ego-strengthening before progressing to remedial measures. The following case illustrates both these points, along with some of the hypnotic applications that can be brought to bear on cases of chronic PTSD.

Jimmy the Worm

In Mexican American communities, children are often dubbed early with an *apodo*, or nickname. As a young child, Jimmy (who came to see me at age age 58) was tagged with *gusano*, or "worm," since he was short and wiry and adept at squirming away from the grasp of his parents and older siblings. At 58, Jimmy carried dual diagnoses of chronic PTSD and depression, and for years he had been stable on sertraline and klonopin. He visited his psychiatrist every six months, and was followed in primary care for asthma. He had quit drinking 20 years earlier and had retired from his electrician job one year before coming in. He had adjusted well to retirement and assisted his wife in looking after their grandchildren during the day. He prided himself on his cooking abilities and golfed when it was not too hot. When I read his history, I expected him to be the picture of tranquility.

Instead, I was faced with a short, thin man who was sweating profusely and wringing his hands. His eyes darted about the room. He was the paragon of a client who was wracked by guilt and anxiety.

"So, you've been referred for hypnosis," I ventured. "What?" he answered distractedly. "You seem nervous or worried or something," I tried again. "I wonder how I might help you."

He jerked a thumb at the video camera on a tripod by the desk. "Is that thing on?" he asked. "No. Do you want it on?" I replied. "Of course not!" he spit. Just then, he jumped to his feet and said, "Listen. This is all a big mistake. I came here because my doctor told me to, but I really don't want to be here. I'm just wasting your time." He quickly left.

Two months later Jimmy was back. He was more gaunt and equally anxious. "Well, it looks like you're back," I queried. "Tell me something I don't know," he answered. Still hostile, I thought to myself. Jimmy explained that his wife had ordered him to get some help, "or else she's kicking me out. Life is just a sour enchilada." "Okay, Jimmy, please start at the beginning. I'll shut up and listen," I said.

In the Tunnels of Cuchi

Jimmy talked about being happy and well adjusted early in life. He had been a fleet running-back on the high school football team. Then he had enlisted in the army in 1965, and that was when life changed.

Being short and thin, he was tapped for tunnel "rat" duty in Vietnam. At that stage of the war, the enemy operated out of a complex of hundreds of kilometers of interconnecting tunnels in the country's Cuchi District. Unbeknownst to the Americans and their allies above ground, down below the Vietnamese had command centers, hospitals, kitchens, and ordnance factories. Tunnels connected to other tunnels, which in turn connected to a dozen villages in the district. Until the tunnels were discovered, the occupying Americans could be kept under constant observation. The Americans were mystified by the enemy, who would pop out to kill, only to disappear again underground. The Americans pumped liquid napalm into the tunnels they discovered. Others they blew up. They bladed the surface with bulldozers. They finally resorted to carpet bombing by B-52 aircraft, and this essentially destroyed the tunnels. However, long before the B-52s were called in, it was the job of "tunnel rats" to go in after the enemy.

Jimmy talked about descending into a tunnel with a flashlight and a .45 pistol. "You could only go ahead or back. There was no place to turn around," he said. Trapdoors or enemy corpses might be booby trapped with explosives. Sometimes the enemy would hastily bury their dead in the tunnel walls. "A decaying foot in the wall brushed my cheek. I still dream about that foot," he mentioned wanly.

Down in the tunnels it was "damp and smelled rotten. I didn't have that smell in my nose for many years, but lately it's back," he stated. In one chamber he found a cache of pilfered U.S. carbines and ammunition, "along with blood-stained bandages, a banana peel, and a *Little Lulu* book, of all things. That was the only time I laughed out loud down there." Several of Jimmy's buddies lost their lives in the tunnels. Some of their bodies were never discovered. He described having ropes tied to his feet before going in. "Once when I got back up, the two who were holding the rope were dead," he said.

He continued to talk about his experiences in the tunnels. As horrifying as it was, I knew that he was holding back to some extent; people who endure such catastrophic stressors seldom tell all early on.

His shirt became soaked with perspiration. He had been crying and laughing and talking nonstop. Finally, I reluctantly said, "Jimmy, we're about out of time here." He jabbed a finger at a saint candle and a small container that said "anti-jinx powder" on it, which I had on my shelf. "Do you believe in that?" he asked. "I've seen some people who say they've been cursed," I answered. He was silent as he eyed me cautiously. I then added, "Yes, there's plenty of evil out there." "Like I said, life is just a sour enchilada," he said. As we made a follow-up appointment, I contemplated this strange food metaphor he kept using.

When Cursed Together You Stay Together

About once a year I have someone who makes a serious inquiry into the saint candles and anti-jinx powder on my shelf. Most who pick them out among the clutter in my office tend to chuckle, perhaps regarding them as a curious affectation from a bygone era, much like a jukebox or buggy whip. It is there for that once-a-year individual or family who notice it and then risk mentioning that they have been cursed. One elderly Mexican American couple knew for certain that the wife's family had hired a *bruja*, or "witch," to harass them because they hated her husband. The harassment ranged from hang-up telephone calls to a dead chicken on their doorstep. This had gone on intermittently for 25 years. Their daring to risk this disclosure in therapy led to a *curandero*, or "healer" (who was also a professor at Arizona State University), going to their home and performing a *limpia*, or "cleansing ceremony," with burning sage. The next day, the couple reported a palpable lifting of pressure—"a new lightness," were their words. The harassment suddenly ceased, and as if to underscore their new life they discovered a family bible that had been missing for 20 years. Needless to say, the marital conflict for which they had been referred evaporated, and I never saw them again.

Since the mid 1980s, I have encountered many similar cases in Tucson. So, when Jimmy responded in the way he did, I knew this was something worth pursuing.

The Next Session with Jimmy

Jimmy opened with, "Call me crazy, if you like, but someone laid a curse on me, plain and simple. That's when all this started. My wife doesn't believe in this stuff. She says I should go to a priest, but I don't trust priests." He told me that one morning he had picked up the newspaper in the driveway and it had a white powder smeared on it. Then the phone calls started, along with a dead cat hung on his fence. He continued, "When 'You die G.I.' was painted in red on my sidewalk, that put me over the edge. I don't know who would do this."

During sleepless nights he would pace about, "walking the perimeter." Then his wife burned herself on the stove and one of their grandchildren was diagnosed with leukemia. "My wife says it's all my fault for the affair I had 30 years ago," he continued. "You sure someone doesn't have it in for you?" I asked. "Yup," he answered. The session was about up. "Jimmy, let's come up with a game plan here," I said. I explained how I could teach him self-hypnosis and gave him a rationale for ego-strengthening. "Let's go for it," he said. "But we might have to bring in bigger guns," I noted. He realized where I was going and answered, "But I don't know any *curanderos*." "Neither do I," I said. He and I both knew that you don't just open up the Yellow Pages or do a Google search and find a list of curanderos. For every benign and well-intentioned healer there are dozens claiming to be legitimate. We would have to leave the healing up to trancework in the forthcoming sessions.

The Third Session

Jimmy appeared to be just as distraught as he was in the previous session. He mentioned the "sour enchilada" again. He told me that his doctor had started him on Zyprexa, which he took "when I remember." He admitted to feeling much more calm from the medication, though from an objective standpoint he looked anguished.

I quickly went over the trancework preliminaries. I learned what his naturalistic trance experiences were by asking, "What pleasant activity do you do where you lose track of time, when a minute seems like an hour, an hour like a minute . . . ?" "Listening to Tex-Mex music," he answers. I let him know that today's session will be similar, but even better, as he'll have a guide. (Addressing control issues with every client is important, especially for those who are new to formal hypnosis, and likening hypnosis to a naturally occurring experience helps the client feel more secure. Another technique that lessens apprehension is bringing the client out of trance, realerting briefly, and then inducing trance once more.)

. . . Jimmy, looking at that spot out there, that's the way . . . and you can close those eyes at any time . . . [eyes blink, but remain open] or just leave them open and become more and more immersed in that spot as you listen to my voice, or perhaps you will find your attention fixated out there and not even hear my voice, or maybe all your concentration will be arrested by that spot out there and my voice will drift in and drift out . . . and speaking of out, that's one thing most people with PTSD are very good at, spacing out, and that ability we can put to use now . . . but before you go even deeper, I want you to come out of trance for a moment, so I'll count from one up to five, and before I reach five, please open your eyes and tell me what you're thinking about . . . 1, 2 . . .

dissociative language

suggestion covering all possibilities

reframe

realert

"Jimmy, what are you thinking about?"

"Nothing, just kind of blank."

"Blank is good, we like blank. Now, you may close your eyes and we'll continue."

I continued with a permissive, conversational induction, counting-down deepening, and a version of the "Three Lessons" story (see Appendix 4; Wallas, 1985). He was realerted and debriefed. He showed that he had experienced time distortion, tingling in his hands, and no amnesia for the story. Objectively during the procedure I had observed *facial mask, lack of swallowing,* and *immobility,* all signs of a moderately deep trance. Had he experienced intrusive phenomena he might have showed eye flutter, or arousal and spontaneous realerting. He had enjoyed a comfortable respite from his symptoms. Most of all, his initial trancework experience was positive—a good foundation for future therapy.

The Fourth Session

Jimmy reported that the harassment had continued, but it bothered him less. He was getting along better with his wife, who had started taking a class called "Vietnam Wives," in which she was learning various facts about the war, PTSD, and its treatment. I offered to have another therapist see them for couples counseling, but he declined. In my experience, many of these men reveal little of their wartime experience to family members. "Some wives *want* to know, Jimmy. To them, that's real intimacy. You don't have to tell everything, maybe just five percent," I said to him. However, he wasn't interested. Later, I would reframe this as protecting his wife, and I would continue to push him to disclose to her.

Jimmy responded well in these two sessions. One time he was told the "Greenhouse" story (Gafner & Benson, 2000; see Chapter 2), an ego-strengthening story, and I install an anchor, or associational cue, near the end of the session.

> . . . *You have done an excellent job here today, Jimmy, slowing down your mind, and slowing down your body, not something that is easy to do, and in a moment I'm going to count from* one up to five,   realert
> *and when I reach five you can awaken alert and refreshed, but before that, you have* those *hands of yours out there, and*   dissociative language
> *with* that *right hand I'd like you to slowly touch the thumb and forefinger together, forming a circle . . . that's the way. And you can know that this circle is your anchor, or reminder, for when you need to* slow   suggestion covering all
> down, take stock *of things,* be strong, *or*   possibilities
> *for* some other *good reason, as this anchor you will always carry with you. . . .*

He was then realerted, and by accident I realerted him by counting from five down to one instead of the reverse. He was slow to open his eyes and he had a "punch-drunk" or dazed look on his face. His experience was indeed pleasant, and he was amnesic for both the story and the rehearsal of the anchor. I know that with other clients, when I have announced the 1 to 5 realerting and then purposely done the reverse, amnesia is sometimes effected. Possibly that was what had happened with Jimmy.

I said, "Jimmy, it's fine if you don't remember the story, but I do want you to remember the anchor," and the rationale and its use was again explained. I repeated that he had within his power to *do something different*, and that the anchor could help.

The Fifth Session

Jimmy came in, sat down in the recliner, cranked up the foot rest, and closed his eyes. I asked him to open his eyes, and I say, "How sour is that enchilada these days?" "Still pretty damn sour," he notes. I explained that today in trance we would be establishing ideomotor finger signals, an idea he found intriguing. By now I knew that trance could be induced much more economically, and that all I would need to say was:

Jimmy, just let those eyes close and let that feeling of complete relaxation develop, slowing down both your mind as well as your body, that's right . . . and I'll be quiet for a few minutes . . . and, taking as much time as you need just let yourself drift off as deep as you need to go in order to do the work you need to do, and *when you're there, you will know and I will know because you'll find yourself taking one big, refreshing breath. . . .*

linking suggestions

He breathed deeply after about 45 seconds. He was asked ahead of time to have his hands out on his lap so I could see them.

Jimmy, there are many ways to communicate in trance, *which you now recognize as an* entrance *into another state, and one important way is with your fingers on* that *right hand. Years ago there*

pun

dissociative language

was this ad for the Yellow Pages that said your fingers could do the walking—*or was it* talking? *Beginning now, I'd like the front part of your mind to occupy itself with the chair supporting your body, the sound of my voice, or something else* out *there while at the same time*—inside— *the back part of your mind drifts and dreams, and when your mind selects a yes finger, one that can* communicate yes *with me, that finger can twitch and develop a lightness all its own and move up into the air. . . .*

confusional suggestion

apposition of opposites

liking suggestions

ideomotor signalling

Jimmy's right index finger moved almost imperceptibly. I then continued to establish two more responses on the same hand, one for "No" and one for "I don't know/I'm not ready to answer yet." I asked him to take one more deep breath and settle even more deeply into a nice, peaceful, comfortable trance.

I then told him "Beethoven" (Gafner & Benson, 2003), another ego-strengthening story, and then probed for unconscious acceptance of the metaphor:

> *That's the way, Jimmy, doing just fine. Now, I want to ask a question of the back part of your mind, and you may answer with one of those fingers. The question is, "Can your unconscious mind put to use that story I just told you?" Taking as much time as you need, you may answer with one of those fingers. . . .*

His little finger, the one that represents "I don't know/I'm not ready to answer yet," twitched, but on his left hand! I paced the behavior with, "That's fine, Jimmy." I waited a few more minutes and then realerted him. This time he remembered the story and the three responses on his right hand, but had no recollection of any finger moving. I praised him for his hard unconscious work, and then I handed him something I had written out ahead of time:

Vegetarian Enchiladas

2 tbsp. olive oil

1 clove garlic, minced

2 tbsp. flour

1 jar chili paste

2 1/2 cups hot water

1 tbsp. oregano

10 corn tortillas

16 oz. cottage cheese

1 can sliced black olives, drained

3 green onions, chopped

1 cup Monterey jack cheese, grated

He looked at it and said, "I'm not vegetarian." I responded, "Never mind, Jimmy, the main point is that it's an enchilada recipe that I tried once. I figured you wouldn't need the directions. I want you to use this to make me a really *sour enchilada*, something I've never had before." He gave me a strange look, and the muttered "Okay."

The Sixth Session

Jimmy entered, sat down in the recliner, and put up the foot rest. He sat back and closed his eyes. "Well?" I asked. I saw that he was not carrying anything. "I did it, but I threw it out in back for the rats to eat." "Oh. How did you make it sour?" I asked. "Vinegar, a cup of vinegar," he said, before adding, "My wife now thinks you're crazy, too." He looked very sedated today, so I opted for just talking.

He said that the harassment had continued, telephone calls, another dead cat hung on his back fence. I then led him in a discussion of Mexican shrines in the area. He closed his eyes and showed facial mask and all the signs of being in trance. "I've been to El Tiradito shrine, the 'Little Castaway,' I'm sure you know it." He nodded. "There's also that one outside of Patagonia, the one erected by the rancher whose son was kidnapped by Apaches in the 1800s." He nodded again. I stopped talking and just observed him. Soon he was fast asleep.

The Seventh Session

He returned after two weeks. He looked haggard, unshaven, and agitated. He didn't remember what we had talked about the last time, but said he had gotten "shit-faced drunk" three nights before, climbed the steep stairs to the shrine near Patagonia, and passed out. "I woke up in the morning. I'd spent the night with my face next to those burning saint candles. I'm lucky I didn't burn myself up," he added. "You still drinking?" I asked. "No, but my wife left. She says she might divorce me," he noted.

"Okay, Jimmy, here's what we need to do today," I explained. I outlined the amplifying the metaphor technique. "In trance I'll have you come up with a symbol for the problem, and a symbol for the absence of the problem, and then there'll be other instructions. I think this will help, although it might be tough emotionally," I said. "I don't want my wife to divorce me. Let's go for it," he answered. "I don't need you to fall asleep now, Jimmy. Try to stay awake for this," I said.

Trance was induced and soon he was in deep trance. I noticed a marked eye flutter for the first time.

Jimmy, your unconscious mind has many resources, and that part of you can help you now when you need it the most. In a moment I'm going to ask the back part of your mind to come up with a symbol or representation for the problem. It can be anything you like—a sound, a color, a concept, an image—anything you like. For example, one time another man, *sitting right there, came up with the sound of dragging a shovel down a sidewalk, and you know what that sounds like. Let your mind drift and dream right now, and when you have a symbol or representation for the problem, you will know and I will know because your yes finger will lift. . . .*

metaphor

After a few seconds his yes finger moved. I then asked him to generate a similar representation for the absence of the problem, and he signaled after a few moments.

> *Very good, Jimmy. Now, returning to that symbol for the problem, in a moment I'm going to ask you to amplify it, exaggerate it, make it strong, while I count to three . . . one, two, ...*

He grimaced and perspired, squirmed in his chair. The eye flutter was now very pronounced.

> *. . . three, very good, and now just let it go. . . .*

I waited a while to let him collect himself before continuing.

> *Now, returning to that symbol for not having the problem, for the absence of the problem. In a moment I'm going to ask you to exaggerate it in the same way, and while you're doing so, I want you to make that circle, that anchor with your right hand . . . one, two, and three, and now, just let it go. . . .*

He shuddered, and then his right hand relaxed again on his lap. I praised him for his hard work and then realerted him. He looked dazed. "What did you select for the problem?" I asked. "Enchilada, what else?" he answers. His symbol for the absence of the problem was more abstract. "Peace of mind at home," he said. "Keep practicing that anchor. I'll see you in a couple of weeks," I said.

The Eighth Session

Jimmy's wife accompanied him this time. After he introduced her, she said, "I'm glad that medication is finally starting to work." He was much improved, she noted, and he verified this. The harassment had diminished. "Only one telephone call all week," he said. "I think you'll be fine now, Jimmy," I said. "Call me if you want to come back." The two of them held hands as they walked down the long hallway to the exit.

Final Thoughts on Jimmy

Jimmy never called again. I still see him in the waiting room when he visits his psychiatrist every six months. As with many cases, several questions remain unanswered. Who was harassing his family, and why did it stop? Was the medication chiefly responsible for improvement? Perhaps it was, although I like to think that a lot of hard work on my part also had a role. One thing I know for sure is that ever since then I taste something extra in enchiladas.

Another Look at PTSD

In developed countries we are accustomed to the broadening of psychiatric classifications, especially PTSD, so that currently the diagnosis may be assigned to people who have undergone surgery, for example, or endured other events that formerly were regarded as being within the realm of normal experience. I wonder if this tendency toward inclusiveness may invalidate the disorder in people who have experienced traditional stressors like war, sexual assault, and natural disaster.

Those of us who spend time and energy treating PTSD must remember that not everyone is so keen on PTSD treatment, especially as it applies to survivors of torture in Third World countries. Summerfield (1999) was highly critical of what he called a "globalization of Western cultural trends toward medicalization of distress." He called PTSD a "pseudocondition," as it reframes the understandable suffering from war into a technical problem that can be cured by Western techniques like psychotherapy. He decried these experts who define the problem from afar and show up in places like Bosnia and Rwanda to force these techniques on people. He noted that such treatment may be disrespectful of peoples' own traditions and capacities to mourn, endure, and rebuild.

Physical Movement and Cognitive Processing

Psychiatrist and PTSD researcher Bessel van der Kolk was on hand in 1989 to lend his expertise in the aftermath of Hurricane Hugo. He observed people *actively* putting their lives back together, cleaning up debris, repairing their homes, and helping each other *until* the Federal

Emergency Management Agency (FEMA) told everyone to stop what they were doing so that various bureaucracies could assess damage and organize financial aid. All activity immediately ground to a halt, and that's when rioting, looting, and assault broke out.

Van der Kolk emphasized how important it is after a trauma for people to overcome their sense of helplessness by actively *doing something*. He advocated a similar approach at his trauma center when he refers clients to things like dance therapy. In other words, he gets them *moving*. Doesn't this sound just like Milton Erickson whose goal was to break up a dysfunctional pattern by getting the client *to do something*? (Wylie, 2004)

I recall a client in my own pro bono practice at the refugee clinic at the University of Arizona. Marwan had endured torture in three prison camps in Bosnia in the early 1990s. This torture, which was independently verified by the European aid organization, included breaking nearly every bone in his body, mock firing squads, having to sleep with cadavers, and even being forced to watch as his captors slit the throats of 200 children! Marwan, age 40, looked to be age 75, and he had the worst case of anger that I have ever seen. He could tolerate none of the medications that doctors tried, but eventually he allowed physical therapists to touch him, and during these sessions a type of bodywork called "zero balancing" (see below) began to provide him with some relief. As one of the languages Marwan spoke was Italian, and Italian-speaking counselor began to work with him, and he got him to *do something*. Marwan learned English and began to visit classrooms in the public schools, where he *told his story*. Also, he learned how to operate a computer, and via the Internet began to *communicate* with his countrymen around the world. Now, he has fewer nightmares and is much less angry. I am still amazed at how much this client improved—-solely as a result of nonconventional treatment.

When an Icon Strays

Van der Kolk is considered one of the most accomplished experts on trauma in the world. He writes prolifically on subjects such as dissociation and the efficacy of EMDR, he is a university professor and director the The Trauma Center in Boston, where 15 researchers and 40 clinicians work with clients ranging from incest survivors to immigrants who have been tortured. He introduced neurobiology to the trauma field, and Judith Herman of Harvard Medical School calls him "one of the most generative and creative minds in the trauma field" (Wylie, 2004).

Van der Kolk's influence is pervasive and his popularity enormous. So, when such a titanic figure deviates from empirically supported treatment, the outcry from his peers is hardly insignificant. Even though he has received a fierce backlash for embracing treatments like EMDR, thought field therapy, and the somatic therapies, van der Kolk is determined to infuse heart and soul into treatments that traditionally hide behind science and neutrality and avoid vital moral issues. In his talks, he often reminds his audience of the reality of human evil, and the scope of cruelty and inhumanity in the world (Wylie, 2004).

Somatic Memory

In the early 1990s van der Kolk legitimized what physical therapists and others have known for many years—i.e., "the body remembers." He demonstrated how trauma disrupts the stress-hormone system and becomes "stuck" in the brain's nether regions—the amygdala, thalmus, hippocampus, hypothalmus, and brain stem—where they are not accessible to the thinking and reasoning parts of the brain. "We're much less controlled by our conscious, cognitive appraisal than our psychological theories give us credit for being," he explained in an interview with the *Psychotherapy Networker* (Wylie, 2004).

So, if approaches like CBT and EMDR have limited utility, what can therapists do to help people regulate these "core functions"? Well, you have to *touch* the body. Touch is not within my scope of practice, and may not be in yours, nor is it in van der Kolk's. He turned to Peter Levine, the developer of an approach to trauma treatment called "somatic experiencing." Levine calls PTSD a fundamentally highly activated, incomplete biological response to a threat that is *frozen in time* (Wylie, 2004). His goal is to begin a *thawing* of this process, a goal that is very similar to other bodywork approaches, like zero balancing.

Zero Balancing Combined with Hypnosis

Zero balancing (ZB), a gentle, hands-on bodywork system whose goal is to balance the structural body and the energy body through touch.

It was developed in the 1970s by physician Fritz Smith, who combined Western concepts of anatomy and osteopathic medicine with the Eastern principles of energy and healing in the treatment of chronic pain (Hamwee, 1999). Designed to enhance physical and emotional well-being, ZB focuses on the relationship of energy and structure, specifically bones and key joints in the body. The "energy body" is not visible, but is palpable and perceptible through temperature changes, tissue softening, or movement of tissue beneath the physical therapist's fingers. ZB practitioners believe in "tissue memory." Years after a physical trauma, the tissue may have healed, but the vibration of the trauma is still present. By applying gentle lifting, or curved pulls, to key areas of the body, and holding these areas for a few seconds, the physical and energy bodies suddenly become relaxed and quiet, and healing begins.

Several years ago at the refugee clinic we began to employ hypnosis with ZB. We quickly learned that these two modalities highly complement each other, and serve to hasten recovery. In a typical session, the client is lying on the physical therapist's table, and as the bodywork begins, I begin a hypnotic induction and deepening, which is typically followed by an ego-strengthening story. The client is instructed in the use of an anchor, and then realerting and debriefing follows. Sometimes clients experience intrusive phenomena, such as flashbacks. These experiences are briefly processed—verbally—and then we return to what we term our "combined treatment."

This combined treatment has become our preferred treatment for people who have been tortured. For a complete description of the procedure, see "Touching Trauma: Combining Hypnotic Ego-Strengthening and Zero Balancing" in *Contemporary Hypnosis* (Edmunds & Gafner, 2003).

Selecting Techniques

Some people can offer you many techniques. However, let's remember to always let the client's responses be our guide, and not allow our interest in a particular technique to direct us. If you've seen a client for a long time and there's little improvement, maybe you need to do something different. Perhaps recommend a break from therapy. Maybe therapy not so frequently. Maybe no therapy at all.

Maybe a fitness or spiritual route. Maybe reconnect with family. Or, as I sometimes tell clients, "Don't do *anything* for at least two months." Never underestimate the value of straight talk.

Age Regression

The practitioner has a wide range of techniques to choose from for anxiety and other disorders. Employing age regression early on may help identify under-utilized resources,—e.g., past mastery or competence, or ways of coping that can now be tapped into. Phrasing an age regression need not be complicated—e.g., "Right now I want you to drift back in time, at your own pace and in your own way, to a time in the past, any time at all, where you successfully coped with anxiety, and *when* you are there, you can nod your head one time." For clients who have not experienced age regression previously, it is helpful to first age regress them to something "easy," (like what they had for breakfast today), before proceeding to something more difficult. You always want to gain the client's permission before attempting age regression or age progression.

Age Progression

Yapko (2003), who frequently employs age progression, sees the technique as an extrapolation of one's motivations, feelings, behaviors, and interactional patterns. This technique is especially useful for identifying goals and anticipated outcomes. The phrasing is similar to that of age regression. I often age progress the client two or three times within the session to compare and contrast responses. I also like to use age regression and age progression within the same session. This can result in both valuable client data as well as an increased depth of trance, with heightened time distortion.

Embedded Suggestion, Interspersal, and Story

The technique I use most frequently is embedded suggestion, which hopefully is evident in every chapter of this book. In treating anxiety, for example, a story about someone driving down a road, (both speeding up and *slowing down*), bypasses resistance and hurls a barrage of indirect suggestions at the unconscious.

Interspersal similarly bypasses resistance and affords the therapist an eminently useful indirect technique. The easiest way to employ interspersal is to simply toss in the suggestion within a story. For example, within an ego-strengthening story or even in a long, boring purposeless narrative (like a passage from a statistics textbook), you intersperse, or insert, *just slow down* with a slight vocal shift. Two or three times should do it. Anymore than that may unnecessarily activate the client's critical evaluation.

I have many stock stories and, of course, I can't remember them all, so I often just read them. There is no better route to *la via regia*, or the royal road, to the unconscious. There are many variations of story, such as alternating stories, story within a story, story without an ending, and story where the client supplies the ending or outcome (Gafner & Benson, 2003). Remember that it is important for the client to *consciously* integrate what occurs in therapy. To this end, I encourage clients to keep a journal in addition to discussing what they wish during the session.

Hypnotic Phenomena Revisited
The response of the client during the initial sessions will provide us with much of what we need in order to tailor therapy to the individual. In this regard, our best friend is hypnotic phenomena. If, during debriefing, the client with social anxiety says, "It felt as if my feet belonged to someone else," such dissociation is employed and amplified in future sessions. For example, she can be given the suggestion ". . . and at the party you can leave the nervous part of you parked outside by the curb." I strongly recommend that practitioners ground themselves solidly in all hypnotic phenomena (dissociation, time distortion, catalepsy, etc.), as this, possibly more than anything, can move therapy along.

Clinical Comments
The field of trauma treatment is currently in great flux. Even though conventional psychological treatments such as CBT, EMDR, and hypnosis may provide immense relief to sufferers, clearly, these treatments have their limitations. Other approaches, such as dance therapy or martial arts training, may foster needed cognitive processing—and emotional healing—if they are added to conventional treatment. Approaches that incorporate physical touch may hold much promise.

The application of computer technology may also hold promise. Rothbaum and colleagues (1999), in a case study, demonstrated that a virtual Huey helicopter experience greatly ameliorated the PTSD symptoms of a Vietnam veteran. As these nonconventional approaches continue to work their way into everyday practice, we may see their impact on other anxiety disorders in addition to PTSD.

One must look beyond anxiety and trauma—to the cellular level— to see even vaster applications of hypnosis. Wood and associates (2003) confirmed their hypothesis that hypnotic induction followed by ego-strengthening and other suggestions could differentially modulate T-cell subsets of the hypothalamo-pituitary adrenal axis. Rossi (2000) showed us some of the possibilities in his seminal article, "In Search of a Deep Psychobiology of Hypnosis: Visionary Hypothesis for a New Millennium." Keep an eye out for further work by Rossi for more exciting developments in this area.

Chapter 8
Depression

Nothing can wear us down like clients with depression. Chronic depression need not be seen differently than any other symptom or posture that is sorely in need of perturbation. If we succeed at matching the client's mood and experience, and if we utilize extant hypnotic phenomena, therapy can often proceed to a successful conclusion.

Is "Depression" an Inadequate Term?
In an eloquent account of his own experience with depression, William Styron (1990) rued the substitution of the word *depression* for *melancholia*, believing that the former in no way did justice to the human suffering it was intended to describe. In his assault on the term Styron remarked:

> . . . for over seventy-five years the word has slithered innocuously through the language like a slug, leaving little trace of its intrinsic malevolence and preventing, by its very insipidity, a general awareness of the horrible intensity of the disease when out of control. (p. 37)

Indeed, those whose practices contain elderly clients may still hear the term *melancholia*, as in, "Melancholy has descended on me like a dark cloud," or even, "You ask me how I feel? *Melancholic*—that's how I feel."

Early Terminology

Jackson (1986) traced the evolution of *depression* and *melancholia* from their Greek and Latin origins. *Melancholia* first appeared in English writings in the 14th century. It was derived from a Greek term, *melaina chole*, and translated into Latin as *atra bilis* and into English as "black bile." These translations were in line with the presumed etiology of the disorder, an excess of black bile. Depression, devised originally from *deprimere* ("to press down") entered the English language in the 1600s (McMullen & Conway, 2002). Burton (1621/1990) is credited with the earliest entry of depression in its current form in the *Old English Dictionary*, when it connoted "to bring into low spirits, cast down mentally, or dispirit, deject or sadden." Burton (1621/1990), in his *Anatomy of Melancholy*, provided us with one of the earliest recorded reframes when he reassured sufferers that "hope refresheth, as much as misery depresseth."

Client Metaphors

In treating depression, we may listen for metaphors provided by clients, such as, "I am in the dark," or, "a shadow has engulfed me," or, "I feel heavy, weighted down, and slowed down." A metaphor thus provided may serve for diagnostic purposes as well as a paper-and-pencil depression inventory. In my practice I listen very closely for such descriptors and often return to them during the course of therapy. If, for example, in an early session, a client notes, "I have the world on my shoulders," I may in later sessions return to this index metaphor and ask:

> *That world on your shoulders, does it still feel as heavy?*
>
> *On a 1 to 10 scale, how would you describe that weight at this moment?*
>
> *That world on your shoulders, is it still supported evenly by your neck and back and both shoulders, or has it shifted?*

By employing a depressed client's metaphors in therapy we match, or model, their experience, and the meta-message inherent in such message is "I'm listening closely to you and I understand some aspects of your suffering." Contrast that with therapist-provided metaphors, which not only might not match their experience, but also might be interpreted as intrusive or disrespectful. And what do we do if clients provide *no* metaphors? First, in my experience *most* clients will offer metaphors, and because they represent affective experience clients will usually mention them in the first few minutes of the first session. Maybe you were too busy scribbling notes or thinking about next weekend and you missed the client's metaphoric offerings. you have to begin the session intending to *listen* for them. Some clients want to check you out first, and maybe they will feel comfortable giving metaphors the next session.

In the rare case of the client who offers none, I often float some trial balloons. For example:

> *One person one time likened her depression to* darkness. *Another said, "I am* blue." *Still another said she felt burdened or* weighed down, heavy-hearted, *even* trapped, *as if her freedom of movement was restricted, and I've heard other people who know their depression is hardly a decent thing, and* descent *is what comes up, or most often down, as in, "I feel* low," *or, "It's hard to climb back up."*

As I'm floating those balloons I'm closely monitoring nonverbals, which will be evident before she says, "Yes, I feel low." Will the nonverbal response be a glint of recognition, a slight nod of approval, or something more subtle, like increased vitreous fluid in an eyeball, a flaring of one nostril, a tic-like behavior, like a cough or a twitch, or something else that is reflexive? Remember, metaphors are unconscious communications, and clients will usually answer unconsciously and nonverbally before you hear any words. We *listen* for a client's metaphors, maybe with our third ear, which often entails going into trance briefly ourselves. *Listening* may merge fleetingly with *seeing* in order to pick up vital communications from the client.

Images of Descent

Two linguists in Canada, McMullen and Conway (2002), followed the course of therapy of 21 clients, audiotaping 471 psychotherapy sessions in order to determine which metaphors depressed clients employ to describe the disorder. Four main metaphors were present in their data: *darkness, weight, captor,* and *descent.* Interestingly, *descent* accounted for 90 percent of metaphors reported. Descent metaphors included "spiraling down," "having a downswing," "going through a nosedive," "sinking low," "getting mired down," "needing to work one's way back up," etc.

"Going down" may entail "going below the surface of the earth," as in "backsliding into a dismal pit," "hitting rock bottom," or "in the dumps," with the implication that the further one descends, the harder it is to go back up.

Lakoff and Johnson (1980) noted that orientational metaphors (up-down, right-left, front-back) structure a whole system of concepts that are fundamental to Western culture in terms of spatial orientation. In hypnosis, think of the pivotal role of **apposition of opposites** in hypnotic language and the *induction of trance.* In this regard, McMullen and Conway (2002) emphasized that *up-down* may be the most common orientational metaphor. Being up is associated with happy ("He's on top of the world"), being conscious and awake ("She's an early riser"), healthy ("*peak* physical condition"), and having control and power ("*top* of the ladder").

Each up example we commonly employ may be counterbalanced by down to designate the opposite condition—e.g., "dropped dead," "bottom of the heap," etc. In short, up is desirable and good, and down is neither. Furthermore, our daily-life experience reinforces this orientation, such as when we are *upright* we are healthy, awake and alive, and when *prone* we are ill, sleeping, or dead; an erect posture is associated with happiness, and a drooping posture with sadness; and culturally *up* is associated with high status and control, and *down* is not. Furthermore, *descent* is often associated with two domains of the dead, the grave and hell (McMullen & Conway, 2002).

Not Always Down: Cultural Considerations

What metaphors for depression do you hear from your clients? I bet *descent* will far outpace *dark* or *weight* or any other image. Certainly *descent* predominated in Midge, a client who will be discussed shortly. However, as you surmised early on, this topic is strongly influenced by culture. McMullen's and Conway's subjects were white, middle-class Canadians. In my practice I usually hear *weight* to describe depression among Hispanics, as in, "My heart is heavy," just as American Indians often cite *darkness*, as in, "Every day is a dark day." In my work with refugees, I seldom hear *descent* from people from African countries or Central America. Their experience is often expressed more somatically, as in having loss of spirit or soul, or sadness trapped in the body, usually in the heart or viscera. Of course, physical pain and psychological distress may compound each other, so that people who have been tortured may evince depression and anxiety as pain in bone and joint, which then may be the place to begin treatment (Edmunds & Gafner, 2003).

To be sure, people from cultures that place value on balance and neutrality may give little priority to the up-down orientation. Also, many from non-Western cultures may not share our independent view of self. Accordingly, they may describe their depression *not* in terms of descent, weight, captor, or darkness, but instead as not feeling one with nature or cut off from their interdependence with others.

Many people in other cultures may only be concerned with survival and day-to-day existence, while in Western cultures, pursuit of *happiness* is considered a standard goal in life. Isn't pursuit of happiness mentioned in the United States *Declaration of Independence?* *Up* is the norm, and sad is abnormal, unwelcome, and not easily tolerated. *Down* costs billions of dollars in lost work time and antidepressants, and people devote whole chapters like this one to the dull topic. However, when treating a depressed person from a culture other than your own, try to understand other things besides their figurative language. I have seen many people who regard extreme misfortune in life—as well as depression—as normal, something to be expected. People who come from countries where genocide and civil war went on for *generations* may see life much differently than Americans do. One woman from El Salvador saw her husband and four children killed, and then she was brutally raped. Remarkably, she had reframed the experience as "it was bad but it happened to everybody," and three years later she was doing well. For others, their life might be a train wreck every day since the trauma. I remember asking one young man why he felt nervous (he had severe posttraumatic stress disorder [PTSD]), and he said, "Because of that pill they gave me in Guatemala." It was readily apparent that any *Diagnostic and Statistical Manual-IV* psychoeducation would be lost on him. So, try and find out how *they* see it. You might be surprised.

The Illusion of Empirically Supported Treatments

Yapko (2001) has aptly noted that researchers of empirically supported treatments for depression miss a major point. Their assumption is that what is therapeutic lies in the techniques alone, and they omit vital personal, interpersonal, and contextual variables. In other words, the validation of the *techniques* of therapy, even scripting session-by-session protocols to follow, totally ignores the therapeutic *relationship*, the foundation from which therapeutic change happens. Yapko (2001) pointed out that techniques are no substitute for clinical judgment—the ability of the therapist to recognize and respond spontaneously to salient client data. In fact, Ablon and Jones (1999), who studied clients finishing therapy, have noted that it is the therapeutic *alliance*, not the specific techniques, that are valued by clients. To Yapko (2001), this is a potent "strike one" against a singularly technique-orientated approach.

Even though techniques—and the validation of empirically supported groups of techniques—are important, psychotherapy has always been more art than science. Complicating factors, such as comorbid conditions, the occurrence of significant life events (such as divorce), and variable personality traits are all largely ignored in efficacy studies. To Yapko, this is "strike two" against manualized protocols.

Yapko certainly values the contribution of science, as he never mentions "strike three." However, he takes a strong stand against any technique or procedure that is rote and prescribed, including hypnosis. Even hypnotic procedures, if similarly ritualized, ignore clients' individual differences in information processing and response styles. He emphasizes that any clinician who employs hypnosis in the treatment of depression or any other problem needs to remain responsive to individual needs. He notes that hypnotic applications will have the greatest likelihood of success only if the clinician considers the same personal and interpersonal variables as in any psychotherapy.

Procrustean Beds

This is precisely what Erickson reminded us of time and time again, that therapy must be based on the unique needs of the individual rather than the person tailored to fit in a "Procrustean bed" of hypothetical theory and behavior. Remember that cruel fellow Procrustes from Greek mythology? He was the robber who waylaid travelers and "fit" them to his special bed. If they were too short, he stretched them to fit; and if they were too tall, he cut off their legs. Procrustes didn't last as long as empirically supported treatments, as only a few years passed before Theseus killed him.

To individualize treatment, does this mean that we should *not* read an induction, or that we shouldn't use a favorite story with more than one client? Of course not! None of us are as wise and creative as Erickson, and none of us have either the time or inclination to reinvent the wheel with each new client. We work within our own limitations and we employ approaches and techniques with which we are comfortable and practiced, and yes, ideally we stay abreast of the literature and incorporate what is empirically validated or "evidence-based." We also use what might make sense to us, or lend itself to our own clinical interests, as well as the population with which we work.

If you've seen a demonstration by masters like Lankton or Zeig, you may marvel at their facility for adapting their hypnotic patter to the orientations and ongoing behavior of the client. However, don't think for a minute that Michael Yapko or Joyce Mills or Carol Lankton don't rely on stock phrasing, metaphor, and other techniques that *work for them.* When you're practiced at what you do well, your confidence translates strongly to clients, whose reflexive thought will be, "This therapist knows what she's doing, and if she believes I *can* get better, I can get better!"

The Case of Midge

Midge's speech was redolent with *descent*, which mirrored her chronic depression. She said, "I've been trying to climb out of a deep hole for a long, long time." Midge was a 39-year-old woman who was the only child in a strict household in Mississippi. Her father was a Baptist minister and her mother a homemaker. Her ten years in the Air Force were an "exhilarating experience . . . the highlight of my life," in a life that was otherwise a downhill slide. She was twice divorced by two husbands who cheated on her, drank heavily, and occasionally beat her. Of her three children, one died in a motor vehicle accident, one was a suicide three years previously, and with the other she had little contact, as "she was turned against me by my husband." Both parents died of cancer, and she was the caregiver for both in their final months.

She had not worked for three years, lived alone with her dog, and she was supported by a family inheritance. Her goal in therapy was to "build a bridge to my daughter," and to "study computers so I can return to the workforce." She did not drink or use drugs, nor did she smoke, and she had no personality disorders—four rather rare plus factors in a normally highly problematic population. She was on a mood stabilizer, and had been on a variety of medications to date. Her general health was good.

Early Sessions with Midge

In the first session, Midge cried from beginning to end, using up nearly an entire box of Kleenex. Midge was the paragon of grief and misfortune, and someone for whom I felt deep sadness and sympathy. As I was thinking, "She sure is a total mess," she remarked between shudders and sobs, "I know I'm a complete mess." She recounted her psychotherapy history, which included participation in a multicenter CBT study. She stated rather acidly, "Don't tell me I'm a ruminator. Been there, done that. Frankly, I just want supportive therapy. I don't need someone else to help me with my disordered thinking."

She completed a depression inventory and scored well into the severe range. I saw her three times during which I did a lot of listening, threw in some reframes when I could, and added some ego-strengthening anecdotes (Mauseth, Kiesling, & Ostolaza, 2002), such as the following.

THE SAMAIPATICERUS

In the highlands of central Bolivia, we find the Samaipaticerus cactus, which supports itself in an interesting way. As a branch grows it eventually rests on the branch of a tree, and the tree then does all the work of supporting it. The cactus then produces a weaker wood that lacks fibers. As it produces weak wood, the energy it saves can be used for further growth.

GYMNOCALYCIIUMS

The gymno cactus in South America grows only in very rocky soil. Inside the branches are tubes that are lined with bark, and inside that bark is another layer of bark, a healing bark. When the plant detects a wound, it activates its healing cells to produce a layer of healing bark, which also provides further protection for the plant.

Midge made no comment when these anecdotes were presented to her, nor did she wish to discuss them next session. These were presented to her for ego-strengthening and instigating purposes, but I also had something else in mind. I was testing for any resistance to unconsciously directed interventions, and also setting a foundation for hypnosis, which I had not yet introduced.

During these initial sessions I strongly encouraged social contacts, and I also urged her to begin a walking routine, something she summarily dismissed. When she returned next time I began the session with a story from Matt Weyer, a psychologist in Phoenix, Arizona (Gafner & Benson, 2003).

THE WOK

Midge, let me read you this story before we actually begin today, and mind you, it may not really be pertinent to your particular situation.

Someone told me once about a man named Bruce, the best cook he ever knew. Bruce went to different schools to be a chef, and he even worked at several fine restaurants, though he never quite cooked up to his potential But things began to change for him one day when he *discovered* something. To his great surprise, way back in the cupboard among the various pots and pans, he found his old *wok*.

That *wok* was covered with rust and had not been used for many years. He remembered the trouble he always had with Asian dishes, but at the same time his classmates at chef school had become quite adept at *woking*. "You notice a lot of things about cooking when you get lost in *woking*," they told him.

In his kitchen Bruce began to experiment with his wok, first with one kind of oil, and then another; and first on low heat, then on medium heat, and eventually on high heat. He did a lot of thinking when he worked with his *wok*, but mostly he contemplated, deep inside, "I can do this, really I can." The dishes he prepared were absolutely marvelous, and employment in a five-star restaurant soon followed.

Midge contemplated the story for a bit and then said, "'Wok-walking,' very clever. Well, what other surprises do you have for me today?"

"Midge, I think the time is right now to begin hypnosis. What do you say?" I asked.

"I'm for anything that can help, though I don't know about those weird stories you tell," she responded.

Beginning Hypnosis

Midge harbored no negative stereotypes about hypnosis and showed no control issues. Naturalistic trance experience consisted of stroking her cat on her lap, ". . . and sometimes listening to music." I reiterated to her the goal of therapy, as I understood it: to return to the workforce and to reestablish relations with her daughter. I began with a conversational induction and counting-down deepening, and ended with the "Three Lessons" story (Gafner & Benson, 2000, 2003). Debriefing yielded a heaviness in her hands, some **time distortion**, no **amnesia**, and an overall pleasant subjective experience. I explained that I would like to continue with a combination of talk therapy and hypnosis, which would concentrate for now on ego-strengthening. She agreed to this plan, where we would meet every two weeks.

When she returned next time she reported she had purchased a stationary exercise bicycle and was using it 15 minutes every day. "Wonderful," I thought, "behavioral activation has begun. What can we do here to push that along?" We had rehearsed the associational cue, or **anchor** (a circle made with her right thumb and index finger) to trigger relaxation and to break up negative thinking, and she said she was practicing this on a regular basis. Also, Midge was now becoming accustomed to stories, and following induction and deepening I opted for one I sometimes use with depression, one that may further match the depressed person's experience. An instigating suggestion is interspersed throughout the story.

DARK JOURNEY

I want to tell you a little story that was adapted from a Western novel in the 1920s, a little book called *Avalanche* by Zane Grey (1928). The cowboy's name was Jack, and he started out on a journey, and he called it his Dark Journey. As he rode along slowly on his horse he felt enveloped by his surroundings—the overcast sky, and the gloomy and forbidding late afternoon. The cold wind was raw, and as he crossed a creekbed his horse's hooves trampled on brown leaves in the freezing mud. Jack was in the midst of a bitter feud with his brother, and morbid fantasies and harsh words resounded in his mind. He heard words in his mind, and it was as the words reverberated off nearby granite walls that he heard in his mind: "*Something must happen when I see a light.*"

Jack climbed through thickets of mesquite and manzanita and into the somber pines. He dismounted and led his horse up the steep slope. Dead manzanita broke like icicles against his legs. Suddenly the trail plunged down and he rode through tall grass, sear and brown, down into a canyon abyss. He heard the words again, loud in his mind: "*Something must happen when I see a light.*" He gazed upon a vast amphitheater framed in saw-toothed gaps. It was miles across, a riot of colors, dark red sumac, ragged gold maples, and dusky greens. Yellow crags leaned over a void of looming escarpments, and caves peered out of the cliffs like black eyes.

Far down was Black Gorge, so inaccessible that few bear or deer had penetrated within. The basin lay deep in shadow and had a most sinister aspect, and the setting sun gleamed an angry red. Jack passed through a thick mat of brush and vines. He crossed a depression that had once been an outlet for a stream. It was now choked by a splintered cliff. He recalled the words again in his mind, "*Something must happen when I see a light.*"

And now, Midge, please note that when I went to sleep last night I had a dream, and when I woke up most of that dream I could not remember.   amnesia

I'm going to count now from one up to five, *and when I reach five you can feel alert and refreshed as if waking up from a* realerting *nice, pleasant nap*, five, four, three, two,   confusion and one.

Is It a Stab in the Dark?

Midge looked a disoriented when she opened her eyes. "Something about a *woman* on a horse" was all she could remember about the story. That meant that the interspersed suggestion, *something must happen*, was lolling around in her unconscious, and that this "something" was tagged to seeing a light. Okay now, is this getting far afield for you? Are you saying, "Yes, I see the contingent suggestion, but isn't that way too general and open to interpretation?" You bet it is. You might also be thinking, "How can we *know* it's sitting there in her unconscious?" Well, I *know* very few things for sure, but what I do after such an unconsciously directed suggestion is wait and *observe* a behavioral or attitudinal change during the next two weeks or so. In my experience, if something is to happen, it will usually occur within a few days to two weeks. Not immediately and generally not after two weeks. That is generally in the same timeframe as paradoxical prescriptions delivered in talk therapy, as they seem to "take" within one to two weeks (Shoham-Salomon & Rosenthal, 1987).

Can you just give the suggestion (*something must happen*) without tying it to a behavior that is likely to occur? Of course. Try both ways. The likelihood of success is more with the latter. Erickson often used "when you see a *flash* of light." Try "when you feel a smooth surface," or "when you hear the voice of a dear friend." I prefer the visual. Does this always work? Of course not! It works maybe half the time. As a general rule, the deeper the trance and the more amnesia experienced, the more this technique is indicated. Making the switch from 1–5 to 5–1 at the end of realerting serves as a very good distraction for fostering amnesia.

Continued Progress

Ten days later Midge began to compose a letter to her daughter. Was this a consequence of the suggestion? I'll never know. Did the decision happen when she saw the neon sign of Acme Pest Control, or when she glimpsed the light of the TV during the evening news? I'll never know. I'm fine with *not knowing*. I appreciate and respect science, but frankly, I hope some things remain art.

Blending Approaches

Midge no-showed once and cancelled twice before being seen again six weeks later. She had felt depressed over the holidays and one time she had called her daughter, who hung up on her. She was keeping up her daily exercise and she had completed some CBT worksheets on automatic thoughts and core beliefs. "What did you learn from those worksheets?" I asked her. "That I think I'm a loser, but I already knew that." "What else?" I asked. "That I can interrupt bad thoughts with my anchor," she noted. She said she was now ready to continue therapy.

I saw her ten more times over the next three months. I continued to reinforce her CBT work at home, and during hypnosis sessions I continued ego-strengthening stories and employing hypnotic phenomena, such as catalepsy, to match her experience.

Catalepsy

Nothing matches a depressed person's experience like catalepsy, which can be defined as "involuntary tonicity of the muscles" (Kroger, 1963), or as a "suspension of voluntary movement" (Erickson & Rossi, 1981). For a long time Midge had been mired down with depression, physically, behaviorally, mentally, in all ways. To date, I had induced trance conversationally and indirectly, and one time I switched to the **arm catalepsy** induction, a highly directive technique. Midge was asked to extend her arm straight out, and I gently held her hand for a moment before letting it go.

Midge, let that *arm float out there,* all by itself, *and right now I'd like to direct* those *eyes to a spot on the back of your hand, and when you've selected a spot,* anywhere at all, *let me know by nodding your head one time.* . . .	dissociation permissive suggestion
Isn't it most curious how that hand just floats out there independently, *all* on its own, without any conscious effort or intention . . . and *I wonder if that hand will want to* drift up *to your face, or* descend *to the comfort of your lap* . . . *That rigidness and immobility, we call it catalepsy, and there's nothing* feline *about it. It's not unlike some psychological states that seem like granite, but I take for* granted *your arm won't remain out there unmoving, but will choose to go up at its own pace,* down *in its own way, or maybe it will* twitch *or shake with inclination in one direction before finally settling on some* north *or* south *orientation of its own choosing* . . . , *and now that your eyes have closed you don't even have to listen to the words.* . . .	dissociation linking word permissive suggestion distraction bind of comparable alternatives

With that technique, a major meta-suggestion has been communicated to Midge: You don't have to stay the same. Why not use this early on in the first few sessions? Because she wasn't ready for it. Some people, like Midge, experience fear and loss of control at seeing their hand suspended out there involuntarily. The last thing I wanted was to scare her off. After several sessions had passed, sufficient trust had been built. Another obvious contraindication for this induction is a medical problem, such as cervical pain or peripheral neuropathy.

Time Distortion

Like catalepsy, *time distortion* lends itself nicely to the treatment of depression. Early on, Midge reported feeling that her depression had *always* been there and that it would *never* leave her; in other words, she was stuck in this timeless, negative void. Also, after her initial hypnosis session she reported feeling time *contraction*, or the sense that only a short time had passed between closing her eyes at the beginning of the induction, and opening them again at the start of debriefing. The following induction was used with Midge.

TIME INDUCTION

Back in 1959, two researchers in hypnosis (Linn & Erickson, 1959) conducted various experiments on *time distortion*, that phenomenon that has to do with experiencing time either as speeding up or slowing down, when a minute can seem like an hour, or an hour like a minute, something that everyone experiences at one time or another, either when absorbed in something pleasant, or immersed in an activity that is boring or uninteresting. Certainly such experiments might qualify as something rather tedious or boring. In fact, many people who have read those 1950s experiments in 1980, 2000, 1960, or even now, tend to feel rather sleepy by the end, if not earlier.

In these experiments, the researchers showed their subjects two gray circles on a white background, something that is easy to visualize with the mind's eye. "What do you notice about these gray circles?" they were asked. "They're exactly the same," responded the subjects, as indeed, both circles were exactly the same in all aspects. "*What* time is it now?" the subjects were asked, and they responded with what they thought the time was, which they could check by the big clock on the wall.

Then, the experimenters flashed the circles on a screen at different intervals, flashing one for a count of 1, 2, 3, 4, and then they flashed them again for a count of 4, 3, 2, and 1, and then they did the same thing again, but faster this time, 1-2-3-4, and 4-3-2-1, to establish an experiential instant, or moment, and then the subjects were asked again, "What *time* is it now?"

We may wonder now, reading about that experiment then, how someone from a primitive culture may have a much different concept of time, perhaps measuring it by sunup or sundown, or by a change of seasons, or even by an hourglass or sundial; while a person in a modern culture may wonder about time in digital seconds, or even nanoseconds, or even thinking about what they had for breakfast this morning, or dinner yesterday evening.

The scientists next studied the relation of one gray circle to the other, again in terms of experiential space, relation of course, not meaning aunt or uncle, or even distant cousin. Then they were asked again, "What time *is* it now?" Observing a gray circle flashed ever so quickly, or very slowly, on a white background, over and over again, can get very boring, even in an interesting experiment, as present experience can become extended, or contracted in experiential space and time. While this was occurring one subject glanced up at the big clock on the wall, and counted the sweep of the second hand through all 60 points, noticing that each interval was equal, each arc being six degrees. One subject wondered and imagined about the overall experiment, taking satisfaction in knowing that this was a timely contribution to someone's advanced degree.

The same subject, when asked, "What time is *it?*" let her mind drift to geologic time as opposed to clock time, time required to freeze, or thaw, orange juice concentrate, or how long a fossil has been in a rock. Just then the experimenters introduced another element, a loud noise, at different points in the process, either while flashing the circles or during the time in between, 1-2-3-4, or 4-3-2-1. She knew what was coming next, the question, "What time is it *now?*" and at that point her mind really drifted off into another state.

Next, the experimenters introduced the idea of image, as well as imageless thought, again, in relation to time on the big clock on the wall. They put a spoon on the table. "Touch it," they were instructed. "What are you thinking of? Don't tell me, just think it, and now close your eyes," they were told, and while their eyes were closed the images were again flashed and the counting continued, 1,2,3,4 and 4,3,2,1. The experimenters banged the spoon loudly on the table and asked them again, "*What* time is it now?"

Up to that point, which came sooner to one subject and later to the other, everything in the experiment had been pretty concrete and straightforward. Next, however, the scientists introduced the concept of *meaning tone*, yes, meaning tone, which is almost like *sound symbolism*, such as when you hear a spoon bang on the table, you can feel the *meaning*, or know what is meant by the sound tone. One subject, upon hearing this, thought about when you think a word in your head over and over again, such as "four-fore-four-fore-four-fore-four-fore," and how the exact opposite of meaning tone may be reached along with a blankness or neutrality that can be a pleasant respite from noise and words. Both subjects were caught off-guard this time by the question, "What time is it now?"

The most important part of the experiment followed next. One experimenter said, "Beginning now I'd like you to briefly review in your mind, as well as in your body, the items we've covered today—gray circles, white background, 4-3-2-1 and 1-2-3-4, clock on the wall, loud noise, four-fore-four-fore-four, and spoon, as well as the question about time, and precisely now just *let go* of all that, and let yourself drift off into a nice, peaceful trance, sleeping soundly and deeply for several minutes until you are realerted at a point to be determined in the near future . . . that's the way. . . .

So, by utilizing what is naturally occurring, *time distortion*, we are doing two things: matching the client's experience, and ratifying trance experience. Both of these further cement the relationship and make it more likely that treatment will be successful.

Other Ways to Use Time Distortion

Other ways that I employed this phenomenon with Midge were in the deepening. In a counting-down deepening a non sequitur set up a suggestion:

9 . . . 8 . . . in airline parlance "overdue"	non sequitur
and "late" mean quite different things . . .	
you can go deep . . .	suggestion
7 . . . on a commercial airliner the pilot	non sequitur
can get through immediately on the radio,	
and slower on the data link . . . you can	suggestion
go deep.	

Or, you can match the impatience one feels in waiting for depression to lift by mentioning naturalistic examples of time distortion. In therapy and in inductions and stories I threw in things like the homily, "a watched pot never boils," or casually asked, "Midge, did you ever watch the second hand on an old clock? The more you watched it, the slower it seemed to go?" Or, likening what Midge is currently experiencing to being in line at the airport, or any other number of activities.

Finishing Therapy

Midge was now doing much better. She was going through vocational rehabilitation, sleeping well, and had begun to date a man she met on the Internet. She was evasive regarding my queries about her daughter, so I left that topic alone. She asked to be seen only once a month, and after three months she returned one day in distress. She wore no makeup and was sobbing. She felt "downright awful" and didn't know why. I suggested we do some unconscious exploration, which she agreed to.

We had previously set up ideomotor finger signals on her right hand, one for *yes,* one for *no,* and one for *I don't know/not ready to answer yet.* I asked her to let her unconscious mind drift and dream for a few minutes while I was quiet. Then, I asked:

> *Midge, I want to ask a question of the deepest part of your mind . . . Is there something in the past that's causing your suffering to continue? You may answer with one of your fingers . . .*

Her *yes* finger twitched, and then she muttered something that I didn't understand. "Repeat that with your words," I said. "Gift," she said more clearly. Not knowing what was going on, I followed up with:

> *Midge, that which has to do with this* gift *. . . is your unconscious mind now willing to let this go so you can move on in life . . . you may answer with a finger signal. . . .*

Her *yes* finger lifted again. I eagerly realerted her so I could learn more about this gift. She sobbed, body-wrenching sobs for several minutes. Then she composed herself and explained, "I forgot all about this. A therapist, it was right after my daughter committed suicide, he told me, 'It's the *gift that keeps on giving.*'"

I was speechless. I had seen the negative effects of posthypnotic suggestions before—even ones like this that were not delivered during formal hypnosis—but this one took the cake. I reminded her of her unconscious commitment this session. She was drained—but relieved—when she left.

I saw Midge in two weeks and she looked great. She said, "Wish me luck. I'm going for ECT next week." Her doctor had been working for months to schedule her electroconvulsive therapy (ECT) in Albuquerque. Though I disagreed with this treatment plan, I trusted her physician's recommendation. At last report she was doing fine. I'll never forget Midge. She learned some things in therapy, but even more, I learned many things from her, about suffering and struggling and prevailing. Most of all, she never gave up on therapy, and I remain grateful to her for that.

Looking at Depression Through the Unconscious Lens

More than at any time in previous years, clients we see are likely to be on one or more medications for symptoms of depression. So, too, depressed clients we see are likely to have had psychotherapy in which cognitive-behavioral therapy (CBT) was a major component. For sure, the appropriate medication and well-focused therapy oftentimes helps people through a tough period and allows them to move on in life. If you yourself have been depressed and not sleeping, you understand what tremendous relief and comfort it is to experience a good night's sleep for the first time in months or years.

For others, though, treatment will not be brief. However, it need not last years. For sure, the client's way of thinking needs to be altered, as do their expectations of themselves and others, just as they may need to build their social skills and problem-solving skills. These "tools" are by and large *conscious*. I argue for directing at least half of therapy at the *unconscious*, the level of *values* and *frames of reference*, which usually underlie thinking and behavior. As discussed in Chapter 1, much of everyone's behavior is dictated *unconsciously*, and not by intentionality or conscious effort. If your clients with chronic, recurrent depression have not improved from CBT, medication, or both, perhaps you need to address your efforts below this surface. Herein is the value of hypnosis, and if not by formal hypnosis, by "working hypnotically." And how does that happen? Because of convincing and rational pages you copy for clients out of that tried-and-true CBT workbook? No. Or, does it happen from your well-crafted stories that penetrate "beneath the radar?" Sometimes. From the medication they started last week? Maybe. From some conventional wisdom they saw on *Oprah* or Dr. Phil last month, or from the latest Dr. Burns paperback? Maybe.

Remember the Dance

All of these things can impact conscious and unconscious change. But most of all, change springs from the *therapeutic relationship*. How does such a relationship happen? Not by our dedication to rote techniques, or flying by the seat of our pants each session, but by planning and hard work. Perhaps more than any other population, chronically depressed clients test our mettle and perseverance. That's where adding hypnosis, or "working hypnotically," can give you an edge. Milton Erickson employed formal hypnosis only 20% of the time (Beahrs, 1973), but he "worked hypnotically" 100% of the time. Michael Yapko (2001), when asked how often he works hypnotically, he, too, said, "One hundred% of the time." By this, Erickson and Yapko meant that they insert stories and anecdotes into the session, and that they make liberal use of hypnotic power words, like *imagine, wonder, notice*, and *appreciate*. But, above all, they meant that they are in sync with the client the whole time, listening closely to his words, and also monitoring nonverbals, pacing, and leading. To Erickson and those who learned from him, this "dance" is the essence of psychotherapy.

One of the best examples of this can be found in *Hypnotherapy* (1979) by Erickson and Rossi. In this book, the authors examine Erickson's tape-recorded sessions with clients, offering analysis and insight on Erickson's pacing and leading. The book shows how much of Erickson's subtle technique would be lost on the reader without vital, ongoing commentary.

Does this mean that "working hypnotically" will cure every chronically depressed client? Of course not. Many of Erickson's cases that we read about were successes. But some were not, and Jeff Zeig (1985a) was careful to make note of these treatment failures. If Erickson's clients did not respond and were deemed "treatment resistant," he simply stopped seeing them. Many of us don't have that luxury, and I, perhaps like you, must continue to supportively see some of these clients who don't get better. It just goes with the job. However, this chapter is about the vast majority of others, those whose suffering is palpable and who are doing their best to try to feel better.

In my practice at the Department of Veterans Affairs, where I see individuals, couples, families, and also do groups, I "work hypnotically" much of the time, but formal hypnosis comprises only about 30% of what I do. With chronically depressed people, of course I "work hypnotically," but I also use formal hypnosis 70% of the time. Why? Because it's what I do well, and like in the case of Midge, I try to make it a major component of treatment. Of course, some people—for a variety of reasons—don't want hypnosis, so that needs to be respected. To turn around chronic depression, I believe you have to practice the equivalent of the full-court press in basketball, or the "full code" in medicine: if the patient's heart stops beating, you bring to bear everything at your disposal to give them a chance at life. Formal hypnosis greatly accelerates rapport and trust, thus cementing a firm therapeutic relationship. But in addition to that, hypnosis affords the therapist a whole spectrum of options for targeting intervention at the unconscious.

Clinical Comments

In practicing hypnosis, I know a variety of inductions, stories, and anecdotes; however, I can't remember every one, and frequently I read a script. This does not detract in any way, and clients become accustomed to the reading. However, when reading, you need to be sure to look up at intervals and be prepared to pace ongoing behavior. If, in the induction it says, ". . . and she took one more deep, refreshing breath . . . ," you anticipate that breath from your client, and when she does so, you make note of it with something like, ". . . very good. . . ." So, too, if you're reading a story, and a part of the story corresponds with the client's eye flutter, perhaps you pace it with something like ". . . you're doing fine. . . ." If it becomes more marked and corresponds with squirming or other obvious discomfort, maybe you need to pace it even more strongly with something like, ". . . and some things may not seem to fit, or maybe there's an uncomfortable feeling somewhere. . . ." You may not want to stop with *pacing*, as you could also *lead* with ". . . uncomfortable feeling somewhere *and* such feelings may mean that increased depth and comfort are just a few more seconds away. . . ." Most often, when I notice eye flutter I make a mental note of what I was saying at the time. Sometimes I will inquire during debriefing. However, many times the client is unaware of it, in which case it is usually best not to draw attention to it. Whatever you do, you're involved in the wonderful dance of hypnosis, something that can't be done on a Procrustean bed.

This chapter demonstrated only a few of the many hypnotic techniques that can be brought to bear on chronic depression. As hypnosis greatly accelerates rapport, you are positioning yourself to have greater influence with both consciously and unconsciously directed interventions. Most of all, in the tradition of Jay Haley and strategic therapists, you're taking charge and *making something happen*, and this proaction alone formidably counters the inertia and negativity of depression.

Chapter 9

Gastrointestinal Disorders

I often think of a river when working with clients who have gastrointestinal (GI) disorders, as this image cues thoughts of movement and flow, time and patience, and process. After all, like any major river, minor rivulet, or even a desert arroyo that is bone-dry except in times of rain, these waterways are likely to experience a multitude of both natural and unnatural changes over the years. These may include banks flooding and eroding the shore, the constant movement of sediment and debris, the concrete channeling of banks, construction of dams and levees, and the introduction of new species of plants and fish, to name but a few.

The Burden of a Chronic Problem

By the time clients with these problems make their way to your office they have probably endured a host of medical assessment and treatment. Just ask someone who has had to fast and then flush out their GI tract by drinking Go-Lightly before a colonoscopy, or, on the other end, someone who endures regular surveillance by endoscopy for a chronic upper GI tract condition, or balloon distension to determine esophageal pain threshold. They also have likely tried various medications, some with nasty side effects, and they may be weary of monitoring everything they eat and planning every outing by where the bathrooms are located. They may also evince the anger, discouragement, and even shame of someone whose life is seriously interrupted by an embarrassing problem. Furthermore, inherent in a referral to you is that "it's all in my head," and that they have flunked out of conventional medical treatment. After all, in today's world, isn't a pill or a surgical procedure supposed to make everything okay?

What Are GI Disorders?

Crohn's disease, gastroesophageal reflux disease (GERD), erosive esophagitis, nonerosive reflux disease, Barrett's Esophagus, functional dyspepsia, and IBS are but a few of the disorders treated by gastroenterologists. To read more, I suggest two books. First, *Hot Topics: GERD/Dyspepsia* (Fass, 2004), which provides a comprehensive review of many of these disorders, and second, I recommend Blanchard's (2001) seminal book on irritable bowel syndrome (IBS), *IBS: Psychosocial Assessment and Treatment*.

Just as we rely on the initial interview, GI doctors live and die by the scope. They put the scope in one end or the other and your clients will experience this essential procedure time and time again. Keep this in mind when you construct stories, or word suggestions. I learned this the hard way with some clients in trance who reacted with eye flutter when I was relating a story whose *periscope* was prominent and in which the *scope* of the problem was *explored*. That one was quickly thrown into my water closet of bad stories. Another client reacted similarly to an ego-strengthening anecdote about a rabbit. Only through much prodding did I learn that her "stool diary" had terms like "green and mushy" and "hard like *rabbit* pellets." Into the W.C. with that one, too.

More than any GI disorder, you are likely to see someone with IBS, a *functional* disorder of the lower intestinal tract. *Functional* means that there is no structural abnormality, leaving only disordered bowel function to account for symptoms. It's like your doctor says that you have *essential* or *idiopathic* hypertension. They don't know *why* you have high blood pressure, you just do.

According to Latimer (1983), the IBS diagnosis is confirmed when the person has recurrent abdominal pain or extreme tenderness accompanied by diarrhea or constipation, which is present for three months or longer, and the doctor has ruled out other problems, such as lactose intolerance or inflammatory bowel disease; and abdominal pain or discomfort is relieved by defecation. There are other criteria involving stool form and frequency, but this is already sounding like the *Diagnostic and Statistical Manual-IV*, isn't it?

Many with IBS don't regularly see their doctor. If I get a call from someone who wants treatment for IBS, and she hasn't seen her doctor in a long time, I say, "After your doctor has cleared you, then I'll be glad to make an appointment."

Prevalence of IBS

If you're not already seeing IBS clients in your practice, I bet you will in the future. A widespread disorder, prevalence rates for IBS range from 8–17% of United States adults. In the United Kingdom, where experts have studied the disorder for many years, it is estimated that 13.6% of adults have IBS. Women are twice as likely than men to be diagnosed, and most individuals with IBS *do not* seek medical help (Blanchard, 2001).

Switz (1976) surveyed gastroenterologists in Virginia and found that 19% of patients had functional bowel disorders (e.g., IBS, functional dyspepsia). In the United Kingdom, Harvey, Salih, and Read (1983) reviewed the charts of 2,000 new patients referred to a GI clinic over a five-year period. They found that 44% had functional disorders, with 23% of the total having IBS. Other studies consistently find that IBS accounts for 20–30% of new patient visits to GI doctors.

If you want to build your psychotherapy practice, my advice is this: Sharpen up your hypnosis and get to know your local GI docs. Their journals are full of articles touting the effectiveness of hypnosis, and they probably want some assistance dealing with these clients.

Medical and Dietary Treatments

Blanchard (2001) reviewed dozens of clinical trials that evaluated various medications, including bulking agents, tranquilizers, antacids, antidepressants, and opioids, and found a 20–70% placebo response. His conclusion: there currently is no effective drug treatment for IBS. However, he added that recent trials involving the antidepressant desipramine are promising.

The primary dietary intervention for IBS is the addition of fiber, usually either wheat bran or psyllium. These can be useful for the patient who is constipation predominant (Blanchard, 2001).

Cognitive-Behavioral Therapy (CBT)

In the first randomized clinical trial to evaluate CBT and IBS (Bennett & Wilkinson, 1985), clients were assigned to two treatment regimens: medical care that included an antidepressant and other agents, or a regimen that involved progressive muscle relaxation (PMR) and cognitive therapy to change self-talk. Results: both groups improved on physical measures, such as abdominal pain and frequency of bowel movements, with the CBT group alone showing improvement in anxiety management.

The first Albany study (Neff & Blanchard, 1987) was a similar study with clients assigned to either treatment or a control group. Results: the CBT group demonstrated greater improvement in most physical measures as well as depression. Various other studies involving CBT (Corney, and associates, 1991; Lynch & Zamble, 1989; Shaw and colleagues, 1991) showed fairly good results in physical and psychological measures. Similar results were reported when these interventions were administered in a group format (Van Dulmen et al., 1996).

Other Therapies

Two randomized clinical trials involving what sounds like a contradiction in terms, brief psychodynamic therapy (Guthrie et al., 1991; Svedlund et al., 1983) reported sustained gains at 12-month follow-up. Other interventions with few supporting studies include bio-feedback, bowel-sound feedback, and bio-feedback of colonic motility (Blanchard, 2001).

A Rose by Any Other Name

Interestingly, almost all of the above studies employed interventions similar to hypnosis. For example, in one of the brief psychodynamic therapy studies (Guthrie et al., 1991) participants were given a *relaxation tape to use at home on a regular basis*. Most of the CBT studies included interventions called "relaxation training," PMR, "guided imagery," "pain management," "stress management," and "stress inoculation."

Hypnosis interventions, such as those described below, incorporate similar suggestions for relaxation and imagery. But they also include suggestions for *ego-strengthening*, and mention the *unconscious mind*. So, is that all that separates hypnosis from, say, guided imagery? Perhaps. We could argue until we're cyanotic about whether meditation is hypnosis. I have a simple rule of thumb: *If you call it hypnosis, it's hypnosis.*

Hypnosis and the Treatment of IBS

We're accustomed to CBT's empirical juggernaut riding roughshod over every other treatment approach for disorders A–Z. Not in this case. Even a very traditional psychologist like Blanchard (2001), who devotes a large portion of his book to CBT, all but admitted that the formidable track record of hypnosis makes it the treatment of choice.

The leader in this field for many years has been Peter Whorwell, a gastroenterologist in England. His impressive initial study in 1984 (Whorwell, Prior, & Faragher) was followed up in 1987 (Whorwell, Prior, & Colgan) by a study of 50 chronic, mild-moderate IBS clients treated with 10 weekly sessions of hypnosis. There were positive results in 42 cases, with many reporting elimination of symptoms. An 18-month follow-up of his first study found that two of the 15 cases had suffered relapses, and a single booster session of hypnosis alleviated the returned symptoms.

Houghton, Heyman, and Whorwell (1996) replicated previous studies with similar results; however, this time the clients had severe, refractory IBS. An interesting finding of this study was that among IBS clients who were on disability because of their IBS, three of four treated with hypnosis *returned to work*, whereas none of the six in the control group resumed employment. In 2002, Gonsalkorale, Houghton, and Whorwell reported results from a study of 250 IBS clients treated with hypnosis at their clinic in South Manchester, England. These clients were given 12 sessions of hypnosis over three months. The authors reported similar rates of improvement in physical and psychological categories. They noted that hypnosis may continue to prove even more cost-effective as new, more-expensive drugs come onto the market. Interestingly, they found that diarrhea-predominant males showed the poorest response to treatment.

Various case reports also confirm the usefulness of hypnosis in treating the disorder. Joseph Zimmerman (2003), a gastroenterologist in Israel, employed the "river" metaphor, which links the altered motility of the digestive system to the emotional contents it may embody. The metaphor is used to evoke both a smooth, coordinated flow through the normal digestive tract and a normal flow in the management of the client's emotions.

In a study that investigated how hypnosis works with this population, Palsson and colleagues (2002) showed that the verbatim delivery of hypnosis, using written scripts, benefits most clients and produces therapeutic gains of at least a 10-month duration. They found that suggestions or imagery specifically directed at reducing intestinal pain sensitivity *were unnecessary*, as they had no measurable effect on bowel-pain threshold or the degree of clinical pain improvement. Importantly, they concluded that *hypnosis alone*, without a CBT component, benefits clients primarily by reducing the somatic focus of attention and *changing beliefs* about the significance of symptoms. So, maybe we can throw those tedious old CBT thought logs into the fire after all!

Functional Dyspepsia

Among GI disorders, the success of hypnosis is not limited to IBS. Whorwell's group (Calvert et al., 2002) randomized 126 clients with functional dyspepsia (a condition distinct from GERD, but which also includes epigastric pain and discomfort) to either hypnosis, supportive therapy plus placebo medication, or medical treatment. Follow-up at 56 weeks confirmed the benefits of hypnosis over the other treatments for long-term management of the disorder.

Combining Direct and Indirect Approaches

In Tucson, Arizona, we use a flexible protocol, in which clients are seen for an average of six sessions over three months. In the first session, clients complete the Beck depression and anxiety inventories, along with a self-esteem inventory, and they give a verbal commitment to treatment, rate their difficulty with IBS on a 1–10 scale, and agree to track their somatic symptoms in a notebook provided for them. They receive a brief explanation of the unconscious mind, and in this session other essential preliminaries are covered: what is hypnosis, negative stereotypes about hypnosis, and an explanation of the procedure.

In session two, we begin by asking the client to perform the Weyer Clasp, in which they place one hand on their abdomen and the other hand on their head. As they do this, we say, "This represents the connection between your symptoms and the unconscious mind, and much of this treatment is directed at the unconscious mind." We tell them that the session will be audiotaped for practice at home, and that ". . . in trance today you will be asked to make a circle, or *anchor*, placing your index finger and thumb (on their dominant hand) together, forming a little circle. This anchor is your friend and ally, something you always carry with you, and something that can help you in times of stress." Formal hypnosis then begins with a conversational induction and counting-down deepening (Gafner & Benson, 2000), followed by an ego-strengthening story, such as "Molasses Reef."

MOLASSES REEF

I was walking along the beach early one morning. It was one of those white-sand beaches—I forget its name—on Florida's Gulf Coast. I was all alone and it was very pleasant, so refreshing, and I can still hear the sound of the gulls and the gentle waves washing up on the shore. Just then I heard someone speaking above the sound of the surf. Off to my right, I saw a man and a woman, seated on a bench, and they were leaning toward each other, conversing in what I can only describe as a loud whisper. The man said to the woman, "*I want to tell you a good story*," and this immediately captured my attention, as I have been fascinated by a *good story* ever since I was young. I sat down in the sand within earshot, but they paid me no heed.

The man was describing a beautiful marine sanctuary called Molasses Reef. He said, "It's off of Key Largo . . . I dove there in the 1940s . . . most people didn't know it existed then. . . ."

The woman seemed to know what he was talking about, and the discussion of Molasses Reef went back and forth. The reef was so named because long ago a ship laden with barrels of molasses had sunk on that spot. "It covers a sizeable area, maybe 5,000 square meters," said the woman. "Yes," said the man. "I still dream about it." Then, they were silent for what may have been several minutes. Still, no one glanced in my direction. The man leaned forward on his cane, deep in thought, and the woman sat back and closed her eyes.

The crash of the surf seemed quieter just then, or maybe they resumed speaking with more volume, although it was still a whisper. The man's eyes opened while the woman remained in her reverie. He said, "If you can imagine the place of your dreams, that was Molasses Reef. A truly enchanted, magical place. The majestic silence, the riot of color and movement of all that lived there."

"I've seen some wondrous things myself," added the woman. "The mouth of the Amazon, the Taj Mahal, the leaves turning in Vermont, the Lakes District of England, the first steps of my grand-daughter, Lake Louise, the lights of Manhattan. . . ."

The man interjected, "Better than all those is Molasses Reef." The woman nodded and drifted off again in her daydream. I was further lulled by the silence and my own mind drifted to this reef and back again. I may have actually fallen asleep, as I was startled when the man's words again penetrated my consciousness. "In 1984 a freighter bound for Portugal sank right on top of the reef. It was a catastrophe. What had taken thousands of years of natural construction was suddenly and irreparably damaged. Or so it seemed, until the Reef Doctor came along." "Yes, the Reef Doctor, I read about him," responded the woman.

"The Reef Doctor, I remember his exact words when he surveyed the damage. He said, 'Much of this reef is pulverized, but we have something that can give nature a jump start *so it can heal itself*," said the doctor. He and his team proceeded to construct several dozen reef replacement structures with hidey holes for fish. Limestone galleries. In no time coral attached themselves to these galleries, and after one year scientists saw shrimp, sea grasses, sponges, and new fish species. The limestone galleries were a remarkable success, and now the reef is *gradually healing itself*, in its own way, in its own time, with a little help from the Reef Doctor."

"That's a very nice story," said the woman. The man looked tired, and he sat back, closed his eyes, and returned to a state of deep reflection. The woman rose and stretched, and stared briefly in my direction before opening a jar of dill pickles. (Davis, 2003)

The anchor is then rehearsed, the client is realerted and debriefed. They are given the audiotape and instructed to listen to it at a variable rate, "at least twice and no more than five times per week." Offering such latitude of choice often leads to more frequent listening.

Session Three

We begin by reviewing the client's symptom log and progress to date as evidenced by the 1–10 scale. The Weyer Clasp is rehearsed, the agenda is set, along with ". . . later on today in trance I will ask your unconscious mind to generate a healing image. This image can be anything at all. For example, some people select a white light, or a walk on the beach. . . ." Hypnosis then resumes with induction and deepening and either of the following scripts adapted from Bryson (1990).

The Great Vowel Shift for Constipation Predominate

Historians of language development have noted that the Great Vowel Shift happened roughage/roughly *around the*   misspeak
time of Chaucer. Exit *discussions with*   suggestion
textbook editors *may* leave *us with the*
impression that people began to pronounce
their vowels one way up until a certain

date, and then another way, suddenly and
swiftly, on the next day, like a leaf drop-   suggestion
ping *from a tree. One historian went so*
far as to push through *his theory at an*
international symposium, his talk being
entitled, "Move Over and Make Way for
Vowel Mastery," though other authorities
recognized that many of the pronunciation
changes *reflected* movement *before the*   suggestion
time of King Alfred. In other words, at an
indeterminate time in the future shove
and move *may be rhyming words.*

The Great Vowel Shift for Diarrhea Predominate

Historians of language have noted that
the Great Vowel Shift stopped/occurred   misspeak
generally around the time of Chaucer in the
5th century. Textbook accounts of of the shift
usually concentrate *on the remarkable and*   suggestion
innate ability of people to smoothly and
gradually make these vowel *pronunciation*
shifts. *Some of the changes remain incom-*
plete today, and lexicographers speculate
that one day words like shove *and* move
may be pronounced the same.

When Chaucer died in 1400, people
still pronounced the e on the end of words,
so that move slower *sounded like* movie   suggestion
goer, *or more precisely,* movie slower,
certainly an entertainment not available   lead away
in those days. But one day— no one
knows exactly when—the e fell silent, as if
suddenly arrested *in the annals of*   suggestion
language.

For whatever reasons, in a relatively
short period of time, Englishmen changed

their values in a fundamental and system-   suggestion
atic way, shoving tense vowels forward
and upward *in their mouths.*

(Clinical note: If your IBS client is a diarrhea-predominant male, you may be wise to employ more techniques such as restraint and leading away, an approach that is advised with other populations when high reactance is present. The one group for whom hypnosis is generally less effective is diarrhea-predominant males with IBS. The reason for this is unknown [Gonsalkorale, Houghton, & Whorwell, 2002].)

Healing Image

The client is then asked to place their dominant hand on their abdomen followed by:

> *. . . and now, [person's name], I'd like your unconscious mind to drift and dream, letting that deepest part of you come up with a healing image . . . and when that image is there, in your mind, you will know and I will know because you'll find your head nodding one time. . . ."* If no head nod is forthcoming, an image, such as a white light, is assigned, and the client is instructed, *". . . just let that image be there for a few moments while I stop talking . . . recognizing that this image is something that can help you now and forever in the future. Many people find themselves turning to this image at home, or while listening to their tape. I knew a woman one time who very successfully controlled her symptoms by using her anchor and placing her hand on her stomach, which automatically brought up her healing image. . . .*

Realerting and debriefing follows.

Session Four

We begin by reviewing progress to date and the Weyer Clasp is rehearsed. Induction and deepening is followed by an ego-strengthening story, such as the following.

EMERSON'S CLEAR CUT

Emerson parked his car off the dirt road. Nothing was so tranquil as his forty acres of New England woods. For a long time he had thought about clear-cutting an acre of his land so he could recreate the serene pasture land of the late 19th century. But just thinking about it caused pangs of guilt and reservation. He thought, "What right do I have to end the lives of innocent pine trees whose ancestors have graced the landscape for thousands of years?"

Eventually he hired someone to cut the trees, and a mule hauled away the logs. Soon he was staring at a barren expanse. "It looks like a wasteland," he mused. "I have let in the light, but why do I experience only darkness?"

Paralyzed by remorse, Emerson chose to do nothing. He watched and waited and soon he saw change. Blackberry bushes appeared, along with grass, cinquefoil, goldenrod, and other plants he could not name. "All this must be good for the wildlife," he thought.

But there were those tree stumps. He had forgotten about them—or just not seen them—until one day he tripped over a stump and fell into a patch of poison ivy. He put in a call to Boyle Excavators, and the owner of the company, Lance himself, appeared the next day at the crack of dawn with his bulldozer. Before sundown all the unsightly stumps had been dug up and buried. Lance Boyle, Jr., followed up with a grater and bladed it bare. For the first time in years, Emerson experienced real peace and silence as he gazed upon the clearing.

He returned to Concord to look after his ailing mother, and for several weeks he forgot about the clear-cut acre. When he returned, he was dumbstruck by what he observed. *An even greater variety of plant life had returned.* The blackberries were back, and so was everything else. Upon closer observation he noted an abundance of wildlife he had never seen before. In his meadow he saw leopard frogs, pickerel frogs, wood frogs, toads, salamanders, katydids, crickets, grasshoppers, and beetles. Some days foxes and skunks appeared, along with song sparrows, tree sparrows, robins, and flickers.

During the day a thought kept repeating in his head. "*So much life has returned* to my clear-cut acre, *so much life has returned. . . .*" At night he gazed up at the stars and sky, and felt the wind blowing against his face. (Mitchell, 1990)

By now, the majority of clients will have responded positively as evidenced by their symptom diary and the 1–10 scale. For some who may need an extra boost, we will add a brief story such as the following.

COLIN AND FLO

She and her husband had just moved to Wyoming, but Flo soon realized that she and Colin had only taken their problems with them. "Like so many bulky steamer trunks," thought Flo.

One night during a heated argument Flo yelled, "Colin, you avoid intimacy. I want to be in you, not outside of you. Let me in so I can be a part of your life!"

"What exactly do you mean?" asked her husband.

"I mean *inside*, in the deepest part of you," she explained, and with those words her reasoning had finally broken through to Colin.

The anchor is rehearsed and realerting and debriefing follows.

Session Five

Practice at home and progress are reviewed. Weyer Clasp precedes induction and deepening and an ego-strengthening story such as the one below follows.

JELLYFISH

Let me tell you a little story that was constructed from notes hastily written down following a discussion with one of our therapists, who overheard two children having a heated discussion in the waiting room of the clinic. The two children, a boy about 10, and a girl of approximately the same age, were debating which was the most powerful fish in the ocean. "It's the shark," said the boy. "No, it's the whale," answered the girl with firm conviction. "Maybe then it's the barracuda," ventured the boy.

The observer, who himself was a keen observer of the natural world, said later, "The discussion went on and on, and I found it quite *absorbing*. At the time it was raining outside, so it was *good to be inside*, and out there in the waiting room I was standing around the corner, but within clear earshot of the children's discussion. Time seemed to *stand still* as I listened, but then my attention took a detour when an elderly woman in an old leather aviator's cap joined the discussion. She was quite a spectacle, but not the first time I've seen human oddities in that waiting room.

There was a rather awkward pause as the woman began to speak, and the boy and girl just stood there as if they were frozen. Then they looked at one another cautiously, perhaps recalling a parent's admonition against talking to strangers.

"It was last summer when it happened," said the woman, and immediately the children's attention was arrested by the woman's authoritative voice. "It was an unprecedented invasion," she went on. "Unprecedented?" asked the girl. "Yes, it had never happened before," answered the woman. "An invasion of jellyfish, perhaps the most powerful fish in the ocean," she continued. The boy and girl sat on the floor, chin in their hands.

"Thousands of lion's mane jellies washed up on shore. I was visiting Cape Cod at the time. People were afraid to go in the water." "Jellyfish sting, don't they?" asked the boy. "They sting more than a fire ant, almost as much as a wasp," said the boy. "Even more, they sting like THAT," answered the woman, as she stabbed a bony finger in their direction. The children sprang back, and their mouths were agape as the woman continued.

"That summer parts of the Gulf of Mexico filled with yellow blobs the size of garbage-can lids. Yes, the blobs were jellyfish, and you know how they sting." "They sting like THAT," said the boy.

"They turned to experts, like the famous Dr. Barbara Burnfinger at the United States Sea Laboratory. She determined that those creatures had stuck themselves on to ships that came through the Panama Canal. Once they arrived, those jellyfish devoured plankton and fish eggs and kept getting bigger and bigger. Her laboratory captured a 60-pound pink jellyfish that had tentacles that trailed 100 feet behind it. And each of those tentacles could sting." "Just like THAT," said the girl.

"Jellyfish don't have a heart or a brain and they can't see, and they are at the mercy of the current or waves, and can be dashed to pieces if they hit anything solid. They can live in shallow tidepools or the bottom of the ocean. You can find them in the warm waters of the equator or under the Antarctic ice pack, and even in freshwater ponds. They can be the size of a pea, or they can be big, big, big. They can grow fast. One can be the size of a grain of sand one day and grow to the size of a dinner plate the next day." The woman was clearly tiring. She took off the aviator's cap and scratched her head.

"What else?" asked the boy. "Oh, there's a lot more," said the woman. "All those oil-drilling platforms out there in the Gulf—well, Dr. Burnfinger said that they attach themselves to those platforms, and all of a sudden, BOOM, they multiply, millions of them. They can't be poisoned or eradicated. There's absolutely nothing we can do about them," continued the woman.

"Now, that's *one powerful fish*," said the boy. The children's mother now appeared. "Time to go," she said. The boy and the girl rose slowly. Their legs had fallen asleep. (Estabrook, 2002)

The anchor is rehearsed and this is followed by realerting and debriefing.

Session Six

Progress is reviewed, the clasp is rehearsed, and induction and deepening are followed by a story such as the following.

OKAY

In a person's experience, which is quite a bit when you think about it, many things can happen. Many things we hear about, things that go together, peas and carrots, *okay* and not okay, right and left, up and down, hot and cold, and all the degrees of temperature in between.

Now with people, some people get along, and some don't. With sibling rivalry, we have Cane and Abel, and we also have brothers and sisters, aunts and uncles, and many things related to one another that aren't relatives, like initials in a person's name. One person was given the initials I.M. at birth, while another was named with the letters U.R., and a person could spend a long time guessing what those letters stood for. The famous naturalist, John Muir, his last name was spelled M-U-I-R, and the origin of that name may be a mystery. I knew a man one time whose sister was named P.I. I asked him, "Does it stand for 'private investigator,' or is it 'principal investigator'?" "No, not even close," he answered. "Then, is it 'Priscilla Inspiration'?" I asked, and he answered, "You're getting close," and I never did find out what it was.

Two female twins named U.R. and I.M. found themselves separated from each other in a forest on a moonless night. "U.R., is that you over there?" one asked from behind a tree, and the other answered, "It's me, I.M., and I'm *okay*," and with those words they both were immensely relieved. Both U.R. and I.M. were very intuitive with each other. One might say, for example, "When I'm very involved in something time is motionless, as if . . . " and the other would finish the sentence with "as if it, too, is waiting," and both would simply smile and exhale deeply, as no more words were needed.

The twins grew up to become famous lexicographers, and spent their lives immersed in the study of words. "It's something a person can immerse herself in to a maximum degree," commented I.M. "I agree with you, but just up to a point," said U.R., who added, "Total and complete absorption in anything may not be a good thing." Her sister then added, "If my attention is arrested by, or otherwise fixated by, one particular word, say the word *time*, then I'm more likely than not going to in fact lose track of time, which can be a rather pleasant thing in itself." "And you're *okay* with that, it sounds like," her sister commented. "Yes, I am," she answered.

I.M. and U.R. attended different graduate schools, but both did their dissertations on the origins of the word okay, and the topic often occupied their discussion whenever they got together. One might venture forth with, "*Okay* is all around us, so much a part of us, like, *O.K.* Corral and *O.K.* Cleaners, or *O.K.* Auto Parts," and the other one would answer, "I.M. *okay* and U.R. is *okay*, too," "But we knew that already," responded her sister. "That reminds me of the short story called 'Graphite Delirium,'" said the other, who definitely was the more distracting of the two.

"Let's not forget linguistic pockets and regional dialects," said I.M. "You're talking about a linguistic layer cake?" asked her sister. "No, just boundaries for dialects," said I.M., who added, "Remember that in any country we have north, south, east, and west, and let's not forget about time. In one century, dear sister, you may have said, 'You were born in a barn,' but during the next 100 years you would have pronounced it, 'You were barn in a born.'" "If my midwife was in that barn, so was yours," answered her sister."

U.R. continued: "If you want the freshest vegetables, you'd go to *O.K.* Market, right?" "No, I'd go to Better Market or Best Market for the freshest," answered I.M., who continued with, "The word *okay* started in the U.S. as an abbreviation for Obadaiha Kelly." "No," said her sister, "It started with President Martin Van Buren, whose nickname was Old Kinderhook. In 1840 they had the Democratic *Okay* Club, solely because of the president. In those days they stamped "O.K." on crates and barrels." I.M. asked, "I guess that designated quality or reliability?" "I'm *okay* with that," answered her sister.

U.R. noted, "The word is possibly taken from the Choctaw Indian word, *okeh*, or else it came from the French term, *aux cays*. "I can be *okay* with that, too," answered I.M., "but then you also have to consider what was attributed to President Andrew Jackson, who said, "Oll korrect." "Well, so much for military men who go on to high office," said her sister.

I.M. said, "One time I was addressing a class of undergraduates about this very topic. There were about 30 in the class, all sitting in concentric circles, and I asked them to turn to the person on their right and say, 'You're *okay*,' and sure enough, one student was unable to do it. So, I sat down next to him and showed him how to do it. I looked deeply into his eyes, which made him kind of nervous, and I slowly mouthed the words, '*Y-o-u a-r-e o-k-a-y*.' I don't know if he believed me, but then he said the words, '*You are okay*' to the person on his right, which was me."

"But he was addressing you, I.M., and you already knew you were *okay*," said U.R.

"Yes," she answered, "but then the next week someone else was on his right, as well as his left, because each week they sit in a different chair, and everyone said it and accepted it just fine."

"I'll have to try that out in one of my classes, but where I teach all the chairs are in rows," said her sister.

Following realerting and debriefing, the self-esteem, depression, and anxiety measures are repeated. Clients are reinforced for their hard work, and reminded to keep up their practice. They understand they can return for a booster session in the future if they feel the need.

Other Issues

I handle problems of noncompliance the same way with all clients—by cutting them very little slack. If they don't keep their symptom diary, or say, "Oh, I forgot" when asked about practice with the tape at home, I'll immediately cut the session short and say, "Call me when you've completed these things and we'll set up another appointment." If they fail an appointment, or cancel twice in a row, they're going to have to convince me that they're serious about therapy before we proceed.

With some IBS clients, anger is palpable, and it must be addressed before you can proceed. If they have responded well in hypnosis, I might first try techniques like "pile of rocks" or the amplifying the metaphor (Gafner & Benson, 2003). If they haven't responded well I will use a traditional anger-management procedure that includes an anger log, time-out, etc., and hopefully get back to the hypnosis procedure after a few weeks.

Some people have a history of abuse and may have coped poorly for years. People with childhood sexual abuse in their background may respond less to this approach. So, too, with borderline personality disorder. Clients such as these need to be reminded that your job is their GI problem, and that other issues need to be addressed with their regular therapist, if they have one.

Clinical Comments

For some clients, especially the lesser educated, the "Okay Story" may come across as too "busy." Some therapists new to ego-strengthening have difficulty fathoming that a story about jellyfish could be unconsciously incorporated and that an increase in self-efficacy could result. If you feel more comfortable with a story that has to do with a tree or animal that survives adversity and prevails, or even a story about a *human being*, of all things, who suffers and survives, knock yourself out. I bet you'll come around to jellyfish sooner or later.

Feel free to substitute the stories in this book with other ego-strengthening stories, such as those found in our first two books (Gafner & Benson, 2000; Gafner & Benson, 2003). We have experimented with ego-strengthening anecdotes and short-burst ego-strengthening with IBS patients, and although these techniques seem to be nearly effective, stories alone lend themselves better to a scripted procedure or research protocol. Although we have not conducted a formal study with these techniques and IBS, our results are similar to those reported by others, whose techniques are more direct than ours.

Noncardiac chest pain (NCCP) is a common condition with the esophagus being the primary source of symptoms. As with IBS, there currently is no effective drug treatment for the condition. NCCP has never been subjected to a research protocol involving hypnosis as a treatment condition. We are currently beginning a formal study entitled "The Effect of Hypnotherapy vs. Supportive Therapy on Symptoms of Patients with Functional Chest Pain of Presumed Esophageal Origin: A Randomized Trial." It is funded by the American College of Gastroenterology. Thirty participants are randomly assigned to either six sessions of hypnosis, or six sessions of supportive counseling. Instead of placing their hand on their abdomen while they generate a healing image, as is done with IBS, clients are instructed to place their hand on their breastbone. An upper endoscopy will be performed to exclude an esophageal mucosal injury. If endoscopy is negative, participants will undergo 24-hour esophageal pH monitoring to exclude abnormal acid exposure. Various psychological measures are employed along with pre- and post-esophageal balloon distention to determine perception thresholds for pain.

Appendices

Ego-Strengthening Anecdotes

When do you use an ego-strengthening anecdote and when a story? That's like asking, "How many people are dead in that cemetery?" and the answer is, "All of 'em." Story, anecdote, short-burst, ego-strengthening—I judiciously mix techniques, as many clients badly need a boost in self-esteem. But don't ignore the social and behavioral. They may *feel* better, but until they actually *do* something different, improvement may be specious.

245 Feet High

In 1826 David Douglas began to explore the forest south of Fort Vancouver. Local Indians noticed this man wandering through the woods, collecting plant specimens and certain seeds. Douglas was determined to find the mysterious pines with huge cones of Indian legend. He had traversed the unexplored territory for weeks when he came upon an immense sugar pine that was 18 feet thick and some 245 feet high. (Arno, 1999)

Prolific Producers

Sugar pines become prolific producers of cones when they reach 150 years of age. While still green, a single cone weighs four pounds. The sugary resin forms crunchy crystalline deposits, which were a prized delicacy of Indians in the area. Indians also employed pitch from the trees for repairing canoes and other uses. (Arno, 1999)

THICK BARK

Once it has passed through the vulnerable sapling stage, the Ponderosa develops a very thick bark, which makes it resistant to fire. Large trees may have blackened wounds caused by a sequence of forest fires. The tree seals its fire scars with pitch, which prevents decay by damaging organisms. One 400-year-old tree discovered recently on a ridge in the Bitterroot Mountains showed that it had been scarred by fire 21 times between 1659 and 1919. Nevertheless, the tree remained very much alive, vigorous, and vital. (Arno, 1999)

LODGEPOLE PINE

Lodgepole pine grows on a thin layer of soil and develops a rather shallow root system. The tree's seeds are so small that it takes about 100,000 to make a pound of seeds. Often the seeds are enveloped by the branches and become completely encased in wood. In one study, the naturalist William Inskeep found seed from a 150-year-old cone imbedded in the tree. Inskeep discovered that seeds from this cone were still viable. (Arno, 1999)

CONICAL FRUIT

The hard conical fruit of the Pitch pine sometimes stays on the tree all winter long, sometimes even for years. It is prickly and strong on the outside, covered with pitch, and inside are the dark-brown seeds in pairs, each pair occupying a separate compartment. A thin membrane or wing extends from each seed, and wind can transport them a great distance, on the back of a deer, or on a passing truck or railroad car. The more impoverished or rocky the soil, the more cones they bear. (Thoreau, 2000)

LILLY

When the seed of the white lilly first leaves its pod, first it floats, and once its protective coating is washed away, it sinks to the bottom, where it takes root. (Thoreau, 2000)

ACORN

Acorns are more likely to sprout beneath pines rather than oaks. They may lay many years in the soil before sprouting. If there are warm rains in November they may sprout *before* wind blows them to the ground, where squirrels or birds may carry them off. (Thoreau, 2000)

TOUCH-ME-NOT

The seeds of the touch-me-not flower may shoot off like a pistol at the slightest touch. That is how they escaped from gardens and achieved a reputation for stealth. However, they were transported from England to America by a different route. (Thoreau, 2000)

BIRCH SEEDS

Some have mistaken the seeds of the birch tree for tiny brown butterflies. The winged seeds are designed for flight, floating and gyrating in the wind, quickly disappearing from sight. That is why the Indians dubbed them "no-see-ums." It is also why Thoreau found them beneath willows and alders and maples, even though no parent birch was to be seen. (Thoreau, 2000)

GRAY GOOSE

John Muir called the common gray goose the wariest of large birds. They were very devoted to their flock, and they were also exceedingly cautious and circumspect. They often flew several times around adjacent thickets and fences, checking for danger. (Teale, 1982)

VONNEGUT

Kurt Vonnegut waited 20 years to write *Slaughterhouse Five*, an anti-war classic based on his experience as a prisoner of war in Dresden, Germany, when the city was destroyed by waves of incendiary bombs dropped by British aircraft. The war in Vietnam was the catalyst that caused him to put pen to paper.

EPIPHYLLUM I

In the lowlands of Bolivia we find the epiphyllum cactus, which has adapted both strangely and wonderfully *above* soil and down below where the conditions are too wet. Its seeds are carried by birds to tree branches where they germinate, and the epiphyllum spends the rest of its life clinging to tree bark, and its stems project in all directions, capturing all available air and sunlight. (Mauseth, Kiesling & Ostolaza, 2002)

EPIPHYLLUM II

No tree bark holds water for very long. After a light rain, the leaves of a tree may remain moist, with the bark remaining dry. In a heavy rain water runs down the bark, where some of it is captured by the epiphyllum's thirsty roots. But those roots must be quick, as the bark quickly dries out. (Mauseth, Kiesling, & Ostolaza, 2002)

EPIPHYLLUM III

The epiphyllum cactus is not much to look at. Among the tangle of dead branches you will find one or two live ones. This is actually a sophisticated adaptation. In times of drought, why should the plant maintain its entire self instead of redirecting available water to one or two vital branches? (Mauseth, Kiesling, & Ostalaza, 2002)

EPIPHYLLUM IV

If you can locate it, in the highlands of Bolivia, near the confluence of two rivers, you will find two adjacent valleys very different from one another: green vegetation and brown, alpine and low habitat, meadowland and desert, moist and dry. On the wet side is a sole tree, and in the tree is an epiphyllum cactus, filled with fruit. (Mauseth, Kiesling, & Ostalaza, 2002)

SAMAIPATICERUS

In the highlands of central Bolivia we find the samaipaticerus cactus, which supports itself in most interesting way. As a branch grows, it eventually rests on the branch of a tree, and the tree then does all the work of supporting it. The cactus then grows a weaker wood that lacks fibers. As it produces weak wood, the energy it saves can be used for further growth. (Mauseth, Kiesling, & Ostalaza, 2002)

HAAGEOCEREUS TENUIS

The haageocereus tenuis cactus survives in extreme conditions in northern Peru. It grows on its side, branches splayed forlornly, its base decaying in the loose sand. The sides of the stems produce roots that store water, which is rarely available. It may experience moisture when a fog rolls off the ocean, or when it rains only every two years. (Mauseth, Kiesling, & Ostalaza, 2002)

NEORAIMONDIA GIGANTEA

The neoraimondia gigantea cactus is a true giant, with 30 stems, each 18 feet in length. It concentrates its resources in only one stem and the rest of the plant must do without, receiving just enough to keep it alive and functional. However, it continues to grow. Once the favored stem reaches a particular length, its supply of nutrients is restricted, as resources go to another branch. (Mauseth, Kiesling, & Ostalaza, 2002)

NEOPORTERIA

The neoporteria is difficult to transplant. However, every once in a while we see a seemingly moribund plant that has been withering for months in the greenhouse, and all of a sudden it will return to life, thriving, happy, and healthy. This transformation is a mystery. However, scientists surmise that the neoporteria, accustomed to extended periods of drought, experiences a dormancy when uprooted, and that a certain amount of time must pass before water will stimulate it to grow again. (Mauseth, Kiesling. & Ostalaza, 2002)

THE GREAT WALL

In northern China, a portion of a village abuts part of the Great Wall of China that was built in the 1300s. Some houses are carved out of the Wall itself, so the homes have walls that are 20-feet thick. Mr. Wang said of his house, "Warm in the winter, cool in the summer." (Hessler, 2003)

WILD WATER

Buhner (2002) talks about what passes in silence between people, and what also passes between people and the natural world. He remembered his grandfather reaching into a glassy pond and cupping some water in his hands. "Here, have you tasted this," asked grandfather. Forever after, Buhner remembered his first taste of 'wild water.'

BUDWORM PROTECTION

The Douglas fir tree demonstrates a sophisticated chemical response to attacks by the spruce budworm. During times of peak budworm infestation, the tree releases volatile oils, or terpenes, from its needles, and during June and July terpene production increases 600 percent. (Buhner, 2002)

DISPERSION OF SEEDS

Someone was talking one time about growth and new learning and I'm not sure exactly what she meant, but she likened it to the dispersion of seeds in the wild, and how things happen automatically, but not always predictably. Of the uncountable seeds produced by any plant during its lifetime, most will never germinate. However, some indeed do, and then begin a life of their own.

STRAWBERRY

Thoreau once talked about the wild strawberry, finding a plant growing in a ditch, barely detectable, so close to the ground. He thought, "How did it find its way to such an unfavorable place, in knolls and swells, in sandy hollows, or in a cow path? I would never look for it there." But it was well worth it, it's vernal fragrance, and then there was the taste. Very few know where to discover the early strawberry, as if it were Indian knowledge or secret tradition. (Thoreau, 2000)

PITCH PINE

Pitch pine disperses its seeds all winter long. The seeds are not only blown through the air, but *slide* over snow and ice. In the fall its seed would be detained by grass and bushes, but in the winter it travels far and wide, on the crust of snow, or the glaze of ice, and even years later it springs up along a shore, a mile or more from parent trees, or on a sandy railroad embankment. Of course, some sprout on land recently plowed or burned over, and others are spread by squirrels, buried or carried off to a convenient place. One time Thoreau observed a single squirrel carrying three cones at a time. (Thoreau, 2000)

Appendix 2
Instigative Anecdotes

In doing hypnosis I'm usually doing two things: planting seeds (seeding) and perturbing. Clients come to therapy and however their problem is defined, they are *stuck*—on an unconscious level—and perturbation is indicated. Instigative anecdotes in trance may trigger unconscious perturbation. Oftentimes I will tell the client two or three instigative anecdotes, perhaps with some fluff in between, and then ask for unconscious acceptance. For example, "I told you some little stories today. Are they something your unconscious mind can put to use? Taking as much time as you need, you may answer with one of your fingers. . . ."

TELETUBBIES

Anne Wood, creator of the popular PBS children's TV program, *The Teletubbies*, was negotiating with network executives on details of her new series, *Boohbah*, whose purpose is to teach exercise skills to toddlers. Against a dreamy pastoral backdrop of green lawn and distant trees, two giggling six-year-olds snapped their hands like lobsters and bobbed up and down. Before each new exercise, one child would exclaim, "Look what I can do!" The executives were adamant that the phrasing should be a call to action, and changed to, "Look what I can do! You can do it, too!"

Anne Wood was equally adamant, saying that such an explicit invitation was not necessary, adding, "You don't want to set up anxiety on the part of children who *don't* want to do it. This leaves it up to the child," and allows them to feel confident rather than put upon. Anne Wood prevailed, demonstrating both the *law of parsimony*, and the notion that gentle, open-ended permissiveness may be more persuasive than *explicit direction*. (Dominus, 2004)

A Path

A path that led to a blank wall. Does the trail lead to an entrance nobody knows? (L'Amour, 2002)

Automatic Writing

When the Irish poet W. B. Yeats married his second wife in 1917, he purchased a 13th-century Norman tower house. In that house he witnessed her special talent, the gift of automatic writing. (Storr, 2000)

Ladybugs

Most people don't realize that the larvae of ladybugs, or more correctly, ladybeetles, consume more aphids than adults. An adult might eat 200 aphids before it lays its eggs and passes on, while a larva will consume 600 aphids. Horticulture experts tell gardeners that the real benefit from ladybeetles comes *after* they lay their eggs. Unfortunately, that is exactly when some gardeners want to apply insecticide. (Heffernon, 1991)

Ladybugs in Arizona

In southern Arizona, when ladybugs have consumed available aphids in peoples' gardens, they fly straight up until they reach a layer of air that is 50 degrees Fahrenheit. Then, they either fly on, or let prevailing winds carry them to the mountains. It is a mystery why they congregate only on certain mountain peaks. (Heffernon, 1991)

Robert Parker

Folklore has it that the American mystery writer Robert B. Parker was talking once about his "rules for detectives and private eyes." He said something like this: "If you're not sure what's going on, sit down and have a cup of coffee and see what comes up."

Overdeveloped Memory

These moments of reverie are refreshing mirages sweetening the world's inexorable drought. Life has ceased to be inflected in the present. Boualem is one of the people suffering from a new malady: an *overdeveloped* memory. (Djaout, 2001)

Barbara Kingsolver

The American writer, Barbara Kingsolver, reportedly said one time that truth is a close relative of memory, but not a twin.

Beautiful Flower

Marilyn Ferguson (1980) mentions an incident in Kenya where a scientist pointed out what appeared to be a coral-colored flower made up of many small blossoms, like a hyacinth. However, on closer inspection, each oblong blossom turned out to be a wing of an insect. The thousands of insects in the colony had created a flower that deceived the eyes of the hungriest of birds. The scientist shook the "flower" and the insects filled the air. In a moment they returned to the twig in no particular order, and for an instant the twig was alive with the movement of scrambling bugs. But the movement was not random. In a moment the scientist again gazed at the stillness of the beautiful flower.

Orson Welles

American movie director Orson Welles was asked about the dreamlike but seemingly connected rooms in his film, *The Trial*. "It came from my dream," he reported. (Van de Castle, 1994)

MUSICIANS

Sullivan composed *The Lost Chord* in a dream, but could only remember the first few bars when he awoke. Handel heard the last movements of *The Messiah* in a dream, and one of Wagner's operas was composed entirely in a dream. He remembered it all when he awoke, and told a friend, "Now you are going to hear my dream." (Van de Castle, 1994)

GOLFER

The American golfer Jack Nicklaus had fallen into a terrible slump. In his dream he saw himself holding his club differently, and when he applied this new grip in his waking life his scores improved dramatically. (Van de Castle, 1994)

MARK TWAIN

Mark Twain once remarked that the greatest of all inventors is accident. (Chowder, 2003)

ACCIDENTAL INVENTIONS

In 1991, Tim Berners-Lee, a British physicist, was experimenting with a way to organize his research files. He developed a software program for just that purpose, and in doing so, invented the World Wide Web. (Chowder, 2003)

In 1928, Alexander Fleming was working with a petri dish of staphylococcus bacteria. Some mold happened to drift through the window and landed in the petri dish. Fleming observed the effect, and the then-miracle drug penicillin was born. (Chowder, 2003)

When Eli Whitney observed a cat pulling feathers through a bird cage, he got the idea of how to comb cotton mechanically. Thus, the cotton gin was born. (Chowder, 2003)

POPPING CORN

Percy Lebaron Spencer, a developer of radar, was walking through his lab at the Raytheon Company in Cambridge,

Massachusetts, when he stopped briefly by a magnetron—the tube that produces the high-frequency microwaves that power radar. A "strange feeling" came over him. He suddenly reached in his pocket and realized that a candy bar in his jacket pocket had melted. He decided to put some popcorn kernels in front of the magnetron, and soon the corn began to pop. The microwave oven was born. (Chowder, 2003)

How do such creative accidents happen? One is the observed event, where the "invention" is the way the mind seizes upon an inconspicuous occurrence. "Chance favors only the prepared mind," said Louis Pasteur. The unintended event is one thing; quite another is the creative way it is used. (Chowder, 2003)

LENSES IN A TUBE

Hans Lippershey, a 17th-century Dutch eyeglass maker, noticed that when he looked through two lenses at a time distant objects were greatly magnified. When he put the lenses in a tube, the world's first telescope was born. (Chowder, 2003)

MATCHES

In 1826, John Walker, a pharmacist, not a scientist, was mixing potassium chlorate and antimony sulfide together with a stick. The mixture stuck to a stick, and when he tried to remove it by scraping it off a stone floor, the stick burst into flames. Soon he produced for sale the first friction matches. (Chowder, 2003)

FROZEN ON A STICK

In the early 1900s, Frank Epperson was an 11-year-old boy when he accidentally left a mixture of soda powder and water out on the back porch on a cold night. In the mixture was a stick he'd used as a mixer. The next morning he found the soda water frozen on the stick. Twenty years passed before he realized that if he added some flavoring, he had a frosty treat on a stick. He called them Eppsicles, which eventually was changed to Popsicles. (Chowder, 2003)

RUBBER

For many years, Charles Goodyear tried to make something useful out of a substance from Brazil called rubber. The amateur inventor tried mixing it with many chemicals without success, until one day he blended it with sulfur and dropped the mixture on a hot stove. Once it had cooled he realized that the rubber had suddenly become more solid, and was also very flexible. Today this vulcanized rubber is used in many things, from automobile tires to golf balls. (Chowder, 2003)

POST-IT NOTES

Post-it sticky notepaper happened when a 3-M Company researcher, Spence Silver, needed to make bookmarks for the hymnals for his church choir. (Chowder, 2003)

TEFLON

In 1938, a 27-year-old chemist, Roy Plunkett, was trying to create a new kind of refrigerant, when he happened on a most slippery material, Teflon. (Chowder, 2003)

DIAL TELEPHONE

In 1888, a Kansas City undertaker was losing business to another funeral parlor, whose wife was the town's telephone operator, and often the first one to hear about a death. Upset at his disadvantage, the undertaker, Almon Strowger, invented electromechanical switches to direct calls, and thus, the dial telephone was born.

GLACIER BAY

John Muir fared forth into the wilderness alone, unarmed, unafraid of danger and hardship. "I have chosen the lonely way," he once remarked. He was the first to explore Glacier Bay in Alaska. (Teale, 1982)

AFTER THE POND

Edwin Way Teale was editing an edition of Thoreau's *Walden*. As he checked the writer's journals he discovered that a large proportion of the entries were made *after* Walden left the pond. (Zwinger & Teale, 1982)

SCHOPENHAUER

Philosopher Arthur Schopenhauer said that life and dreams are leaves of the same book. (Van de Castle, 1994)

D. H. LAWRENCE

The American writer D. H. Lawrence never could decide if his dreams were the result of his thoughts, or whether thoughts were the result of his dreams. (Van de Castle, 1994)

HELEN KELLER

Helen Keller looked forward to passing through what she called the "portals of sleep," where her dreaming mind let her experience "clear seeing all night." (Van de Castle, 1994)

FILM DIRECTOR

One famous American film director said he would prefer two hours a day awake and 22 hours in dreams. (Van de Castle, 1994)

HAVELOCK ELLIS

American writer Havelock Ellis once noted that the infinite knows no bounds in dreaming, when time and space are suspended, and a person can have a deeper communion with nature. (Van de Castle, 1994)

RED VIOLIN

Joshua Bell purchased a violin that was made in 1713 during Stradiveri's "golden period." The young violinist said, "This is the closest thing to the Red Violin that I've ever seen."

The violin was formerly owned by a Polish virtuoso who lost it twice. The first time was in 1919 when it was stolen from his hotel room in Vienna. The second time, it was stolen from his dressing room at Carnegie Hall in 1936. He never saw it again.

For the next 50 years, the thief, Julian Altman, played the violin in elegant New York martini clubs. He coated it in black shoe polish so no one would recognize it. Altman made a deathbed confession to his wife in 1985, and the violin was returned to Lloyds of London. (Steinberg, 2003)

LABYRINTH

Our English language is very flexible, but it also may promote confusion. Consider the five ways we have of making *labyrinth* into an adjective: *labyrinthian*, *labyrinthean*, *labyrinthal*, *labyrinthine*, and *labyrinthic*.

PIG FARMER

This is one of those anecdotes that I use judiciously, and with very few clients.

In Italy in 1938, a pig farmer, who was also a psychiatrist, noticed the dazed look on his pigs after he prodded them with his shocking device. He decided to try it on one of his depressed patients. He shocked the patient, who sat bolt upright and demanded, "Don't do that again, or you'll kill me!" The doctor shocked him stronger next time, it induced a seizure, and electroconvulsive therapy, or ECT, was born. (Freeman, 2004)

Appendix 3
Ego-Strengthening Stories

Why is it that clients so often self-reference a metaphor and incorporate it in their own unique way? For an answer, we need not look beyond the hypnosis session itself. There you have a client in some degree of distress who is probably *ready* for change. He believes he may be helped by the therapist and is receptive to her intervention. He is in a comfortable, quiet room with a therapist who is confident in her abilities. This is not the first time she has followed and induction and deepening with "The Greenhouse," a story that many other clients have incorporated into their personal situations and then have begun to feel better about themselves. In the story, her voice lwers an octave as she says, "strong root system."

MATCHSTICK GIRL

Fewer and fewer doctors today are born with a silver spoon in their mouths. Take the real-life case of Kelly, who today is a confident and articulate psychiatrist, superbly competent and appreciated by her peers. More than with other doctors, clients warm to her and sense an instant connection. People don't know the reason for this bond; it's just there. You see, in many ways, Kelly is just like them. She, too, suffered immensely, and she knows, just really knows. . . .

Kelly said, "I used to think I had evil in my family, but now I see it for what it was, an illness, a sickness that ran deep and affected every one of us." She died her first painful death at age four when her innocence was stolen, and the deaths continued for many years. Her mother and sister took their own lives. She saw no sunshine. "I was the little matchstick girl left out in the cold," said Kelly.

She had an imaginary friend who asked her every year on her birthday, "Kelly, are you strong?" "*Just enough,*" she would answer.

Years of help from a trusted counselor helped her come out of the cold. It was a secret—no, not really a secret—that she shared with her counselor. At the end of the hour the counselor always asked her, "Kelly, are you strong?" "*Just enough,*" she would answer.

She married only once. "It lasted 14 months and five days too long," she says. Years later she ran into her former husband in a restaurant. "Time wounds all heels," was all she had to say about him.

She introduces herself to a new client. Her big smile illuminates, warms, and embraces. She will never be completely whole, but she is happy, and inside her head she still hears the question from her imaginary friend, and she breathes deeply and answers, "*Just enough.*"

A psychology intern in the early 1990s, Richard T. Bissett, composed the following story, which he used to help people accept their chronic pain. I have since altered it a bit, and we now use it as one of our stock stories.

THE GARDEN

In a tiny Mexican village lived Eufrasia, a vital and vigorous young woman. Besides her family, the joy of her life was her garden of beautiful flowering plants and bubbling fountains. The garden attracted wildlife of the surrounding countryside—rabbits, lizards, snakes, and javelina. But mostly birds. Birds of all colors and song. Red-breasted birds, were they cardinals? Dusky doves, sleek roadrunners, and quail, bobbing and clucking. They all came to feed and enjoy the warm breezes playing through the leaves, and the steady rain of blossoms onto the garden path.

Eufrasia reveled in her visitors. She planted the most succulent plants for them. She spread seed every morning, poured nectar for the hummingbirds, cut up kumquats and pomegranates for the cactus wrens. Her garden seemed to be in perfect harmony—or so she had every reason to believe. She loved to just sit in her garden and take it all in, as it was so peaceful and relaxing, so utterly tranquil and relaxing. As she sat there she listened to the bubbling of the fountain. Every ripple of the water coursed through her. She heard or felt nothing else, for during those timeless moments she was part of the fountain.

One morning while enveloped in the ambience of her garden, Eufrasia was distracted by something. It was a pigeon, a common city pigeon, dull, dirty, and gray. "A rodent with wings soiling my garden," she thought, and she immediately rose to her feet and tried to shoo it away. But the pigeon only flew a short ways and returned again. And who could blame it for being lured to this wonderful garden.

Day after day she awoke to find the pigeon befouling her garden. Bathing noisily in the delicate marble bowl intended for finches. Pecking at other birds, eating their food, and soiling the jasmine. This was too much for Eufrasia, and she became quite discouraged. Soon, her garden ceased to provide the joy she had known for so long. Why set out seed if it will only be eaten by that pigeon, she thought. She spent much less time in her garden, and stayed inside, where she caught herself sighing, small sighs at first, and then longer ones. "I am sighing my life away," she yelled one day in desperation.

One morning she awoke to a strange premonition. Something was different. Perhaps it was the sound of the garden.

She listened . . . and like music, the cooing of the doves and cluck of the quail filled her ears. The gurgle of the fountain, there it was again! She rushed to the window. No pigeon! She said aloud, "I mustn't get my hopes up. It might come back." However, it did not return. One week passed, then a month. She worked in her garden every day and restored it to its former beauty. Ah, the gurgle of the fountain, the scent of the jasmine, the soft petals drifting down. She was really, totally, wonderfully happy once again.

As the weeks passed something deep inside percolated, and soon it was more palpable, surging within her. And then she realized it: she missed the pigeon. No, she didn't just miss it; she longed for it. It buckled her knees, and once again she heard the sighing. She didn't understand it, but one thing was clear. She dearly longed for her pigeon. Yes, she would bake sweet nutcakes and spread them on the garden path. Maybe the pigeon would return. But it did not.

She moved into the garden, slept there at night. She slept beneath the oleanders, and she washed in the fountain. She plucked oranges to eat. Weeks passed, and still no pigeon.

But just as quickly as it disappeared, there it was again! It wasn't dull gray, but luminescent and beautiful. She gazed at it as the pigeon preened its feathers. She felt a sense of peace, an inner contentment. She returned to her bed at night and fell into a deep sleep. Maybe tomorrow the pigeon would still be there, maybe not. She drifted and dreamed.

TIME

He had seen and done a lot in his life, and had a particular, if not peculiar, perspective on time. Charles Ditmas's job was inspecting clocks, all kinds of clocks, at Harvard University. Each time he made his rounds, Charles wore an Edwardian-style checkered suit, a black hat, and a fitted coat with a luxuriant fur collar. His meticulously dyed hair fell down to his shoulders, and no one would have ever guessed that he was 90 years old. With his walking stick and black leather bag he made his rounds once a month. He was the honorary keeper of the clocks, a position he occupied from the early 1940s until his retirement in 2002.

While many of us would be most interested in the outward appearance of a watch or a clock, Charles occupied himself primarily with a timepiece's inner workings. Any clock anywhere in the University was his domain. One time the president entered his office with a wealthy alumnus who was contemplating a donation of 100 million dollars to the university. They were discussing details of the potential gift, and as they entered the president's suite, the donor exclaimed, "I want history to remember my name for a long time," and before the president could answer, they encountered Charles peering into the office's historic regulator clock.

"Stop, gentlemen," Charles commanded. "Let's suspend discussion of mere external phenomena for a moment while I examine the inside of this clock." The bewildered donor, mouth agape, was quietly ushered outside by the understanding President, who whispered, "We refer to that odd fellow as Father Time. He'll be done before you can count to a hundred, and then we can go back inside."

Once, during a faculty meeting, Charles burst in wearing a checkerboard detective cape. He climbed up on a chair and began examining a big clock on the wall. "Carry on, ladies and gentlemen, I'm just here to examine the inside of this clock. In a few moments you shall either forget I am here, no longer notice my presence, or otherwise have your attention re-arrested by this august faculty meeting." The meeting promptly resumed, though a few of the faculty continued to be distracted by the keeper of the clocks. Aware of their attention, Father Time whispered without looking up, "Animals in the forest, bears and boars in the wood, boring tasks and necessary distractions, a few pairs of eyes boring into that checkerboard, something that soon becomes very boring, as your attention is re-absorbed in nontemporal matters." One of the faculty stopped as if frozen, hand in the air, while others yawned. The chairwoman resumed her monologue, and some listened, though most heard nothing.

Sooner rather than later all present forgot he was there. After half an hour on most clocks, Father Time promptly exited the room, muttering, "I should hope that the department head will one day wind his own clock."

Charles only worked on *real* clocks, no electric or battery clocks. "All clocks have their own personalities," he was heard to say. "And I'm not talking about their walnut casing or brass mounts, or some carving of Atlas and the phases of the moon up on top. I'm talking about *inside, deep inside.*" Often he would remove pieces and work on them at home, pinions, gears, cranks, and wooden hands. "In there, that's my domain," he was prone to remark.

Once inside a clock, time on the outside ceased to exist for Charles. One time someone observed him bending over the famous Temporal Abatement clock in the chapel. He had a small flashlight in his mouth and precision tools in both hands. "Most curious," he remarked as he noticed dried candle wax from a previous caretaker's candle light. The observer called his name, but he didn't hear. She then tapped him gently on the leg, but he did not feel the touch. After an unknown number of minutes, someone accidentally knocked over his walking stick that had been leaning against the wall. With the resounding crack he extricated himself from the clock and yelled, "What the deuce?!" (Grann, 2002)

THE CONTEST

Justine was lost in a daydream as she gazed out the window of her house. Her husband, asleep on the couch, had dozed off 30 minutes ago, or was it longer? Her own eyes closed and she drifted and dreamed, pleasantly immersed in the quiet and comfort of nothing to do, or know, or think about. Was it like seeing the silence between the leaves on a tree? She remembered that poem about the young girl lying on the lawn, and how every blade of grass was a different shade of green.

She awoke with a start as she heard the mailman's truck out by the curb.

Justine Forte could not believe her eyes as she re-read the letter. She had actually won! Yes, the makers of Self-Care Bubble Bath had selected her as a finalist in their big contest. She was to report next Saturday night to the banquet in the Emperor's Ballroom of the Sargent Hilton Hotel, and rsvp only if she required a ticket for her husband. Just think: she was in the running to win the grand prize, a Lexus SUV and the dream vacation in Hawaii.

Saturday evening finally arrived. Her husband had not returned on time, so she drove alone to the banquet, where she met the other finalists. Mary Knoll was very nice, about her age, as was Mayvis Strong. "I'm not strong like my name, and besides, my maiden name was Meeker," said Mayvis. Betsy Beefheart, also in her early fifties, made a joke about her name, and said she was a vegetarian who'd been on cardiac medicine for years. Her husband, nearby in a wheel-chair, wore a look of sour inconvenience. "The stress of it all, I don't know how I manage," remarked Betsy Beefheart. Justine Forte knew exactly what she meant.

The area manager for Self-Care products was the MC. He announced, "We have a special surprise for tonight's contestants. We are going to hook each one of them up to a polygraph, and the one with the best answer to our question will win the grand prize."

Mary Knoll went first. She was asked, "How did you like Self-Care Bubble Bath?" She nervously answered, "Frankly, I forgot all about it. It's still in the bathroom cabinet." The audience loosed a critical murmur.

Mayvis Strong was next. She answered, "I was just too busy to use it, doing everything around the house and worrying about my husband." This time the audience groaned.

Betsy Beefheart was especially nervous. She took a long time to spit out her answer: "I used it, but only to clean the cat box." The audience laughed.

Justine Forte went last. She answered proudly, "I didn't get to try it, but my husband did. I used up the whole box on his baths in three weeks, and he said he loved it." Again, laughter rippled through the audience.

After conferring with the judges, the MC announced the winner: "Regrettably, there is no winner. We have learned from this experience that we'll have to screen our finalists better next year."

THE VOYAGERS

In the Canadian north woods in the early 1800s, some were interested in pure exploration, and tried to discover the fabled Northwest Passage. Others took part in the flourishing fur trade. They hired a hardy lot of men to carry their cargo through this uncharted terrain. This story is about those French Canadians, who were known as "the voyagers." *Onward they moved, ever forward.*

The voyagers were a rugged and stalwart lot with their big row boats called York boats. Loaded with cargo, they had only a compass and crude maps as they navigated a labyrinth of rivers and lakes, portaging, or carrying their boats and cargo overland to the next navigable water. *Onward they moved, almost ceaseless forward motion.*

They worked only from the first of May until the end of September, the precious time between spring thaw and autumn freeze. The rest of the year their route was blocked by ice and snow. They went 1,000 miles north with a cargo of trade goods, and 1,000 miles back with a load of pelts. The Indians helped them find their way, as the paths had been used for centuries by moccasined feet. How did they know which river flowed northwestward, or to the southeast, or which had unpassable rapids? They paddled upstream against strong currents, portaged through treacherous swamps, and lay exhausted by their campfire at night. *Ever forward, onward they moved.*

Each York boat carried 10 men and one and one-half tons of cargo. On the Grand Portage trail, each voyager was required to carry eight bales uphill to the Pigeon River, the first waterway on the route north. If a man took the normal load of two bales, or 180 pounds, that meant four roundtrips, a distance of 72 miles. Some could carry more. A man named George Bonga carried nine bales, more than 820 pounds, one mile uphill. Uphill they went, taking one last look at civilization. Then the trail plunged into the forest, and they emerged eight miles later at the Pigeon River. Their journey was underway. *Onward they moved.*

Paddle and portage, portage and paddle, day in and day out. There were long vistas of blue water. An osprey plunged into a lake. They heard the screech of a bald eagle and the haunting wilderness sounds at night. The northern lights danced and mingled with the midnight sky. The next day held towering pines, glimmering white birches, cliffs and promontories, and places unknown. (Knauth, 1972)

TURN RIGHT HERE

A man came into my office one time—I forget just how long ago it was—and he started talking. I listened very closely to the words, but at the same time I watched his body language while taking in fine nuances in meaning, and whether it was how he moved in the chair, the way he said the words, or the content of his monologue, I readily became absorbed in the entire process.

His talking went on and on, and I was past being immersed in anything, as by that time I had become rather bored. He must have picked up on my own body language, and it was just about then that he started to emphasize the word *right*. "I was *right* about that," or "the country made a *right* turn back there—" those were just some of the things I can now remember. My attention was just becoming arrested by his use of that word, when he asked, quite innocently, "Is *this* something that can induce trance in me?" "What?" I answered, taken aback. "That," he said, pointing out the door and down the hall, which was to the right. "After all, I am not a good trance subject. Someone told me exactly that a long, long time ago," he said. "I suppose so," I answered. Then he continued talking, mentioning things like *right* up ahead, you can *write* that down, and *righting* the ship of state.

The more I listened to him, the more I noticed that this man really had very little appreciation for anything except his own words, which must have had a calming effect on him. I thought to myself, "I wonder if I can help him to appreciate *something?*"

Fortunately I had had three cups of coffee that morning, as I picked right up where he left off, and began in with the following induction, most of which has been lost and forgotten, except for some quick notes jotted down afterward.

His name was Les Irksome, and I said, "Les, a person can write in the drawing room, or stand in the sitting room, or do something post haste in the ante room, is that not right?" Les nodded almost imperceptibly, and that nod told me I was on to something good.

I continued. "Les, when I go home at night after helping people like you I tell myself, 'When I get off the Interstate at the Prince Road exit, *right here*, I'm going to leave the day behind,' and that's something that has worked just fine for a number of years. After all, once a person learns how to ride a bicycle he never forgets, does he, Les?" A more demonstrative nod from Les was apparent this time. He had closed his eyes by now, and he was either drifting and dreaming, or dreaming and drifting, I couldn't tell for sure.

"Going down any road I can turn right here, or I can turn left there. Before I turn right there I can look down here, or up over there, but not for very long, as a person needs to keep his eyes on the road ahead, not to mention the road behind, either in the rearview mirror, or one of the side mirrors, but in my car there are several blind spots, so I usually turn and look, not totally trusting any mirror." By this time Les was rather deep in trance. He also may have fallen to sleep, I wasn't sure at the time, so I said to him in a hoarse whisper, "Les, I wonder what you will be able to *notice* from today's experience. . . ."

"Even before grade school I knew that I wrote with my right hand. 'Don't write with your left hand,' said the second-grade teacher, and she was often right more than she was wrong. At any rate, I remember buying a house in 1992, and at that time I had a new Chevrolet *Capris*, something I was rather proud of. 'Don't act like the nouveau *riche*,' said my wife, who would often rad*iate* with confidence after saying something like that. 'I appreciated our home all by myself,' she said, adding that it was her idea to upgrade the carpet, to put in drip irrigation, and to install solar panels. 'I congratulate you for appreciating our home, dear, but it usually takes two to appreciate something as big an investment as a home,' I answered. She quickly followed with, 'Appreciation isn't quite that simple, you know, as it depends on what comes back from the appraiser when the time comes to sell this place.'

"Her uncle, who is hard of hearing but soft on his niece, happened to be there that day, and he offered these conciliatory words: 'An honest appraisal of this situation confirms your mutual appreciation,' and although he was a bit off the mark, his words, as well as my wife's, helped me to toe the mark in the future."

I was not yet done with Les, and I realized at the time that the *law of parsimony* means less is more, but I continued anyway, even though by now it was quite clear that Les had pleasantly drifted off into another state. "Back on that road, Les, all the time being in the driver's seat, a person can adjust his position, swiveling left while looking right, which may be a bit awkward, or notice something going by on the left while thinking about turning right just up ahead. Or, he can imagine, just imagine, any combination of doing and thinking in terms of left-right-right-left, front or back, and still continue down the road, always staying right between the lines.

Appendix 4

Instigative Stories

Sometimes clients, when realerted, say things like, "That was a strange story" or "What was that supposed to mean?" Others have little or no recollection for the story. I don't discuss instigative stories with them, as it would be like discussing a koan. I'd rather spend our time talking about what they can do to improve their life or what they can do to give back to society. If they are so intrigued by a story I will give them a copy of it. Dwelling on it consciously certainly may reinforce unconscious perturbation.

Included in the appendices are "Three Lessons," adapted from Lee Wallas's (1985) story of the same name, and "Balloons." In most cases I use "Three Lessons" because the therapy component of the first hypnosis session, as it tests response and embeds the suggestion that clients have resources within themselves that can aid them. "Balloons" is useful for anxiety, anger, and for any client who has difficulty letting go.

SLOT CANYON

The following account, dated September 10, 1955, was discovered among the papers of Arthur Sliceman, a psychiatrist who moved to Arizona from Iowa in the 1930s. Dr. Sliceman is long deceased, and the client's name in this account is omitted for reasons of privacy.

"I have been in therapy for my problem for the past seven and a half months. I am writing this report for my therapist, Dr. Sliceman. I undertook an assignment for him, and thinking back on it now, I believe that the objective of this assignment was accomplished.

"I was bogged down in life, in therapy, in all ways, and Dr. Sliceman hounded me to take a journey, an arduous journey, to a place of my choosing, where I would discover an answer to my problem. I chose to try and find the Secret Pass in the Black Mountains in northwest Arizona. I had read various accounts of this area, which has seen lost Spanish missionaries, vengeful Indians, and Union soldiers turned miners defending their veins of gold.

"I drove my '54 Oldsmobile as far as I could and got out to walk, and I had not gone 10 feet when I felt as if in a dream. I found myself in a steep gully choked with loose rock and thick brush. I slid down, hoping to find another ledge. I can still hear the cries of cactus wrens. The collared lizards moved, but I could not hear them. There were large boulders all around as I continued my descent. Soon, I was in a winding sandy wash, with 100-foot red granite walls, and there were caves way up in the walls. I could barely see high desert greenery way above.

"I continued walking and soon I encountered a massive sandstone cliff face split by a curious dark, narrow slit. Undaunted, I squeezed my body into the aperture. It was both dusty and moist. I had only a canteen, no flashlight, and I was not prepared for total darkness on a blazing bright day. I inched along, first on hands and knees, and then on foot. I tripped on something. I could tell it was shredded canvas and bone. I continued on, not certain if I should turn back or forge ahead. Could a precipice await me?

"I lost my sense of time as the path wound deeper into the cliff. Thinking back, I had suddenly lost my fear, and during that time I contemplated my problem and the reason for undertaking the venture. A tremendous fatigue came over me, I crouched down, and my eyes closed all by themselves. Some time later I awoke to the loud thumping of my chest, and a rushing sound in my ears. My mind swam in disorientation, and I now moved forward, or was it back?

"After what may have been seconds or many minutes, the darkness gave way to a veiled physicality, then a filtered light, and soon marvelously tapestried walls surrounded me. I had wandered into a slot canyon, a wind-and-water-fashioned sanctum of dancing shapes and swirling colors. Jagged edges of rock blended with soft curves. This was a visual symphony. No, it was a sandstone symphony!

"I remember the quiet, the silence. Deep purple changed to red and tan, and soon I was walking in another sandy wash. I shaded my eyes from the intense glare of the sun. I had lost both my canteen and sunglasses along the way.

"Dr. Sliceman had given me instructions that were both explicit and general. I was to go alone to a natural place of my choosing, and some time during the journey I would discover something important about my problem. Well, if only I possessed words to describe what I experienced in that slot canyon. How could my problem *not* have changed as a result?" (Taylor, 1992; Fatali, 1991)

LOST AND FOUND

I can remember reading about—or maybe it was on TV—a lost city somewhere, maybe off the coast of Greece, or perhaps it was a mythical lost city, Atlantis, or some other place. Throughout history there are many lost things, lost languages, some plant that ceased to exist, or the passenger pigeon.

Certainly we all lose things, like our keys, or feeling in a hand or foot, or maybe it's a matter of discovering that curious feeling or sensation after it occurs, just happening all by itself. That's how it was with Hyacinth Absentry, who had an experience something like that. Normally a very vigilant woman, she decided one day to try being inattentive and forgetful, just for one day. Now this wasn't easy for her, but she just put it out of her mind, and then she arose one morning, and her eyes strayed across the room to the big clock that said five minutes before six o'clock. It seemed like an abstraction, that big clock, the small hand beneath the big hand, and the minute hand was absent, removed, or just vanished long ago, Hyacinth had no idea.

She remembered glancing out the window before she went to bed. Her neighbor, Lois, was supposed to be moving that night, relocating to another state. Hyacinth heard the sound of a truck out there, and there it was, backing up in Lois's driveway. On the side of the big moving van it said "Time Movers," a rather curious name for a company that was to move Lois, and her many things, to some place else, but probably in the same time zone.

As she sat on the edge of the bed, she noticed how she felt in her body—hands, feet, and other places, seemingly regions far away from anywhere in particular. The hands on that clock were now straight up. It was 6:00 exactly, and her special experience began precisely *now*. She covered the clock with a blue towel, tucking it in neatly so there was no way it could fall off. She would go about her day, never leaving her home, and never glancing at the clock again. No radio or TV or computer, nothing that would tell her the time, and then, when she determined, in her mind, when she *guessed* it might be 6:00 again, the small hand and the big hand making one revolution each, she would then yank that blue towel down, and glance at the hands of that clock one more time. She said to herself, "I won't think about time at all as I go about my day, busy doing inattentive things."

After a leisurely breakfast, she couldn't help but notice her to-do list on the refrigerator. It said, in bold letters, "Find the pillow and footstool." After reading those words, she immediately forgot about it, and returned to wondering why she had bothered to undertake this special experience in the first place. Her eyes fixed on Proust's *Remembrance of Times Past*, and she went from there to her dresser drawer, which she yanked open. Many timepieces were in there, her grandfather's seven pocket watches, Mickey Mouse and Spiro Agnew watches, the batteries long since expired, or never wound for many seasons. The miniature hourglass. That had been missing for quite some time. She turned it over, and watched the sand.

Living in a warm climate, sometimes you forget if it's fall, or spring, or winter, and in summer the air conditioner clicks on at intervals, something a person can count on. Nevertheless, all that really doesn't matter anyway, she thought, and then again outside came to mind, driving, from here to there, passing something, and then wondering later whether she had really driven by that something, or if it was simply a figment of her imagination. Many other things from the past crossed her mind as she drifted and dreamed. "Don't forget to pay attention," her mother had told her as she left for school. Just what should she pay attention to now? What was the task at hand, she thought, as she sat on the edge of the bed, absorbed in the back of her hand, and then she closed her eyes. The day passed, and she wondered what she would do next to pass the time.

THE PIANO

Let me tell you about a person who came to me once with a rather interesting problem. This man—let's call him Ernie—he said he was having difficulty distinguishing reality from fantasy. I eagerly asked for more details, as this was starting out to be one of the more interesting problems I had heard in a long time.

He told me that it was becoming increasingly difficult to tell if something was real, or if it was just a dream. Now, Ernie did not mean that minute-to-minute he could not tell fact from fantasy, and he was not talking about daydreaming, nor was he, like some people, who believe that if they dream something it is bound to come true later on. "Give me a for-instance," I said to him.

"Well, the other day before going to work, I was thinking about this piano. And the more I thought about it, the more

I got into the details, and the more I got absorbed in this piano, the more I lost track of time, and I forgot all about having to go to work that day. And the more I think about it now, I don't know if all this really happened or not.

"The strange thing is that I don't play the piano or any instrument, but I do appreciate nice music. Anyway, in the middle of the night I was driving out into the desert with this grand piano—a Steinway—on the back of a flatbed truck. It was a magnificent piano and had a shiny black-lacquer finish. I don't know how far I drove, but it was way out in the desert, on the way to the Mexican border. There weren't any houses or streetlights or telephone lines or anything out there on that washboard dirt road. No moon, no stars, just real, real dark. All I could see was my headlights bouncing out there on the road ahead of me.

"I was just going along on autopilot, not really aware of purposely doing anything, but at the same time the whole thing was rather curious . . . amusing, like I was watching myself in my dream, which I guess is what was really going on at the time, but I still wonder. The farther I drove the more interesting the road became, and the more I just got lost in the whole journey. Finally, I took a side road for a couple of miles and then stopped next to a dry riverbed. I grabbed a shovel and dug this huge hole in the riverbed. After a while the soil became very hard and I needed a pickax. I must have been digging that hole for hours because it was starting to get light when I finished that hole. There was a winch on the back of the truck, and with that winch I lowered the piano down into that hole. Very gently. Then I worked as fast as I could to fill in the hole. The piano was probably two feet below the surface when I finished. I was just exhausted when I drove back home.

"Now three years passed and every once in a while I thought about that piano, deteriorating in the desert sand. I know that during those three years we had a lot of rain, so that dry riverbed must have filled with water I don't know how many times. One night I went to bed real early, about

7:00, and I awoke with a start at 9:00. The next thing I realized I was in that truck heading out in the desert, down that same dirt road, out in the middle of nowhere, the beam from the headlights bouncing out ahead of me. After driving a long time I got to where I had buried that piano. I remembered the spot exactly because it was near a big mesquite tree, the only one around. I dug up that piano and winched it up on the back of the truck. There was a full moon out and I can still see that piano on the back of the truck. The odd thing was that the piano looked exactly like it did when I buried it. The black-lacquer finish was brilliant. The legs were firm. I opened up the keyboard and hit the keys, two at a time with my two index fingers, starting at the right and the left, and even though I don't have a trained ear, the piano sounded like it was in perfect condition. I continued to plink those keys with my fingers, two at a time, and as I neared the center of the keyboard one of the keys didn't work at all . . . and that's all I can remember from that dream, which seems so very real to me even today."

Well, after Ernie told me that story he began to realize things about himself, useful things, things that just came up from inside him, and after a few times I told him, "Ernie, you don't need to come back anymore. I believe you'll do just fine."

"But I still can't tell fantasy from reality!" Ernie answered.

"Oh yes, you can, Ernie. Just keep on dreaming those dreams."

UNHEEDED

Winston Inskeep had just purchased an automobile. It was a 1979 Chevrolet, now three years old. "It still looks brand new, like it just came off the showroom floor," remarked Winston. Today, he was fine-tuning his driving skills on the icy roads of rural Minnesota. His aunt, Sally Goodwin, occupied the front passenger seat. She muttered something about the high snowbanks and icicles every-where, and how the heater didn't work on this car, but Winston didn't hear, as he was completely absorbed in his driving experience. "When you skid to the right, turn the wheel in the same direction," commanded Sally. She knew how to drive on icy roads, as she had been doing it for a long, long time.

The Chevrolet was a real pleasure to drive, and it continued down the road, seemingly all on its own. Winston enjoyed his car summer and winter. Jimmy Carter was now President, and Margaret Thatcher was Prime Minister, but Winston paid the news no heed, as he continued behind the wheel, enjoying the air conditioner in summer, and ignoring the cold in winter.

The years passed and the Chevrolet changed owners. Among them was Pun Lexifer, who changed her driver's license to Pun Wittingly after she wed Sam Wittingly. The car needed new tires and brakes now and then, and rust spots on the body were patched and painted. However, the heater never worked properly.

Before Pun and Sam purchased the car, Sam said to his wife, "But it's unheated, dear." She just ignored him. During their first winter in the car, Sam complained fervently about the broken heater. "I told you before we bought it. As always, I go unheeded," he told her. "Unheated doesn't bother me one bit," she responded.

One time when Pun was out of town on business Sam took the car into a repair shop and bought a new heater. They sold him on a new brand, the Unheater. Sam picked his wife up at the airport on a frigid night. As he started the engine, he announced, "Mrs. Pun Wittingly, let me demonstrate a fine new addition to your fine old car." "No doubt it won't warm up for several minutes," responded Pun critically.

"But it's the best heater on the market, this Unheater," noted Sam. "A tepid concept at best," answered Pun. Pun continued to mock his purchase. "Oh, it must be like 7-Up, the 'uncola,'" she said. Sam ignored her, as he surmised that for the first time in its long life the Chevrolet was no longer unheated.

The Focus Group

He grew up in Gila Bend, a remote, dusty town in the Arizona desert, and the story goes that his parents weren't sure what to name him when he was born. However, as his mother opened the door of their trailer home one morning and gazed bleary-eyed at the searing heat, she exclaimed, "We'll name him Ojinaco," as the name just came to her as she rubbed the sleep from her eyes. "Okie what?" asked his dad. "O-hee-NAH-ko," she answered, so Ojinaco is what they put on his birth certificate.

Ojinaco eventually had a home of his own in Gila Bend, but no family of his own, and no job, and as money was lacking, he perked up one day while reading the newspaper, when he saw that he could be paid for taking part in a focus group over by San Diego.

It was a long drive to California, and as he drove, his mind drifted in his own special dream world. His hands, as well as his feet, operated independently and he became absorbed in the scenery, such as it was, and it seemed that he arrived in no time. He got to the meeting and sat down with a dozen other people in the cool room. After a brief orientation, the woman passed out cups of orange juice. "This is a double-blind study, so you don't know, and I don't know, if you're getting brand A or brand B. But it really doesn't matter, as there's nothing to know or do or think about. Just drink it down without any conscious or purposeful effort, fill out the brief questionnaire, and pick up your check. Very good, we'll see you in a week," she said in a voice that was low and melodic, really rather soothing.

"This sure is an easy way to get a check," thought Ojinaco.

As he exited the room, a man took him aside. "I'm Les Irksome," said the man in a disembodied voice. A woman quickly approached. "Les is more of a bother to deal with than I am," said the woman in a mere whisper. "I'm Shirley Knott. A third person approached quietly from behind. "Shirley is a very agreeable person, though Les is not, but listen closely to me, Ojinaco. I'm Batt Guano, stepbrother of Matt Guaiac," he said. Ojinaco, very distracted by now, found the words slipping out of his mouth. "Does everybody here have a funny name?" he asked. "Ojinaco is not like any other Norwegian name I've every heard of," said someone. His eyes were now very blurry and he viewed all three people as if through a rain-soaked windshield.

"What will you find on the way home?" one of them asked. "What?!" answered Ojinaco, who was starting to feel uncomfortable. He began to speak, and his mouth moved, but no words appeared. He turned on his heel and headed for the glowing red of the exit sign.

Soon he found himself outside in the parking lot, and before he knew it he was driving back through the Arizona desert. The sun had dropped well below the horizon and a glowing magenta filled his rearview mirror. He didn't know why—or precisely when—but he remembered the darkness as he eased his car off the road. He inhaled deeply and got out. He walked and walked, first over yellowed newspaper, discarded tires, and thriving prickly pear cactus. He knew it when he saw it, an old orange-juice-concentrate container. He picked it up and looked inside.

Tyranny of Ten

When she was younger, Betsy Tierney went to the gym five days a week, always arriving at the same time, week in and week out, tote bag over her shoulder, broad smile on her face.

"We could set our watches by you, Betsy," called out the personal trainers behind the counter. She answered, "Everybody just calls me 'Tierney,' and if your watches need a new battery, think of me as your dependable power source, but only if it makes you feel better, something that may best be forgotten." They just smiled as she strode away, knowing that it was just another Tierney-ism that left them lost in the words, or maybe the meaning, or somewhere in between.

Tierney remembered that conversation, as she forgot very little, and now that she was older and visited the gym only three times a week, she occupied her mind at home with less-strenuous pursuits, like boiling water for her tea. "I put it in the microwave for exactly two minutes, and I watch the clock tick down, 9 . . . 8 . . . 7 . . . , and when it's done, I put in the tea bag, and I watch it for a precise amount of time before I taste it, counting the seconds, 10, 9, 8, . . . but I don't want to bore you with such details."

Frank often saw Tierney at the gym. He said to her once, and only once, "Well, watching you, and how methodical you are, many similar things can happen, like becoming transfixed by the details, or having my attention arrested by the overall precision of the operation."

"Yes," answered Tierney. "My mind does indeed become immersed in the process. Perhaps there's something in your own experience where you routinely feel near total absorption. That can be very pleasant and enjoyable, and beginning now, Frank, you can simply ignore me and turn your attention on yourself." Her words gave pause to Frank, who then watched her stride away to the back of the gym.

He watched her at the leg-press machine, 10 repetitions precisely, followed by a brief rest period, and then exactly 10 more, up, down, up, down. . . . Tierney definitely had her routine. At the dumbbells, she flexed her grip 10 times on each bar, and then hoisted them, up and down, up and down, 10 times, and then waited five seconds, and then another five seconds, and repeated the procedure. She hollered out to Frank: "Ten seconds in between, you catch that, Frank?"

Frank just stood there, fixated by her precise routine, and she continued, hoisting each 15-pound weight 10 times, waiting five seconds, and then another five seconds, and beginning all over again until she had completed 10 sets of 10 on each side. "My arms never get tired," she whispered to Frank. "But what about your mind?" asked Frank. "My mind's only getting warmed up, and when my mind's warm or cold, I see the number 10, a big one and a big zero—quite distinct imagery," she responded, wiping the sweat from her brow 10 times with each hand before slinging the towel over her shoulder and striding off to a large barbell.

She lay down on the bench, scratching the back of her head one time with her right hand, and then reached back there with her left hand for nine more deliberate scratches. She was catching her breath now, and then, inhaling and exhaling but two times, she followed with eight more quick inspirations before reaching up and grasping the bar, flexing her hands five times on the left, five times on the right, and then five again with each hand.

"Hey, don't you think you should slow down?" asked Frank. "After all, you're not 25 anymore." "No, my years total twice 25, and that's 10 times five if your calculation is slow," she told Frank. She was now back at the dumbbells, and snatched 25-pounders this time.

"How about 20 repetitions with one arm and none with the other, or six on one side and seven on the other?" asked Frank. "That's an interesting proposition, Frank, maybe even curious," she answered, as she began the same routine, flexing, then releasing 10 times, right and left, and lifting 10 times 10 on each side.

Quite exasperated by now, Frank asked, "Tierney, when you're a hundred years old, will you still have the same routine?" Tierney responded before he had finished his sentence. "I did this when I was 10, probably will when I'm a hundred. "But by then you'll be underground, six feet under," noted Frank quite smugly. "No, 10 feet under, not a mere six, it's prearranged, and all paid for," answered Tierney.

She was once again immersed in her routine, and Frank's mind drifted off to something else, tent worms and sand flies. He ignored the itch behind his left shoulder and soon he became absorbed in his own routine.

<u>SLEEP</u>

For the next several minutes I would like to read an account of a now-famous lecture to a room full of doctors one day before the dawn of the current century. It was 1:00, right after lunch, and the doctors, from the departments of pharmacy, anesthesiology, neurology, and pulmonology of a renowned hospital, were assembled in the large conference room. The room buzzed with eager anticipation of hearing Dr. Drempt Lavender, recipient of last year's prestigious M. Drowser award for research in sleep apnea and related disorders.

Rather bizarrely, a thin man in the front row approached the podium and whispered to Dr. Lavender, "I have narcolepsy, and if I doze off during your talk, please don't take it personally." "By all means," responded Dr. Lavender.

Without waiting to be introduced the speaker began, "Ladies and gentlemen, this talk will last somewhere under an hour, which for some of you might be a long time, and for others the time will pass quickly. I don't expect any of you to fall asleep—with the exception of one of you—and if I catch anyone nodding off . . . and it reminds me of a time when I gave a similar lecture to neuropsychologists, and I said, 'Sleep-inducing phenomena may be present in the words, in the way it is said, or even inherent in the overall implication of physically slowing down or mental inertia; however, if I catch more than one of you dozing off due to sheer boredom. . . .'"

A woman in a white lab coat in the back quietly exited through a side door. She had expected a lecture on sleep-walking. The rest of the audience showed a marked levity to Dr. Lavender's comments. Nervous chuckles and murmurs rippled through the conference room. Dr. Lavender glanced down at the man in the front row. "I wonder if he's putting me on," he thought. Just then a woman in the back turned off all the lights in the room. The red exit signs glowed. "Pardon me while I take a nap in the dark," joked Dr. Lavender. Momentarily, bright lights filled the room, and then the lights were dimmed. "Nap time is over," chortled the doctor, as he aimed his light pointer at the first Powerpoint slide, a person in deep slumber by the hearth.

The man in the front row suddenly dropped off to sleep, chin on his chest. He listed to the right, where a woman nervously supported his body. His breathing was even and regular, his face peaceful and serene. As Dr. Lavender resumed his remarks, the man in the front row snapped to attention, transfixed by the words that now filled the screen. People in the back row found their eyelids closing, and others blinked, as the words had become blurry. Dr. Lavender's lips moved but no sound came out. He tapped on the microphone, and soon his rich baritone again filled the room. "Those words are supposed to be sharp and clear," he said curiously, and the man in front was again fast asleep.

A garbled overhead announcement penetrated the haze: "Will the owner of a purple minivan, license plate 37 K-N-A-P, please return to the vehicle." The announcement was repeated and something was said about the car being locked and the motor running. The man in the front row stretched and then exited the room. Three people in back yawned, and one of them said, "My foot has fallen asleep." Another said, "My arm did, too," and another remarked, "My arm is-did-also." "The right one?" "No, the other one." It was hard to see who was saying what. "That not attached feeling." "Numb and number." "Past tingling." "Not unpleasant."

Dr. Lavender continued his remarks. It was now close to 2:00, and the man in the front row had returned to his seat.

BALLOONS

Back in the late 1950s, Maria graduated from a small high school in rural Texas. In those days women Maria's age were expected to stay close to home, marry, and raise a family. However, Maria was independent and adventurous, and against all advice she enrolled at the University of Wisconsin, where she got a scholarship to study biology. People back in in Texas continued to be surprised by Maria as she went to medical school and later became a renowned researcher, but that really has nothing to do with this story.

As a freshman in Madison, Wisconsin, money was tight. Maria worked whenever she wasn't studying, and among her jobs was selling concessions at University sporting events. It was now late October, and the day of the homecoming football game, and the boss said to Maria, "Come with me. I have special duty for you down on the field."

Down there, in the corner of the end zone, she gazed at hundreds of thousands of small balloons of various colors, that were straining beneath a gigantic net. The boss said, "Maria, your one job is this: When the players come back on the field to start the second half, you pull hard on this cord and *let all those balloons go*." Maria nodded, as it was a very easy job.

Maria had never been much of a football fan, and she ignored the game and the cheers of the crowd. Unaccustomed to cold weather, she vigorously rubbed her hands together, stamped her feet, and through her cold breath she observed the mountain of balloons under the net. Being a curious and imaginative person, Maria began to wonder what it would be like if *that one red balloon* were released ahead of all the others. She toyed with the net by that one red balloon, and soon there was enough room for it to escape. As she *let it go*, it rose up in the frigid air and soon the swift currents carried it out of the stadium. She went around to the other side of the net and did the same with a certain blue balloon, *let it go*, and up it went. No one in the stadium noticed what she was doing, as the Wisconsin Badgers were driving toward the other end zone with less than two minutes until half time.

Maria giggled as she reached up and *let go* a particular white balloon. She immediately walked half way back around the net and released two red ones. Then two blue ones and a white one down there, just *let* them *go*. She continued in this way, different combinations of colors, two here, five there, up, down, around the other side, delighting in just *letting* them *go*. She went on and on, losing track of time, totally absorbed in *letting* those balloons *go*. As she continued, quickly moving from here to there, a minute could have been an hour, or an hour could have been a minute, as she was totally unaware of the passage of time, which really didn't matter because everybody knows how two minutes of clock time in a football game can drag out to ten minutes or more.

All during half time Maria continued to release a red one here, two white ones there, sometimes even daring to *just let* three or four *go* at a time. This continued releasing of balloons went unnoticed by the fans, as they were busy buying hot drinks or moving around to warm themselves. If you're a player or a fan, half time goes by very quickly, but for Maria down by the net, time meant absolutely nothing, nor did the cold, as she was warmly engrossed in simply *letting* those balloons *go*.

At the end of the half, the fans roared as the players streamed back on to the field, but Maria did not hear them. The boss had to yell, "Pull the cord!" three times before he got her attention. She then smiled and pulled the cord, releasing the remaining balloons, thousands and thousands still beneath the net. She just *let them go*.

Three Lessons

One time there was a young man (woman) who lived in another state, somewhere in the United States where it got cold in the winter, and I forget if it was in the midwest or Maine or Colorado, but he heard about a wise, elderly woman who lived deep in the woods, and she was someone who could help him with his problem.

He found out directions to her house, and one Saturday afternoon he set out through the woods. It was early November, a rather chilly day, and he could see his breath. Passing by an icy cold stream he kneeled down and thrust one hand into that cold, cold water. That hand stung at first, and in no time it became very numb. Now, he didn't know if he was there beside the stream for one minute or many minutes or longer, but eventually he rose to his feet and continued on through the forest.

Eventually he saw the wise woman's house in a clearing. He knocked on the door and a voice from *inside* said, "*You may come in,*" and that was lesson number one.

He got *in* there, out from the cold, and he looked around at all the things he saw *in there*. Very soon he blurted out to the wise woman, "I want to know everything you know so I can help myself with my problem," and the wise woman gazed deeply into the young man's eyes and saw that he already knew everything he needed to know, except that he didn't yet know that he already knew *all those things*, which was lesson number two.

The third lesson occurred when he realized it was time to go, and off he went, and everything worked out just fine for him. (Wallas, 1985)

Appendix 5
Favorite Inductions and Stories

This appendix contains two of our stock inductions. "Don't Try Too Hard" is a good general-purpose induction to which many often respond well. The mystifying induction is one we reach for to counteract unconscious resistance. This is one you might try if the client is having difficulty going into trance.

Also included in this appendix are four stories that readers have told us they use time and time again, just as we do. I use "The Pond" in the final session of my eight-week anger management class, as well as at the conclusion of standard therapy. "African Violets" is a handy instigative story with ego-strengthening elements, while "Seeing Things Differently" may be more didactic. I use all four of these in formal hypnosis as well as in conventional individual and group therapy.

(Client's name), don't try too hard to make things happen, and don't try to stop things from happening. *Just allow your* imagination *to wander as you notice things going on, perhaps hypnotic*   bind of comparable alternatives

hypnotic language

238

language interesting *or* curious *thoughts or sensations, maybe on the* inside *or the* outside, *or* both at the same time. *You don't have to think, or reply, or try to do anything at all. In fact, it* isn't even necessary to listen *carefully to what I'm saying because your* unconscious mind will inevitably pay attention *to anything important, without any conscious effort on your part. Now, (client's name), perhaps you* thought ahead of time *about this experience today. Maybe it* crossed your mind yesterday or the day before, or maybe you wondered about it today *or in the waiting room a few minutes ago, and perhaps right now* a part of you is observing the process while the rest of you just goes along with the experience, *which is just fine, because beginning now you can* let yourself go *into just as light or deep a trance as you would like.*	bind of comparable alternatives

not knowing/not doing

restraint

suggestion

truisms

hidden observer

suggestion |
| As you hear my voice you can allow your body to relax *as deeply as you can. Now take several deep breaths, just as deep as you'd like . . . very good, that's the way. . . . A deep breath can feel so very comfortable and satisfying.* | contingent suggestion |
| *[If client's eyes are not already closed] You may begin to notice that your* eyes, *and particularly your* eyelids, *may feel very, very* drowsy, heavy, and somewhat sleepy . . . and *as they begin to blink, they may become especially* tired and heavy, *and* when *it is hard to keep them open,* those *eyes may wish to close* all by themselves, *that's the way . . . changing perspective . . . and going inside can be a most* curious *contrast.* | suggestion

linking word
suggestion
implication
dissociation
involuntariness

hypnotic language |

The feeling that you can attain in your body is a sensation of complete and total muscular relaxation . . . *just relaxing into a deep and very* relaxed state . . . *simply listening to my voice* . . . and drifting *into a very, very pleasant state of mind* . . . *a body that is* free from all tension and tightness, free from stress and strain. *As you listen to my voice guiding you into a total and* complete state of relaxation . . . *your mind, your body* . . . *the muscular system, the nervous system* . . . limp, relaxed *muscles* . . . *and your* breathing *is the essence of deep,* deep relaxation. *Your entire body is becoming* completely and totally relaxed, your head . . . your face . . . your neck . . . shoulders . . . back . . . chest . . . arms . . . completely relaxed, *very deeply relaxed, your* mind *and your* body, *relaxed, at ease, free from tension, tightness, stress and strain.*

repetition

repetition

suggestion

repetition

suggestion

Feeling secure and at rest. *Enjoying the sense of* quietness *and calmness. No pressure, no need to rush, no one to please, no one to satisfy. This is just* your *time to* rest and enjoy *a gentle peacefulness. Just letting go, quietly and gently, with nothing to bother you, and nothing to disturb you.*

suggestion

While you sit there *quietly, you can* notice your breathing, *and at the same time you* recognize *you are moving deeper and deeper into relaxation. That's the way. . . .*

contingent suggestion

As soon as your unconscious mind is ready to move deeper into trance, you can raise your right index finger. Good. You know, I once knew a woman who let her

metaphor

unconscious mind identify issues that had been bothering her. As she let her unconscious mind look into the solutions that were already there inside her, she began to feel more and more at ease. And as you allow your own imagination to wander, peering into your own inside issues, your conscious mind may think about solutions, while your unconscious mind considers their implications; or perhaps your unconscious mind will generate some solutions, while your conscious mind wonders what the result might be.

And now, letting that comfort *and calmness flow, out to every part of you. Bringing such a sense of* peacefulness, and quiet, and calm, *that any inner stresses can also relax. Allowing all the stress and strain to* just fade into the background, *and become more and more distant, farther and farther away. . . .*

And now I'm going to give you some quiet time, to continue experiencing a deep level of relaxation, enjoying it in your own way.

embedded meaning/ suggestion for internal search

conscious-unconscious double bind

suggestion

MYSTIFYING INDUCTION

I want to tell you about a rather strange and bewildering experience one of our therapists had as he went about inducing trance in a person in whom it was rather difficult to distinguish what was happening inside him. Accordingly, the therapist resorted to juxtaposing and mixing up various opposite phenomena in order to induce the desired state. All this might not make sense to you right now, but by the time we're done, you may definitely feel in your own way, or sense in your body, the meaning of what follows.

You know how it is when you're glad you do something, looking back on the experience, maybe appreciating it with the perspective of time or distance. Well, we're glad that we tape recorded the exact words that day, which I will read verbatim to you now.

"Bob," his name was Bob, "I know and you know and many others know that you and I and most everybody else has a right hand and a left hand, a left foot and a right foot, a right ear and a left, and a conscious mind as well as an unconscious mind.

"With all those things we have many experiences, even way back there, when we learned to count, one, two, three . . . perhaps experiencing a certain feeling or sensation on one side as opposed to the other, or maybe both at the same time. Now, Bob, one time I was working with a man who insisted on being called by his last name, which was Inskeep, a rather uncommon name.

"I said, 'Inskeep, right now I would like you to imagine, just imagine without any conscious effort, a tingling in your left hand for just a moment, and then imagine that tingling in your right hand. That's the way, Inskeep: don't do it, just imagine it. And now we're going to speed it up just a bit, quick now, imagine a tingling in your left earlobe and then the same thing in your right earlobe, and then a numbness, or a tingling, in the left third of your right hand and a tingling, or a numbness, in the right third of your left hand. Autonomy, independence, out there, that's right. I know all this may sound confusing, but just keep on like you're doing, no conscious effort is required at all, and whatever you feel in any of your extremities is just fine, and pay careful attention with your mind.'

"Inskeep was sitting in a chair just like that, Bob, and he told me that as we talked about his hands he was having a difficult time curling up his toes inside his shoes, interesting as that might sound . . . or feel.

"We continued then: 'Inskeep, cold and hot, hot and cold, and the many temperatures in between, eighty degrees, thirty degrees; seventy-five degrees, forty-three degrees, and no one needs a master's degree to feel any of those things. People can develop a light trance or medium trance or a deep trance, whatever their unconscious mind desires, even though sometimes the conscious mind might try to inter- pose something different. Just imagine, Inskeep, just imagine for a moment a lightness in most of your right hand and a heaviness down there in the bottom part of your left foot. Right hand, left foot, most of up here and bottom part down there, very good, and then a heaviness in a third of your left hand and a lightness in your right foot—not all of your left foot but in just a meaningful part of it. Lightness, heaviness, up here, down there, not all of, just a part of, doing fine, just imagining and knowing that strength means strong mind that *can't not* possibly *not ever* resist not drifting off.

"'Inskeep, going inside, a person can pay attention to outside things at the same time, without even trying, inde- pendently. Imagine a heavy rubber glove on one hand and a soft warm mitten on the other, either the left or the right, and imagine reaching down and touching a part of your foot that has a numbness, or a tingling, or on the other hand, imagine a heavy woolen sock on one foot, perhaps the left or the right, and reaching that foot up there to touch one of those hands that has developed a particular warmth, or coldness, maybe a tingling warmth, or a numbing coldness in either or maybe both. Someone said to me once that extremities have deep meaning, but I know that not knowing, forgetting, or partially realizing in a light or medium way, out there, is something that also provides something worth noticing, and whatever happens in your body is just fine. But, Inskeep, I personally have no authority to permit your mind to drift, so just concentrate on your body.'

"Bob had been paying close attention and by now had experienced many things in his extremities, but he had also

244 CLINICAL APPLICATIONS OF HYPNOSIS

noticed how his breathing had changed almost imperceptibly. He told me later that this experience was not unlike
something he remembered when he was very young, filling
up a plastic bucket on the beach, and the bucket very
quickly filled with sand and overflowed, while the hole in
the ground filled with water, and the more he dug, both the
bucket and the hole overflowed, and all he learned from the
experience was that forever after whenever he met
someone named Doug he felt almost overloaded—whatever that means.

"Bob also had a teacher in junior high whose last name
was Duggin. Mr. Duggin would catch him daydreaming out
there in the back row and say to him, 'Drift off on your
time, Bob, not mine.'

"'Inskeep,' I continued, 'just imagine my voice is out
there along with your extremities, and we'll go on, but a bit
faster because now we're nearing the end, and paying close
attention now to both outside and inside might take on an
even more curious aspect, or your unconscious mind might
just have fun inwardly.

"'Just imagine, Inskeep, the following: a person's left
third of his right ear can *now* develop a very distinct feeling,
while at the same time the lower part of his left ear can
detect the opposite feeling, perhaps alternately, maybe
together, always listening, while at the same time he listens
inwardly with his third ear, and you know what that is.

"'And while all that is going on with those ears, you can
imagine in yourself a left-right, up-down amusement in
those hands and feet, while that other person's ears—all
three of them—operate independently on their own. Warm-
hand-bottom-third or top half with the other cold, and the
opposite foot numb or tingling-alternately-left-third-yes-
and-rest-of-it-no, or heaviness in one or more parts and one
hand that is different from the lightness already present to
some degree developing in the other hand or the opposite
foot that can't not be taking on a life all its own. Feeling,
independence, autonomy, development . . . .'"

SEEING THINGS DIFFERENTLY

Someone was telling me one time about how he learned to see things differently with the passage of both time and distance.

It was the Fourth of July and he found himself on a boat that was slowly going farther and farther out into the water. It was 3:00 p.m., and he watched various activity on the beach, things that he could see quite clearly, in fairly vivid detail. There was a lifeguard perched way up on the life-guard chair. He had one of those floppy hats on his head, and mirrored sunglasses, and that white stuff on his nose shone brightly in the sun. A volleyball game was going on, off to the right of the lifeguard's chair. All around, people lay on blankets, and the sunscreen on their bodies glistened in the heat of the day. An oversized red umbrella stood out like a crimson flower blossom. Children splashed in the water, and he could hear their gleeful cries above the crash of the waves.

Everything became a bit blurry as the boat got farther from the shore; however, as a telescope was mounted on the back of the boat, he began to watch everything through the telescope, which all of a sudden brought the beach back into sharp focus. The boat continued its journey, out from the shore.

As time passed, the details of the beach—through the telescope—kept changing, ever so gradually. He could see that the volleyball players were still in motion, but he could no longer see the ball. People continued to splash in the water, but he could no longer hear their voices. They may have been children, but they could have just as easily been adults. The lifeguard was still perched on high, but there was no white on his nose. The oversized umbrella was now orange, or was it brown? He stepped back from the tele-scope, closed his eyes, and contemplated what he had seen.

Several minutes later—or maybe it was longer than several minutes—the sun had descended even more, and it was not quite as warm on his back as before. He put his eye to the telescope once again, and everything before him took on a most curious aspect. The lifeguard chair remained prominent, but he could not tell for sure if a person was still sitting on it. The volleyball game appeared to have stopped, just as people may have ceased lying on the sand. He saw only flickers of movement in the water where the children had been playing, and was it the umbrella that was buffeted by a gust of wind? The only sound was the boat's motor. He closed his eyes again and let his imagination drift and dream.

A while later, the sun had gone down even more, and as he put his eye to the telescope once again, the sight before him had become only sea and shore in the distance, water and coastline, as the boat continued out.

Later on in life, he continued to experience many things, with time and distance in between, seeing them one way, and then another, and often he reflected on that journey out from the shore.

African Violets

There was this famous doctor in Phoenix years ago, Milton Erickson, and he was asked to visit a depressed woman who would not leave her house. This Dr. Erickson was very observant as the woman showed him around her big, dark house. She talked about how she hadn't been to church for years but she liked the people there. "Nice people there," she commented.

The house was very, very dark except for one room way in the back of the house. In that room, some light was coming through the window, and next to the window was a table with lovely African violets, beautiful, magnificent violets thriving there on that table.

The woman perked up a bit as she talked with pride about her violets. Then she led Dr. Erickson back through the dark house. As he bid her farewell, Dr. Erickson commented, "I can just imagine . . . how some of those people in your church *might appreciate your lovely violets*." And then he left, and he never saw her again.

Months later Dr. Erickson heard that the woman was doing much better. For some reason, she began to grow more violets. First she set some new violets by one window and opened the curtain, and then she did the same with more violets and other windows, and pretty soon every window in the house had violets. Many people at church ended up with her violets.

The Pond

A man told me one time how it all began with his forty acres back in Indiana. As he began his story, I wondered about its relevance and just how long a story it would be, but finally I just sat back and listened for the words without trying to read any meaning into the content. It turns out that this man had always wanted a tranquil pond in back of his house, a nice pond with plant life and fish, something he could enjoy for a long, long time.

Not caring to do the work himself, he hired a crew of workers, and soon trees were cut down and a place was cleared well back from his house. Next, they brought in a bulldozer and a large excavator. In several hours the man gazed upon a 10-foot reddish-brown gash in the earth's crust. He wondered if the 50-foot by 125-foot hole would ever fill with water, but he knew that eventually the clay-lined hole would fill right to the top.

With the melting snows of winter and the heavy showers of spring, the pond filled up in no time. One day he noticed algae floating in the water, and soon the sound of frogs filled the air at night. In June, various insects buzzed over the water and aquatic plants appeared on the shoreline. He knew that all this life hadn't materialized miraculously, but that it had been borne on the wind or carried unwittingly by the feet of waterfowl.

Eventually the pond looked like a part of the natural landscape. One morning he even saw the tracks of deer, raccoons, and other animals down by the shore. He thought about something he had read once by Henry David

Thoreau, something to the effect of "no sooner will you dig your pond and nature will begin to stock it."

But nature didn't just stock his pond. Nature had seemed to strike a natural balance between predator and prey, parasite and host, each with its proper place in the larger scheme of things. As the man observed it all from his back porch one evening, he proudly contemplated what he had accomplished. "This is the way it's supposed to be," he thought. "This is something I can enjoy until the end of my days."

One month followed another and pretty soon two years had passed. The man paid less attention to his pond, just assuming that its natural balance would always remain in effect, that the pond would always take care of itself. He traveled to Europe and was gone for a couple of months. When he returned in late summer the pond appeared to be clogged with weeds. However, he thought this was only a temporary condition, and he took another trip, this time for six months. While away, he read a book about ponds. The book mentioned that as algae and weeds grow, die, and sink to the bottom, the water becomes shallower, and as more light reaches the bottom, the weeds grow more and more. Rushes and willows on the shore encroach into the open water, which steadily diminishes available water until the pond becomes a swamp, then just a wet spot, and finally what was once a pond, turns into woodland, which is exactly what it was at the beginning.

He hurried home from his trip and feverishly began raking out the algae and weeds. He stocked the pond with a special kind of carp that ate weeds, and planted cattails to filter out new sediment. Pretty soon his pond was again pulsating with life. He even noticed some things that he had not seen previously, an aquatic spider, and tracks left by a fox.

Any trips he took from then on lasted only a month or less and he subscribed to a magazine called *Perpetual Pond*, though he had problems with the title.

Glossary

abreaction Trauma clients may experience intense emotions, such as panic or fear, which may be accompanied by a flashback or intrusive thought. This expression of emotions may occur during direct treatment of the trauma, but may also occur during simple relaxation. In hypnosis, one of several techniques for treating trauma involves *age regression* to a time the trauma occurred, a facilitated abreaction, and *reframing*. This process often provides the client considerable relief and a new understanding of the traumatic experience. This should be attempted only by experienced therapists. Incomplete abreaction of underlying feelings may be a cause of therapeutic failure.

absorption of attention Necessary for successful trance, the client's attention is focused on, for example, a spot on the wall, a story, a bodily sensation, or anything else. *Eye fixation*, eye closure, facial mask, diminished movement, lack of swallowing, and other signs may indicate an absorption of attention.

activate to trigger or stimulate a person or process. With depressed clients the goal may be to get them *doing* something, or behavioral *activation*. To *activate* unconscious problem solving we may employ an instigative anecdote.

age progression Essentially the opposite of *age regression*, clients are asked to imagine themselves in the future, feeling or behaving confident, strong, or in control. The technique is also called *time projection*, among other names.

age regression A technique useful in hypnosis for accessing resources during problem solving and other applications, age regression is experienced naturally whenever someone has a memory or reminiscence. As part of trancework, age regression may be structured and guided, for example, "I want you to ride a magic carpet back through time to age 15," or general and permissive, e.g., "I want you, starting now, to go back in your own way, taking as much time as you need, back to any time in the past that might be important to the problem at hand, and when you get there, let me know by nodding your head. . . ." We should try not to impede clients, as they invariably go back in time much faster than we can guide them.

ambiguous function assignment A technique for both standard psychotherapy and within hypnosis, this strategic task involves having clients go *somewhere* and do *something* which will lead to a *discovery* (that's why it's called *ambiguous*). For example, "Between now and next time I want you to walk up Squaw Peak exactly 48 paces, stop, look down, and the first rock you see, something important about your problem will come to you." To be used when more straight-forward techniques have failed.

amnesia Some practitioners believe that inducing amnesia is necessary for later problem resolution, as amnesia allows unconscious processing to go on without conscious interference. Amnesia can be encouraged with suggestions such as, "Will you forget to remember, or, simply remember to forget?" or "When you go to sleep you dream, and when you wake up you cannot remember that dream." Distraction may also induce amnesia—e.g., the client is realerted and immediately the therapist launches into a story about shaggy dogs. Many clients will have amnesia for some portion of the trance experience even if it is not facilitated.

amplifying the metaphor This technique is often effective with anxiety and anger. It involves permissively generating a symbol or metaphor (i.e., a color, an object, an idea) for both the problem and the absence of the problem. This amplifys both the problem and its absence and anchors the metaphor for the absence of the problem.

anchor Also known as *associational cue*, or *reminder*, this is a technique with which clients themselves can trigger trance. A commonly assigned anchor is a circle with the index finger and thumb.

and A very important word in psychotherapy, *and* leads and links. Following a pacing statement (e.g., "You feel the comfort of that one deep breath") the word then leads (e.g., "*and* you can use that one deep breath to let yourself sink deeper and deeper. . .") It may also link a truism to a directive or suggestion—e.g., "You have experienced the comfort of trance here for the past 30 minutes or so, and you can now begin to employ relaxation at work when you need it the most. . . ."

apposition of opposites An example of *hypnotic language*, this technique juxtaposes polarities or opposites—e.g., "As that right hand develops a *lightness*, your body can sink even deeper into *heaviness* and relaxation." The therapist can experiment with warm–cold, up–down, light–heavy, right–left, or any number of opposites. Hypnotic language is a major tool of the therapist for trance induction and other applications in hypnosis.

arm catalepsy induction Catalepsy means a "suspension of movement." A cataleptic or rigid arm is central to the arm catalepsy induction, an effective, rapid, and highly directive means for inducing trance. It is contraindicated in the person who has cervical pain or related problems.

authoritarian language the therapist who uses such directive language would say, for example, "I *want* you now to drop off into deep trance and *you will* lose your desire for cigarettes." Contrast that with permissive language: "In a few moments you *may* begin to experience yourself drifting off into trance, and I wonder when you *may* begin to see smoking in a different light."

automatic process Synonymous with *unconscious process*, this refers to a mental process that is outside of one's conscious awareness. Techniques such as *metaphor, pause,* and *misspeak* are believed to access this process.

automatic writing a permissive technique for unconscious search, this involves asking the client in trance to write some words—e.g., ". . . with the pencil in your hand and the notepad on your lap, beginning now, just let that hand move all by itself, and who knows what words will appear on the paper?" A similar technique is automatic drawing. Can also be done imaginally, e.g., ". . . I'd like you to imagine yourself standing before a chalk board, and with a piece of chalk in your hand, I wonder what words your hand can write on that board?"

bind of comparable alternatives   Another example of *hypnotic language*, and a potent ally of the therapist, this technique appears to offer the client a choice between two or more alternatives, offering the illusion of choice—e.g., "Today would you like to go into a light trance, a medium trance, or a deep trance?" or "What you learned today might be useful in your personal life, or maybe you can use it at work, or perhaps you can simply incorporate it into your overall experience."

collaboration   see *therapeutic alliance*

commitment   Social psychology ascertains that if people commit to doing something, they are more likely to comply. A vital concept in hypnosis, commitment is a potent therapeutic tool for increasing the effectiveness of suggestions—e.g., "Taking one deep breath can help you in a stressful situation. If this is something you're willing to practice at least once a day, your yes finger will rise." see also *unconscious commitment*

confusion   Employed to counter unconscious resistance, this is a broad category of techniques that interrupt, overload, or distract the conscious mind. In this book, the *non sequitur* is used—e.g., "I wonder why shopping carts always seem to stick together." As the client tries to make sense of the confusing statement, she is receptive to a suggestion—e.g., "You can go deep." In this way an avenue of escape provided by the therapist. Confusion is generally more effective in short bursts, and should always be used judiciously and respectfully. see also *amnesia*

confusional induction   The purpose of any induction is to help the client achieve trance. With most clients a conversational or other straight-forward induction is sufficient. However clients with unconscious resistance that doesn't allow trance to develop may need a confusional induction, like *mystifying*. A confusional induction overloads and distracts, thus allowing the client to escape from the confusion. Usually the client escapes into trance.

conscious-unconscious bind   A bind limits choice, channeling behavior in the desired direction. This type of suggestion helps bypass

conscious, learned limitations by accessing the unconscious mind—
e.g., "An unconscious learning from this experience today may be
developed in your conscious mind as well," or, "When your conscious
mind is ready to provide some useful information about this problem,
you will experience a peculiar sensation in your right hand. If such
information comes from your unconscious mind, the sensation will be
in your left hand."

contingent suggestion Also known as *chaining*, this type of suggestion
connects the suggestion to an ongoing or inevitable behavior—e.g.,
"And as you become aware or that peculiar sensation in your right
hand, you can begin to float back in time." It also works as a *posthypnotic suggestion*—e.g., "When you return here and sit down there in
that chair, just feeling that chair beneath you can be an immediate
signal to allow you to resume that deep and pleasant sense of relaxation." It is believed that it is more difficult to reject two or more
suggestions when they are linked together in this way.

control issues see *issues of control and trust*

debriefing The final phase of the hypnosis session where the therapist ratifies hypnotic phenomena and elicit's subjective experience.

deepening Following the induction phase of the hypnosis session,
trance is deepened, typically by counting from ten to one. Some practitioners employ no formal deepening. The deepening phase precedes
the therapy component.

direct question see *question*

desensitization hierarchy In behavior therapy employing exposure
techniques the goal is to help the client become habituated to feared
stimuli. Accordingly, the stimuli are ranked in a hierarchy from least
feared to most feared.

displacement As used for pain management, the locus of pain is
displaced to another area of the body, or to an area outside the body.
The client may continue to experience the sensation, but in a less
painful or vulnerable way.

dissociation Dissociation is a hallmark of trance and an excellent
convincer of trance. The more clients experience it (e.g., their hand

separated from their body), the more their hypnotic experience is ratified. Whenever possible, the therapist should say *"that* hand" instead of *"your* hand." Employ similar language, especially during induction and deepening. Encouraging dissociation deepens trance.

double dissociative conscious-unconscious double bind Confusional suggestions such as this are complex and interesting. However they are probably the least important type of suggestion to become skillful in using—e.g., "Between now and next time your conscious mind may work at resolving the problem while your unconscious mind wonders about the implications; or your unconscious mind may come up with answers while your unconscious mind ponders the implications." We should always let the *response of the client* be our guide rather than the cleverness of the technique.

double negative An example of *hypnotic language*, it is believed that a double negative may lead some clients to accept the suggestion more than a simple positive suggestion alone. For example, "You can't not pay attention to the warmth developing in the soles of your feet." The two negatives negate each other to form a positive suggestion, and the hint of confusion enhances acceptance. Suggestions such as this should be used parsimoniously. see also *triple negative*

ego strengthening Ego-strength is defined as the ability to cope with environmental demands, and *ego-strengthening* refers to techniques whose purpose is to strengthen the client's self-esteem or self-efficacy. This book describes two types of hypnotic ego-strengthening, *metaphorical* and *short-burst*.

embedded suggestion The client's conscious mind is bypassed when the therapist embeds a suggestion. To encourage an inward focus, the therapist may embed *in* words—e.g., "Going *in*side can be very *inter*esting . . . *in* there where you have your imag*in*ation, fasc*in*ation, *intu*ition. . . ." Also the therapist might suggest *security*, for example, by embedding it in a story that emphasizes *security* provided at a large outdoor concert. A major tool in indirect hypnosis, this is sometimes called *embedded command*.

empathy The therapist shows her empathy to the client by listening, eye contact, and other (verbal or nonverbal) caring behavior.

eye closure Some therapists feel uncomfortable if clients do not readily close their eyes. We can suggest that their eyes will blink, and their eyelids might feel heavy, and that their eyes can gently close whenever they wish. Clients can experience deep trance through *eye fixation* alone, and open eyes permit the therapist an observation of the ongoing process.

eye fixation For clients who fear loss of control, it is helpful to let them focus their gaze on a spot of their choice—e.g., somewhere on the wall, the ceiling, or the back of their hand. Most clients eventually feel comfortable enough to close their eyes.

fluff This refers to meaningless filler that the therapist includes either in the conversational patter in an induction, or in a story. Purposeless, meandering detail is thought to bore the client and deepen absorption. A therapist I work with once said, "It took many years for me to learn to be boring." Too often we may believe that things we say to the client must be purposeful or didactic; however, a few well-placed suggestions inserted amidst a flurry of fluff may be very effective.

Greek chorus With this technique the therapist employs an unseen and often imaginary group of confederates who offer opinions about the case. This technique originated during the days of the one-way window when the therapist would stop at intervals and consult the treatment team behind the window. Its use in conventional psychotherapy—and within hypnosis in the book—involves the therapist's reporting to the client in trance, for example, "Another time and in another place there was a person with a problem like yours, and different opinions were sought from five psychologists. The first one said, "You should definitely do. . . ." Used in hypnosis this technique bolsters the therapist with a host of indirect but potent suggestions. This is an advanced technique that requires preparation before th session and should be used only when more conventional techniques have failed.

habituation In behavior therapy employing exposure, clients repeatedly reexperience feared stimuli for the purpose of reducing negative affect. Negative affect is reduced because clients become habituated, or not so upset by, the feared stimuli.

hidden observer A phenomenon experienced by most people in trance. In preparing a client for hypnosis, we may say, "You have your conscious mind, your unconscious mind, and your *hidden observer*, that part of you that observes the process." It is normal to experience this phenomenon during the first session or two. However, if the hidden observer remains active and impedes the client's letting go, a confusional induction many be indicated.

hierarchy see *desensitization*

hypnotic language In this book, hypnotic techniques like *bind of comparable alternatives, implication*, and *power words* are subsumed under the term *hypnotic language*. see also *bind of comparable alternatives, implication, power words*

hypnotic phenomena Potent allies of the therapist, hypnotic phenomena, when *experienced* by the client, reinforce the trance process. Accordingly, the author's inductions and stories are often replete with suggestions for *dissociation, time distortion*, and *amnesia*. Other hypnotic phenomena are hyperamnesia, catalepsy, arm levitation, automatic writing and drawing, hypnotic dreaming and daydreaming, *age regression*, future progression, anesthesia, analgesia, positive hallucination, and negative hallucination.

hypnotic susceptibility An experimental subject's capacity for experiencing some hypnotic phenomena can be measured by hypnotic susceptibility, or responsiveness, tests or scales. Used mostly in research, these tests have little utility for the clinician.

ideomotor finger signal It is essential that therapist and client communicate during trance. New therapists commonly begin by asking the client to respond with a head nod or verbal report before establishing finger signals on one hand. So that clients have a full range of responses, signals for a *yes* finger, a *no* finger, and *I-don't-know/I'm-not-ready-to-answer-yet* finger are established on one hand.

ideosensory phenomena The more a client *experiences* during hypnosis, the more she will believe in the procedure. A major way to foster this process is to suggest that tingling, numbness, and other feelings and sensations may occur. Their occurrence is a strong ratifier of trance. see also *suggestion covering all possibilities*

imaginal exposure Outside of trance, exposure of a traumatic stressor, for example, would involve leading the client through a reexperiencing of the stressor, or feared stimulus. This could be done, for example, by discussing it or by actually experiencing it—e.g., by riding in an elevator in the case of such a phobia. In trance, clients are led through a similar reexperiencing, but in their imagination.

implication An important method of indirect suggestion, the therapist stimulates trance experience by conveying positive expectancy—e.g., "When you are aware of warmth beginning to spread out, you may nod your head." The therapist does not ask, "*Does* one of your hands feel *light?*" or "*If* one of your hands begins to feel *light*. . . ." Rather, the therapist would ask, "*Which* one of your hands is *lighter?*" In implication, *when* is often the operative word, not the authoritarian *will*, which does not imply or suggest but commands or directs. In accessing unconscious resources, the therapist may say, "Taking as much time as you need, *when* your unconscious mind has selected some strength or resource from the past, your *yes* finger can move all by itself."

indirection To employ indirection generally refers to an unconsciously directed approach. For example, the therapist tells the client an anecdote or story about *someone else* who successfully managed his anger and how he did so, where a *directive* approach with the same client would involve straight-forward instruction. see also *reactance*

induction In this book, the *trancework process* is described as three separate components: 1) *induction*, where the client is put into trance; 2) *deepening*, where the client's experience is deepened; and 3) *therapy*, which could be a story, *age progression*, or any variety of techniques.

instigative anecdote A very brief story that provides clients with a metaphorical example that can be self-referenced and incorporated into their own situation. *Instigative anecdotes* and *stories* are designed to stimulate unconscious activity.

instigative story Similar to *instigative anecdote*, but longer. With both the target is the unconscious mind. see also *instigative anecdote*

interspersal The therapist's hypnotic patter is interspersed with words, phrases, metaphors, or anecdotes to indirectly influence the client. For example, while therapists count backward from ten to one during deepening, they may insert a brief anecdote about another client who experienced a peculiar heaviness in her hand. Words such as *heavy*, *light*, or *deep* may be inserted randomly, or a phrase such as "Just let go." Attention is drawn to an interspersed suggestion that is set apart from hypnotic patter by a pause, and thus it becomes more potent.

intrusive phenomena These are trauma memories that intrude on conscious activity. Also known as *intrusive thoughts*, *cognitive disruptions*, or *cognitive interference*. As therapists work with clients on their traumatic stressors, an increase in such re-experiencing (at least temporarily) can be expected both inside out outside of therapy.

issues of control and trust Clients need to be reassured that they will not lose control during the session. Building rapport and trust neutralizes this fear, as does concrete reassurance—e.g., "You are always in the driver's seat," or perhaps humorously, "Don't worry, I'll tell you if you quack like a duck." Trust is also maintained by discussing the agenda for the session. For example, we would not want to do *age regression* without permission. Failure to attend sufficiently to control and trust is a major reason for poor response and dropping out of treatment.

law of parsimony This "law" holds that the therapist should say or do as little as is necessary to achieve the desired response. A long or elaborate induction is not necessary if the client can go into trance by simply recalling a pleasant scene. With a client experienced in trance-work, this less-is-more approach is manifested by a minimalist induction such as "Just sit back now, close your eyes, and let yourself go into trance. When you are sufficiently deep in order to do today's work, you will find your *yes* finger rising."

lead away A confusion technique, this is used to distract the conscious mind from a preceding suggestion by saying something irrelevant— e.g., ". . . *you can overcome this problem*—and let me tell you what I found when shopping for a new car last week." I use the technique most often after an extended metaphor, such as a story. Techniques such as this are believed to be most effective with clients who show unconscious resistance. see also *pause, amnesia, reactance* and *misspeak*

leading We pace, model, or mirror to show understanding and we connect to a suggestion by leading. For example, "I can see how nervous you feel when you're in social situations, *and* from here on I would like you to employ your anchor when you start to get nervous around people." The operative word is *and*, as it both leads and links.

linking word The most common linking word is *and*. In hypnotic patter we pace and lead—e.g., ". . . you exhale *and* you can release tension in your neck and shoulders. . . ." Or, we may offer a series of truisms followed by a suggestion (see *truism*). In both cases, *and* is the critical word. Some call *and* the most important word in psychotherapy because it links and leads to important suggestions or directives.

matching Similar to *mirroring* and *pacing*. This technique may be applied in a variety of ways: verbally, where you show understanding with feedback; nonverbally—e.g., posture and affect that communicates sadness, in the case of depressed mood; or metaphorically, where your story, anecdote or metaphor demonstrates understanding of content and emotion, e.g., to a couple in marital therapy, ". . . marriage is a tough road, and today you've helped me understand the bumps in the road and how it's affected your lives. . . ."

metaphor A broad class of indirect techniques, the use of metaphor allows the therapist to bypass the conscious mind and tap into unconscious processes, which tend to be represented and comprehended metaphorically. A client's situation or idiosyncratic speech (e.g., "I feel like there is a wall around me") provides the therapist with imagery to be utilized. Stories or anecdotes stimulate self-referencing at an unconscious level.

misspeak To be used sparsely, this elegant indirect technique can be highly effective in communicating a suggestion to the unconscious. For example, ". . . she ceased the umbilical/unbiblical behavior," or "The man changed his behavior across the board/border down in Mexico. . . ." The therapist *appears* to misspeak, the first word is the suggestion and the second word serves to distract or lead away.

modeling Also known as *mirroring*, this technique involves communicating understanding to the client by (nonverbally) leaning forward empathically when a client describes something sad, (verbally) by paraphrasing to the client a summary of what they have said, or (metaphorically) feeding back to the client a representation of their thought and feeling (e.g., ". . . what you describe is very difficult and frustrating, like a dark cloud that has descended on your life.") see also *pacing* and *leading*

multi-level communication When therapists use a word in one way consciously, clients tend to unconsciously evoke other meanings. For example, an anecdote or story that mentions *light* switch, or de*light* may communicate *light* (not *heavy*). Multi-level communication allows the therapist to convey various ideas, or suggestions, simultaneously.

naturalistic trance states Prehypnosis discussion should elicit situations when the client naturally drifts off or becomes absorbed in something pleasant, such as a favorite activity. This establishes trance as a naturally occurring behavior within the client's control. Examples include "highway hypnosis" while driving, immersion in a book, or movie.

negative hallucination Milton Erickson employed *positive* hallucination when he had children imagine a furry animal next to them. Even more useful—and easier to induce—is negative hallucination—e.g., "You will notice the sound of the air conditioner, people talking in the hallway, and my voice speaking to you, and all these sounds may simply drift in and out of your ears, or you may not hear them at all." To achieve a complete absence of something may be unrealistic, while suggesting an alteration or diminution may be more successful.

negative reframe To be used judiciously, a negative reframe is useful for redirecting the client's attention or *perturbing* monolithic behavior. To generalize broadly, a man's reluctance to carry out an assignment can be reframed as passivity or weakness, and a woman's interpersonal conflict can be reframed as uncaring or unprotective. This can be employed both in standard talk therapy as well as hypnosis.

non sequitur Used for distraction or interruption, a statement that is totally out of context can depotentiate conscious mental sets. One of a wide variety of *confusion* techniques, such as statements or stories, a non sequitur can overload or distract the conscious mind. As the conscious mind seeks to escape from this incongruence or dissonance, the client may be receptive to suggestion—e.g., an ego-strengthening suggestion, "You can do it." Non sequiturs can be virtually any phrase or question—e.g., "And the rain fell silently in the forest," or "Do you like dogs?"

not knowing/not doing Actually a suggestion for restraint, this elegant device is very liberating in that it facilitates unconscious responsiveness rather than conscious effort. The therapeutic process may be facilitated if, early in the induction, the therapist says something like, "There's absolutely nothing to do or to know, or to think about, or to change; in fact, isn't it nice to know that by just sitting there and breathing, you can go into trance, and you don't even have to listen to the words." It may also help clients discharge resistance or anxiety.

pacing see *modeling*

paradoxical directive Part of a class of behavior prescriptions in strategic therapy which disrupt fixed habit patterns by nonreinforcement of the existing pattern. Often the client's problem-maintaining solution is the target of intervention. For example, a depressed person who worries excessively about his depression may be provided with rationale and instructions to restrict worrying between 8:00 p.m. and 9:00 p.m., and only in the living room.

pause Believed to be a form of indirect suggestion, the therapist pauses for a second or two at certain times in her patter. When clients hear a pause an unconscious search is begun, and clients are believed to be receptive to the suggestion that follows. For example, in a story "... she was searching for something, and she found it in the morning when (pause, pause) *she saw a flash of light.* A pause can also be used *after* a suggestion, e.g., "... she made an important *discovery* (pause, pause) *which turned out to be quite significant.* A pause can also be used as a suggestion, though less indirectly: "During our session today you will occasionally hear a pause (pause), or a brief period of silence (pause), and you may use these times to let your experience deepen."

permissive suggestion It is believed that many clients respond well when given a wide range of choice—e.g., "You may begin to notice sensations, feelings, or experiences beginning to develop in those hands, or will it be in your feet?"

perturb A good rule for therapists: When stuck, *perturb*, which means to disturb or agitate to help clients break out of old patterns. The therapist's task may be to perturb, especially when clients are stuck in a rigid point of view or dysfunctional behavior. Such clients usually require perturbation that is unconsciously directed (see the "Simple Rooms" story, Chapter 2)

positive expectancy Clients are more likely to be responsive when the therapist conveys confidence and certainty that improvement can be expected. The therapist may express confidence or hopefulness about a successful problem resolution, or during an induction when the therapist suggests hand levitation, both his verbal and nonverbal behavior convey overt positive expectancy.

posthypnotic suggestion This is a suggestion, given in trance, for behavior to occur outside of trance. For example, "When you return here next time and sit down there, the feeling of that chair will be a signal for you to resume the pleasantness and relaxation of trance," or, "At work or at home you will be able to begin to relax when you take one big, deep satisfying breath," or "During the next two weeks when you're going to work on the bus and you cross 22nd Street you will notice something that can help you with this problem. . . ." The last posthypnotic suggestion—notice something—is tagged to a naturally occurring behavior.

power words Certain words, such as *story, imagine, wonder, curious, explore, notice, appreciate, discover,* and *interesting* are thought to activate a sense of wonderment, which may enhance the trance process. In this book, power words and techniques such as *bind of comparable alternatives* are referred to collectively as *hypnotic language.* see also *bind of comparable alternatives*

pre-trancework discussion The beginning of the hypnosis session where the therapist "checks in" with the client and sets the agenda.

question Therapists should remember that punctuating trancework with a question can be quite instigative. A question will focus attention, stimulate associations, and facilitate responsiveness. A question such as, "And the tingling down there in that foot, do you notice it yet?" bypasses the conscious mind and is useful as a probe when the therapist is discovering the client's hypnotic talents, or when resistance is present.

realerting Upon completion of therapy component of trancework, the client is *realerted*—e.g., "Beginning now I'm going to count from one up to five, and by the time I reach five, you can resume your alert and waking state, as if waking up from a nice, refreshing nap." In this book the typical hypnosis session is described as *pre-trancework discussion, induction, deepening, therapy component, realerting,* and *debriefing.*

reframe A new understanding or appreciation comes about because of new information provided by the therapist. By relabeling or wrapping a positive connotation around problem behavior, the client is given hope, along with seeing the problem in a new light. Virtually anything the client brings to therapy may be reframed. The session itself may be reframed as an effort to make things better. When there is little to reframe, therapists may reframe the presumed motivation *behind* the distress or problem in the same way that they may reframe the therapy session itself as an *effort*, or *intention*, to make things better. A reframe also sets the stage for a suggestion or directive, so that it is more likely to be accepted. Reframe is a vital element in all methods of psychotherapy, as virtually any behavior can be reframed as strength, protectiveness, caring, or any other value dear to the client. see also *negative reframe*

reinforcement In this book, *reinforcement* is a component of the *seeding technique* and the final step in the acronym S.A.R: *seed, activate,* and *reinforce.*

repetition Suggestions that are important should be repeated. The therapist may repeat "breathing in comfort and relaxation" several times in an induction. It is also useful to repeat a suggestion in a different way—e.g., "feeling a particular heaviness in those feet" may be followed later by the same suggestion that is metaphorical: "another person felt like he had heavy boots on his feet, and he could barely move them." A general rule of thumb is if it's important, repeat it—but not too much.

resilience The capacity to withstand and rebound from disruptive life challenges. Therapists can help individuals and families to identify strengths and resources to recover and grow from crises.

resistance A client who says, "I don't want to go into trance" displays conscious resistance. A client who says, "I want to go into trance, but I just can't" is showing unconscious resistance. Many clients are keenly aware of their resistance, which may be anxiety, negativity, or feared loss of control. Resistance may be discharged in various ways, including general and *permissive suggestions, suggestions covering all possibilities, not knowing/not doing, metaphor, story, confusion techniques*, having the client switch chairs (so he leaves his resistance in the first chair), and asking the client questions to which he must answer "no," (e.g., "In the winter the temperature in Phoenix is the same as Minneapolis"). Many times clients' resistance will abate as rapport builds, and as they feel more comfortable in therapy.

restraint Resistant clients may become more resistant if we encourage change or adaptation too rapidly. These clients' resistance can be lessened if we restrain or hold them back from moving ahead—e.g., "Go slow . . . change presents uncertainty . . . you might not be ready yet . . . it could be dangerous to move ahead too fast." Early in trancework, inducing trance, bringing clients out of trance, and then resuming hypnosis, holds back something pleasant, builds responsiveness, and enhances client control.

secondary gain If a capable person behaves helplessly in order to gain sympathy we would say his behavior has *secondary gain*. In situations of disability, especially where remuneration is involved, a person who is unable to improve may be doing so because of secondary gain. Secondary gain, also called *the green poultice*, may lie outside of a person's conscious awareness.

seeding A suggestion may be more successful when it has been seeded beforehand. A target suggestion is mentioned, or seeded, and later, mentioning the suggestion again, the target is activated. In prehypnosis, the therapist may mention breathing, slowing down, or deep relaxation, as these suggestions will follow in trancework. If therapists know that they will be offering suggestions to slow down eating, they can cue this idea by appreciably slowing down their rhythm in advance. The acronym SAR is used in this book. *Seed* the idea, *activate* it in trance one or more times, and after formal hypnosis *reinforce* it through discussion.

short burst A term coined by Brent Geary, this refers to a suggestion that is interspersed during the induction, deepening, or therapy component. In this book, it is primarily used as an ego-strengthening suggestion followed by a non sequitur, e.g., ". . . I don't always know why dogs bark . . . and *you can let go.*" It can also be used for other suggestions, without a confusional statement like a non sequitur, and is probably most effective with a slight vocal alteration, which is considered a direct communication to the unconscious.

self-efficacy Often used synonymously with *self-esteem*, the belief that one's behavior will lead to successful outcomes. When hypnosis practitioners boost self-esteem, it is called *ego-strengthening*.

speaking the client's language By incorporating the client's own language, and literally using the words of the client, the therapist's suggestions may conform more to the client's thinking, and be more effective.

story The story is an important indirect technique and a primary means for offering a suggestion that can be self-referenced by the client.

suggestion covering all possibilities This can be especially useful when combined with *metaphor*—e.g., describing someone else's experience in trance: "As a person goes deeper into trance she can begin to notice various sensations starting to develop in her hands. It might be a tingling in one hand; maybe a numbness in the other; perhaps a warm feeling, or a cold one, or some other interesting feeling. One woman one time sitting right there in that chair wondered privately, 'How is it that one time coming in here I can sense a slight coldness up here in my right earlobe, and another time I feel a tingling down there in my right big toe?'" see also *bind of comparable alternatives* and *permissive suggestion*

surprise An example of hypnotic language, the word SURPRISE is thought to stimulate unconscious search—e.g., ". . . and as she found herself walking through the woods, she looked down to her left and found a *surprise* . . . and many months later, she continued to use this new-found knowledge. . . ."

therapeutic alliance Also referred to as *cooperation strategy*, this refers to the "working together" of client and therapist. It is believed that this foundation is necessary for techniques to be effective or for client change or improvement to occur.

therapy component This phase of the hypnosis session may consist of a *story* or *anecdote, age progression* or *age regression, unconscious search, exploration, problem solving,* or other technique directed at the presenting problem.

time distortion This is a common trance phenomenon, as time may seem to speed up (time expansion) or slow down (time contraction) during trance. "How much time do you think has passed since you came in here?" is a relevant question to ask clients when they come out of trance. This ratifies the trance experience and is an indicator of responsiveness.

triple negative If used judiciously, it is believed that a triple negative is received positively by the unconscious mind. A statement such as "Your unconscious mind *never can't not* process this problem between now and next session" may facilitate processing, or it might best serve to give the client a mild confusion or pleasant sense of wonderment. see also *double negative*

truism This is an undeniable statement of fact—e.g., "Everyone has felt the warm sun on their skin." A series of truisms leads to a *yes-set* that builds commitment and acceptance of suggestions—e.g., "Coming in here today on a hot day, sitting for a while out there in the waiting room, walking down the hall, coming in here, and sitting down there, I know that you can begin to let yourself g . . . ," see also *yes-set*

unconscious commitment Therapists may consult the unconscious mind through nonverbal signalling—e.g., "And when your unconscious mind has identified a time in the past when you felt confident, you may signal with your *yes* finger." Unconscious commitment is obtained by a *direct question*—e.g., "I want to direct a question to your unconscious mind: After exploring this problem and understanding it as you do, are you now willing to let go of the problem? Taking as much time as you need, you may signal with one of your fingers." see also *commit-ment*

unconsciously directed therapy A cornerstone of this approach is *metaphor* and *story*, whose purpose is to influence the unconscious mind. An approach such as cognitive-behavioral therapy is primarily concerned with *conscious* intent or purpose. Many other approaches to psychotherapy—like psychodynamic, psychodrama, or Gestalt—employ techniques that are both consciously and unconsciously directed.

unconscious mind Many therapists refer to this construct as meaning virtually any thought or feeling that is outside of the client's imme-diate awareness. With some clients, it may be helpful to refer to this as either *the subconscious mind* or *the back part of the mind*, as that is "speaking their language."

unconscious process Sometimes referred to as *automatic process*, this refers to the mental process that is outside of one's conscious aware-ness. Techniques such as *metaphor, pause,* and *misspeak* are believed to access this process.

unconscious problem solving Some therapists work to foster problem solving on an unconscious level. For example, in trance a client is given the suggestion, "important new information to help you with your problem will come to you when you're at the stop light on Broadway," and then a suggestion for amnesia is given, and the client has no conscious recollection of the suggestion. If, in the next session the client returns with a spontaneous revelation that occurred while in his car, we might presume that unconscious problem solving occurred.

utilization Tailoring therapy, or hypnosis, to the individual takes into account the client's unique motivations, interests, preferences, and use of language. The client's behavior, however problematic, is accepted and suggestions are attached to it—e.g., the client yawns and the ther-apist notes, "Have you ever noticed how even a simple yawn can lead to even deeper relaxation?" The therapist conveys the importance of utterly accepting whatever occurs with the client, then seeks to use and transform it. The therapist follows and then guides the ongoing behavior of the client.

yes-set An ally of the therapist in any modality, this involves mentioning *truisms*, or aspects of undeniable reality, to create a *yes-set* acceptance, thus allowing the client to be more receptive to a suggestion that follows. For example, "You've done very well coming in here for five sessions now, working hard each time, *and* I know that today you can make even more progress toward your goal."

Hypnosis Organizations

American Society of Clinical Hypnosis *www.asch.net*

Australian Society of Hypnosis *www.ozhypnosis.com.au*

British Society of Experimental and Clinical Hypnosis
www.bsech.com

British Society for Medical and Dental Hypnosis *www.bsmdh.org*

International Society of Hypnosis *www.ish.unimelb.edu.au*

Milton H. Erickson Foundation *www.erickson-foundation.org*

Royal Society of Medicine, Section for Hypnosis and Psychosomatic
Medicine *www.vsm.ac.uk*

Society of Clinical and Experimental Hypnosis and International
Society of Hypnosis *ijceh.educ.wsu*

References

Ablon, J., & Jones, E. (1999). Psychotherapy process in the National Institute of Mental Health treatment of depression collaborative research program. *Journal of Consulting and Clinical Psychology, 67,* 64–75.

Ackerman, J. (2003). When the frost lies white. *National Geographic, 203*(1), 88–113.

Allen, S. N., & Bloom, S. L. (1994). Group and family treatment of posttraumatic stress disorder. *Psychiatric Clinics of North America, 17,* 426–430.

Allport, G. (1955). *Becoming.* New Haven, CT: Yale University Press.

Angus, L., & Korman, Y. (2002). Conflict, coherence, and change in brief psychotherapy: A metaphor theme analysis. In S. R. Fussell (Ed.), *The verbal communication of emotions* (pp. 151–165). Mahwah, NJ: Lawrence Erlbaum.

Arno, S. (1999). *Northwest trees.* Seattle, WA: The Mountaineers.

Arnow, B. A., Manber, R., Blasey, C., Klein, D. N., Blalock, J. A., Markowitz, J. C., Rothbaum, B. O., Rush, A. J., Thase, M. E., Riso, L. P, Vivian, D., & McCullough, J. P. (2003). Therapeutic reactance as a predictor of outcome in the treatment of chronic depression. *Journal of Consulting and Clinical Psychology, 71*(6), 1025–1035.

Baars, B. J. (1997). *In the theater of consciousness.* Oxford, U.K.: Oxford University Press.

Bachelard, G. (1971). *The poetics of reverie*. Trans. Daniel Russell. Boston: Beacon.

Bandura, A. (1997). *Self-efficacy: The exercise of control*. New York: Freeman.

Banks, L. W. (1999). Searching for the good spirit of Begashabito Canyon. *Arizona Highways, 75*(3), 4–9.

Barber, J. (2001). Freedom from smoking: Integrating hypnotic methods and rapid smoking to facilitate smoking cessation. *International Journal of Clinical and Experimental Hypnosis, 49*, 257–266.

Bargh, J. A., & Chartrand, T. L. (1999). The unbearable automaticity of being. *American Psychologist, 54*(7), 462–479.

Bargh, J. A., & Ferguson, M. J. (2000). Beyond behaviorism: On the automaticity of higher mental processes. *Psychological Bulletin, 126*(6), 925–945.

Bargh, J. A., Gollwitzer, P. M., Lee-Chai, A., Barndollar, K., & Trotschel, R. (2001). The automated will: Nonconscious activation and pursuit of behavioral goals. *Journal of Personality and Social Psychology, 81*(6), 1014–1027.

Barker, P. (1985). *Using metaphors in psychotherapy*. New York: Brunner/Mazel.

Barlow, D.H. (1998). *Anxiety and its disorders*. New York: Guilford Press.

Barsalou, L. W. (1993). *Cognitive psychology: An overview for cognitve scientists*. Hillsdale, NJ: Erlbaum.

Beahrs, J. O. (1971). The hypnotic psychotherapy of Milton H. Erickson. *American Journal of Clinical Hypnosis, 14*(2), 73–90.

Bennett, P., & Wilkinson, S. (1985). Comparison of psychological and medical treatment of the irritable bowel syndrome. *British Journal of Clinical Psychology, 24*, 215–216.

Bettelheim, B. (1977). *The uses of enchantment*. New York: Vintage.

Blackmore, S. (2004). *Consciousness*. Oxford, U.K.: Oxford University Press.

Blanchard, E. B. (2001). *Irritable bowel syndrome: Psychosocial assessment and treatment*. Washington, DC: American Psychological Association.

Bloom, P. B. (1994). How does a non-Ericksonian integrate Ericksonian techniques without becoming an Ericksonian? *Australian Journal of Clinical and Experimental Hypnosis, 22*(1), 1–10.

Brom, D., Kleber, R. J., & Defares, P. B. (1989). Brief psychotherapy for posttraumatic stress disorders. *Journal of Consulting and Clinical Psychology, 57*, 607–612.

Bryson, W. (1990). *Mother tongue*. New York: Morrow.

Buhner, S.H. (2002). *The lost language of plants*. White River Junction, VT: Chelsea Green

Burton, R. (1990). *The anatomy of melancholy*. (N.K. Kiessling, T.C. Faulkner, & R.L. Blair, Eds.) Oxford, U.K.: Clarendon Press. (Original work published in 1621)

Cade, B., & O'Hanlon, B. (1993). *A brief guide to brief therapy*. New York: Norton.

Calnan, R. D. (1977). Hypnotherapeutic ego-strengthening. *Australian Journal of Clinical Hypnosis, 5*, 105–118.

Calvert, E. L., Houghton, L.A., Cooper, P., Morris, J., & Whorwell, P. J. (2002). Long-term improvement in functional dyspepsia using hypnotherapy. *Gastroenterology, 123*(6), 2132–2135.

Campbell, D. G. (1992). *The crystal desert*. Boston: Houghton-Mifflin.

Cheek, L. W. (1991). Photo-adventuring in Monument Valley. *Arizona Highways, 67*(7), 38–47.

Chowder, K. (2003). Eureka! *Smithsonian, 34*(6), 92–97.

Claxton, G. (1997). *Hare brain tortoise mind: Why intelligence inceases when you think less*. London: Fourth Estate.

Close, H. T. (1998). *Metaphor in psychotherapy*. San Luis Obispo, CA: Impact.

Cochrane, G. (1989). The use of hypnotic suggestions for insomnia arising from generalized anxiety: A case report. *American Journal of Clinical Hypnosis, 31*(3), 199–203.

Cook, F. A. (1900). *Through the first Antarctic night, 1898–1899*. Montreal: McGill-Queen's University Press. (London reprint, 1980)

Cooper, L. F., & Erickson, M. H. (1959). *Time distortion in hypnosis*. Baltimore, MD: Williams & Wilkins.

Corney, R. H., Stanton, R., Newell, R., Clare, A., & Fairclough, P. (1991). Behavioural psychotherapy in the treatment of irritable bowel syndrome. *Journal of Psychosomatic Research, 35*, 461–469.

Cox, P.R. (2003). *From the corner of my eye*. Kearney, NE: Morris.

Dannen, K., & Dannen, D. (1991) Visit the Triassic. *Arizona Highways, 62*(7), 34–43.

Davis, P. (2003). Efforts underway to restore Florida's Molasses reef. *All Things Considered*. National Public Radio, Aug. 25.

Djaout, T. (2001). *The last summer of reason*. St. Paul, MN: Ruminator Books.

Dominus, S. (2004). She speaks 3-year-old. *The New York Times Magazine*, Jan. 4, 18–21.

Edgette, J. H., & Edgette, J. S. (1995). *The handbook of hypnotic phenomena in psychotherapy*. New York: Brunner/Mazel.

Edmunds, D., & Gafner, G. (2003). Touching trauma: Combining hypnotic ego-strengthening and zero balancing. *Contemporary Hypnosis, 20*(4), 215–220.

Erickson, M. H. (1959). Further clinical techniques of hypnosis: Utilization techniques. *American Journal of Clinical Hypnosis, 2*, 3–21.

Erickson, M. H., & Erickson, E. M. (1941). Concerning the nature and character of post-hypnotic behavior. *Journal of General Psychology, 24*, 95–133.

Erickson, M. H., Rossi, E. H., & Rossi, S. L. (1976). *Hypnotic realities*. New York: Irvington.

Erickson, M. H., & Rossi, E. L. (1979). *Hypnotherapy: An exploratory casebook*. New York: Irvington.

Estabrook, B. (2002). Jellies on a roll. *Audoban, 104*(3), 18–23.

Fass, R. (Ed.) (2004). *Hot topics: GERD/dyspepsia*. Philadelphia, PA: Hanley & Belfus

Fatali, M. (1991). Symphony in stone. *Arizona Highways, 67*(1), 22–27.

Ferguson, M. (1980). *The aquarian conspiracy*. Los Angeles: J. P. Tarcher.

Foa, E. B., Davidson, G., & Frances, A. (1999). Treatment of post-traumatic stress disorder: The expert consensus guideline series. *Journal of Clinical Psychiatry, 60*, 1–76.

Foa, E. B., Rothbaum, B. O., & Riggs, K. D. (1991). Treatment of postraumatic stress disorder in rape victims: A comparison between cognitive-behavioral procedures and counseling. *Journal of Consulting and Clinical Psychology, 59*, 715–723.

Fredrickson, B. L., Tugade, M. M., & Waugh, C. E. (2003). What good are positive emotions in crisis? A prospective study of resilience and emotions following the terrorist attacks on the U.S. on September 11, 2001. *Journal of Personality and Social Psychology, 84*(2), 365–376.

Freeman, S.A. (2004). *Update on electroconvulsive therapy*. Lecture, Tucson, AZ, Jan. 8.

Freud, S. (1965). *The psychopathology of everyday life* (J. Strachey, Ed. & Trans.). New York: Norton. (Original work published 1901)

Frey, K. P. & Eagly, A. H. (1993). Vividness can undermine the persuasiveness of metaphor. *Journal of Personality and Social Psychology, 65*(1), 32–44.

Funsten, K. (1986). Adam Clark Vroman and the forest of stone. *Arizona Highways, 62*(7), 28–33.

Gafner, G., & Duckett, S. (1992). Treating the sequelae of a curse in elderly Mexican-Americans. In T. L. Brink (Ed.), *Hispanic aged mental health* (pp. 45–53). New York: Haworth.

Gafner, G., & Benson, S. (2000). *Handbook of hypnotic inductions*. New York: Norton.

Gafner, G., & Benson, S. (2001). Indirect ego-strengthening in treating PTSD in immigrants from Central America. *Contemporary Hypnosis, 18*(3), 135–144.

Gafner, G., & Benson, S. (2003). *Hypnotic techniques*. New York: Norton.

Gafner, G., and Young, C. (1998). Hypnosis as an adjuvant treatment of chronic paranoid schizophrenia. *Contemporary Hypnosis, 15*(4), 223–226.

Geary, B. B. (1994). Seeding responsiveness to hypnotic processes. In J. K. Zeig (Ed.), *Ericksonian methods: The essence of the story* (pp. 315–332). New York: Brunner/Mazel.

Geary, B. B. (1999). Personal communication.

Gilligan, S. G. (1987). *Therapeutic trances: The cooperation principle in Ericksonian hypnotherapy*. New York: Brunner/Mazel.

Gilligan, S. G. (2003). *The legacy of Milton H. Erickson: Selected papers of Stephen Gilligan*. Phoenix, AZ: Zeig, Tucker & Theisen.

Glucksberg, S. (2003). The psycholinguistics of metaphor. *Trends in Cognitive Sciences, 7*(2), 92–96.

Gonsalkorale, W. M., Houghton, L. A., & Whorwell, P. J. (2002). Hypnotherapy in irritable bowel syndrome: A large-scale audit of a clinical service with examination of factors influencing responsiveness. *American Journal of Gastroenterology, 97*(4), 954–961.

Gordon, C. M., & Gruzelier, J. (2003). Self-hypnosis and osteopathic soft tissue manipulation with a ballet dancer. *Contemporary Hypnosis, 20*(4), 209–214.

Grann, D. (2002). A man out of time. *New York Times Magazine,* Dec. 29, 26–27.

Greenwald, A.G. (1992). New look 3: Unconscious cognition reclaimed. *American Psychologist, 47,* 766–790.

Grey, Z. (1928). *Avalanche.* New York: Curtis.

Guthrie, E., Creed, F., Dawson, D., & Tomenson, B. (1991). A controlled trial of psychological treatment for the irritable bowel syndrome. *Gastroenterology, 100,* 450–457.

Haley, J. (1973). *Uncommon therapy: The psychiatric techniques of Milton H. Erickson, M.D.* New York: Norton.

Hammond, D. C. (1990). *Handbook of hypnotic suggestions and metaphors.* New York: Norton.

Hamwee, J. (1999). *Zero balancing: Touching the energy of bone.* London: Frances Lincoln.

Hardin, C. D., & Conley, T. D. (2001). A relational approach to cognition: Shared experience and relationshhip affirmation in social cognition. In G. B. Moskowitz (Ed.), *Cognitive social psychology: The Princeton Symposium on the legacy and future of social cognition* (pp. 3–17). Mahwah, NJ: Erlbaum.

Hartland, J. (1971). Further observations on the use of ego-strengthening techniques. *American Journal of Clinical Hypnosis, 14,* 1–8.

Harvey, R. F., Salih, S. Y., & Read, A. E. (1983). Organic and functional disorders in 2,000 gastroenterology outpatients. *The Lancet, 8325,* 632–634.

Hawass, Z. (2003). Egypt's forgotten treasures. *National Geographic, 203*(1), 74–87.

Heffernon, R. (1991). Killer ladybugs. *Arizona Highways, 67*(1), 12–15.

Hensel, C. S., Sapp, M., Farrell, W., & Hitchcock, K. (2001). A survey of members of ASCH, SCEH, and Division 30, and if they reported using hpnosis to treat depression. *Sleep and Hypnosis, 3*(4), 152–168.

Herken, G. (2002). *Brotherhood of the bomb.* New York: Henry Holt.

Hessler, P (2003). Chasing the wall. *National Geographic, 203*(1), 2–33.

Hornyak, L. (1999). Empowerment through giving symptoms voice. *American Journal of Clinical Hypnosis, 42,* 132–139.

Houghton, L. A., Heyman, D. J., & Whorwell, P. J. (1996). Symptomatology, quality of life, and economic features of irritable bowel syndrome. The effect of hypnotherapy. *Alimentary Pharmacology and Therapeutics, 10,* 91–95.

Huang, M. P., Himle, J., & Alessi, N. E. (2000). Vivid visualization in the experience of phobia in virtual environments: Preliminary results. *CyberPsychology & Behavior, 3*(3), 315–320.

Ingram, D. H. (1996). The vigor of metaphor in clinical practice. *The American Journal of Psychoanalysis, 56*(1), 17–34.

Jackson, E. D., Payne, J. D., Nadel, L., & Jacobs, W. J. (2004). *Stress differentially affects human memory systems involving the amygdala and hippocampus.* Submitted for publication.

Jackson, S. W. (1986). *Melancholia and depression: From Hippocratic times to modern times.* New Haven, CT: Yale University Press.

Josephs, R. A., Bosson, J. K., & Jacobs, C. G. (2003). Self-esteem maintenance processes: Why low self-esteem may be resistant to change. *Personality and Social Psychology Bulletin, 29*(7), 920–933.

Kawakami, K., Dovidio, J. F., & Dijksterhuis, A. (2003). Effect of social category priming on personal attitudes. *Psychological Science, 14*(4), 315–319.

Keane, T. M. (1989). Implosive (flooding) therapy that reduces symptoms of PTSD in Vietnam combat veterans. *Behaviour Therapy, 20,* 245–260.

Kelley, E. J. (1985). The killing of Jack the Ripper. *Arizona Highways, 61*(10), 34–39

Kelly, G. A. (1955). *The psychology of personal constructs.* New York: Norton.

Kihlstron, J. F. (1996). Perception without awareness of what is perceived, learning without awareness of what is learned. In M. Velmans (Ed.), *The science of consciousness* (pp. 23–46). London: Routledge.

Kinetz, E. (2004). A Ziegfeld girl who can't stop dancing. *New York Times,* Feb. 8, p. AR 9.

Kingsbury, S. (1988). Interacting with trauma. *American Journal of Clinical Hypnosis, 36,* 241–247.

Kirsch, I. (1994). Clinical hypnosis as a nondeceptive placebo: Empirically derived techniques. *American Journal of Clinical Hypnosis, 37*(2), 95–106.

Kirsch, I., Montgomery, G., & Sapirstein, G. (1995). Hypnosis as an adjunct to cognitive-behavioral psychotherapy: A meta-analysis. *Journal of Consulting and Clinical Psychology, 63*(2), 214–220.

Knauth, P. (1972). *The north woods*. New York: Time-Life Books.

Koetting, M. G., and Lane, R. C. (2001). Therapeutic metaphor as barrier to the self: A case of an older adult. *Journal of Clinical Geropsychology, 7*(3), 245–250.

Krepps, J. M. (2002). Opening the door on claustrophobia. *Journal of Systemic Therapies, 21*(4), 67–85.

Kroger, W. S. (1963). *Clinical and experimental hypnosis in medicine, dentistry and psychology*. Philadelphia: Lippincott.

Krutch, J. W. (1960). If you don't mind my saying so. *American Scholar, 30*, 409.

La Farge, O. (1957). *Laughing boy*. New York: Signet. (Original work published 1929)

L'Amour, L. (2002). *Haunted mesa*. New York: Bantam.

Lakoff, G., & Johnson, M. (1980). *Metaphors we live by*. Chicago: University of Chicago Press.

Lankton, S. R., & Lankton, C. H. (1983). *The answer within: A clinical framework of Ericksonian hypnotherapy*. New York: Brunner/Mazel.

Latimer, P .R. (1983). *Functional gastrointestinal disorders: A behavioral medicine approach*. New York: Spring Publishing.

Lavertue, N. E., Kumar, V. K., & Pekala, R. J. (2002). The effectiveness of a hypnotic ego-strengthening procedure for improving self-esteem and depression. *Australian Journal of Clinical and Experimental Hypnosis, 30*(1), 1–23.

Levis, D.J. (1980). Implementing the technique of implosive therapy. In A. Goldstein & E. B. Foa (Eds.), *Handbook of behavioral interventions: A clinical guide* (pp. 92–151). New York: Wiley.

Lewicki, P., Hill, T., & Czyzewska, M. (1992). Nonconscious acquisition of information. *American Psychologist, 47*, 796–801.

Litz, B. T., & Blake, D. D. (1990). Decision-making guidelines for the use of direct therapeutic exposure in the treatment of posttraumatic stress disorder. *Behaviour Therapy, 17*, 91–93.

Lynn, S. J., Neufeld, V., & Mare, C. (1993). Direct vs. indirect suggestions: A conceptual and methodological review. *International Journal of Clinical and Experimental Hypnosis, 41*(2), 124–152

Lynch, P. M. & Zamble, E. (1987). Stress management training for irritable bowel syndrome: A preliminary investigation. *Clinical Biofeedback and Health, 10,* 123–134.

Lumsden, A. (1999). Treatment of PTSD utilizing CBT and hypnotherapy. *Australian Journal of Clinical and Experimental Hypnosis, 27*(2), 150–57.

Mauseth, J. D., Kiesling, R., & Ostolaza, C. (2002). *A cactus odyssey: Journeys in the wilds of Bolivia, Peru, and Argentina.* Portland, OR: Timber Press.

Mclintock, J. (2003). Fakahatchee ghosts. *Smithsonian, 34*(5), 24–27.

McMullen, L. M., & Conway, J. B. (2002). Conventional metaphors for depression. In S. R. Fussell (Ed.), *The verbal communication of emotions: Interdisciplinary perspectives* (pp. 167–181). Mahwah, NJ: Lawrence Erlbaum.

Mitchell, J. H. (1990). *Living at the end of time.* Boston, MA: Houghton-Mifflin.

Mjoseth, J. (1997). Hypnosis allies are urging insurers to raise coverage. APA Monitor, May, 22.

Montaigne, F. (1998). Russia's iron road. *National Geographic, 193*(6), 11–33.

Mutter, K. L. (1999). Empowering strategies: The physician's point of view. *American Journal of Clinical Hypnosis, 42,* 116–121.

Neff, D. F., & Blanchard, E. B. (1987). A multi-component treatment for irritable bowel syndrome. *Behavior Therapy, 18,* 70–83.

Neisser, V. (1967). *Cognitive psychology.* New York: Appleton-Century-Crofts.

Nisbett, R. E., & Wilson, T. D. (1977). Telling more than we know: Verbal reports on mental processes. *Psychological Review, 84,* 231–259.

Oliver, M. (2004). Martin Sheridan, 89; Survivor of nightclub fire became war reporter. *Los Angeles Times,* Jan. 12, p. B11.

Orbach, I. (1995). *The hidden mind.* New York: Wiley.

Palsson, O. S., Turner, J. J., Johnson, D. A., Burnelt, C. K., & Whitehead, W. E. (2002). Hypnosis treatment for severe irritable bowel syndrome: investigation of mechanism and effects on symptoms. *Digestive Diseases & Sciences, 47*(11), 2605–2614.

Papp, P. (1983). *The process of change*. New York: Guilford Press.

Pekala, R. J., Maurer, R., Kumar, V. K., Elliott, N. C., Masten, E., Moon, E., & Salinger, M. (2004). Self-hypnosis relapse prevention training with chronic drug/alcohol users: Effects on self-esteen, affect and relapse. *American Journal of Clinical Hypnosis, 46*(4), 281–297.

Perls, F. (1969). *Ego, hunger and aggression*. New York: Random House.

Phillips, M. (1993). Turning symptoms into allies: Utilization approaches with posttraumatic symptoms. *American Journal of Clinical Hypnosis, 35*(3), 179–189.

Phillips, M. (2001). Potential contributions of hypnosis to ego-strengthening. *American Journal of Clinical Hypnosis, 43*, 247–262.

Pittman, R. K., Orr, S. P., Altman, B., Longpre, R. E., Poire, R. E., Macklin, M. L., Michaels, M. J., & Steketee, G. S. (1996). Emotional processing and outcome of imaginal flooding therapy in Vietnam veterans with chronic posttraumatic stress disorder. *Comprehensive Psychiatry, 37*(6), 409–418.

Powell, J. W. (1987). *The exploration of the Colorado River and its canyons*. New York: Viking Penguin.

Rachman, S. (1980). Emotional processing. *Behaviour Research and Therapy, 18*, 51–60.

Robert, B., & Jones, R. (1996). *Great Lakes lighthouses: Michigan and Superior*. Guilford, CT: Globe Pequot Press.

Roberts, B. & Jones, R. (1996). *Western Great Lakes lighthouses*. Guilford, CT: The Globe Pequot Press.

Robles, T. (1990). *Concierto para cuatro cerebros en psicoterapia*. Mexico City: Instituto Milton H. Erickson.

Rodenburg, P. (2000). *The actor speaks*. New York: Palgrave Macmillan.

Rogers, C. (1961). *On becoming a person*. Boston: Houghton-Mifflin.

Rosen, S. (1982). *My voice will go with you: The teaching tales of Milton H. Erickson, M.D.* New York: Norton.

Rossi, E. L. (2000). In search of a deep psychobiology of hypnosis: Visionary hypothesis for a new millenium. *American Journal of Clinical Hypnosis, 42*, 178–207.

Rothbaum, B. O., Hodges, L., Alarcon, R., Ready, D., Shahar, F., Graap, K., Pair, J., Hebert, P., Gotz, D., Wills, B., & Baltzell, D. (1999). Virtual reality exposure therapy for PTSD Vietnam veterans: A case study. *Journal of Traumatic Stress, 12*(2), 263–272.

Rotter, J. B. (1954). *Social learning and clinical psychology*. Englewood Cliffs, NJ: Prentice-Hall.

Saraceno, J. (2003). 30 years later, Cappelleti's tribute has something for everyone. *USA Today*, Dec. 9.

Schoenberger, N. E. (2000). Research on hypnosis as an adjunct to cognitive-behavioral therapy. *International Journal of Clinical and Experimental Hypnosis, 48*(2), 154–169.

Shaw, G., Srivastava, E. D., Sadlier, M., Swann, P., James, J. Y., & Rhodes, J. (1991). Stress management for irritable bowel syndrome: A controlled trial. *Digestion, 50*, 36–42.

Shoham-Salomon, V., & Rosenthal, R. (1987). Paradoxical interventions: A meta-analysis. *Journal of Consulting and Clinical Psychology, 55*(7), 22–27.

Siegelman, E. Y. (1990). *Metaphor and meaning in psychotherapy*. New York: Guilford Press.

Singh, A. R., & Banerjee (2002). Treating panic with hypnosis in combination with rational emotive therapy: A case report. *Sis Journal of Projective Psychology and Mental Health, 9*(2), 105–108.

Skinner, B.F. (1938). *The behavior of organisms*. New York: Appleton-Century-Crofts.

Snyder Sachs, J. (2002). Seeking safe passage. *National Wildlife, 40*(4), 18–27.

Sopory, P., & Dillard, J. P. (2002). The persuasive effects of metaphor. *Human Communication Research, 28*(3), 382–419.

Spiegel, D. (1997). Hypnosis in the treatment of posttraumatic stress disorder. In J. W. Rhue, S. J. Lynn, & I. Kirsch (Eds.), *Handbook of clinical hypnosis* (pp. 493–508). Washington, D.C: American Psychological Association.

Spiegel, D., & Cardena (1990). New uses of hypnosis in the treatment of posttraumatic stress disorder. *Journal of Clinical Psychiatry, 51*, 39–42.

Stanton, H. E. (1993). Ego-enhancement for positive change. *Australian Journal of Clinical and Experimental Hypnosis, 21*, 59–64.

Stanton, H. E. (1997). Increasing internal control through hypnotic ego-enhancement. *Australian Journal of Clinical and Experimental Hypnosis, 7*, 219–223.

Steinberg, M. (2003). 1700s Stradivarius delivers pure bliss on romance CD. *The Associated Press*, Nov. 1.

Storr, T. (2000). Magic and mystery in Ireland. In V. Brooks (Ed.). *Literary trips: Following in the footsteps of fame* (p. 257). Vancouver, BC: GreatestEscapes.com.

Strahan, E. J., Spencer, S. J., & Zanna, M. P. (2002). Subliminal priming and persuasion: Striking while the iron is hot. *Journal of Experimental Social Psychology, 38*, 556–568.

Styron, W. (1990). *Darkness visible: A memoir of madness*. New York: Random House.

Summerfield, D. (1999). A critique of seven assumptions behind psychological trauma program in war-affected areas. *Social Science and Medicine, 48*(10), 1449–62.

Svedlund, J., Sjodin, I., Ottosson, J. O., & Dotevall, G. (1983). Controlled study of psychotherapy in irritable bowel syndrome. *The Lancet, 8350* 589–592.

Switz, D. N. (1976). What the gastroenterologist does all day. *Gastroenterology, 70*, 1048–1050.

Taylor, M. (1992). Secret pass. *Arizona Highways, 68*(3), 40–45.

Teale, E. W. (1982). *The wilderness world of John Muir*. Boston: Houghton-Mifflin.

Thoreau, H. D., & Dean, B., P. (Ed.). (2000). *Wild fruits*. New York: Norton.

Van de Castle, R. L. (1994). *Our dreaming mind*. New York: Ballentine.

Vanderlinden, J., & Vandereycken, W. (1994). The (limited) possibilities of hypnotherapy in the treatment of obesity. *American Journal of Clinical Hypnosis, 36*, 248–257.

Van Dulmen, A. M., Fennis, J. F. M., & Bleijenberg, G. (1996). Cognitive-behavioral group therapy for irritable bowel syndrome: Effects and long-term follow-up. *Psychosomatic Medicine, 58*, 508–514.

Wallas, L. (1985). *Stories for the third ear.* New York: Norton.

Walsh, F. (2003). Family resilience: A framework for practice. *Family Process, 42*(1), 1–18.

Watson, J. B. (1913). Psychology as a behaviorist sees it. *Psychological Review, 20,* 158–167.

Wegner, D. M., & Smart, L. (1997). Deep cognitive activation: A new approach to the unconscious. *Journal of Consulting and Clinical Psychology, 65*(6), 984–995.

Whorwell, P. J., Prior, A., & Colgan, S. M. (1987). Hypnotherapy in severe irritable bowel syndrome: Further experience. *Gut, 28,* 423–425.

Whorwell, P. J., Prior, A., & Faragher, E. B. (1984). Controlled trial of hypnotherapy in the treatment of severe refractory irritable bowel syndrome. *The Lancet, 8414* 1232–1234.

Williams, W. W. (2003). Insider's passage. *Hemispheres,* March, 53–57.

Witztum, E., Van der Hart, O., & Friedman, B. (1988). The use of metaphors in psychotherapy, *Journal of Contemporary Psychotherapy, 18*(4), 270–290.

Wood, G. J., Bughi, S., Morrison, J., Tanavoli, S., Tanavoli, S., & Zadeh, H. H. (2003). Hypnosis, differential expression of cytokines by T-cell subsets, and the hypothalamo-pituitary-adrenal axis. *American Journal of Clinical Hypnosis, 45*(3), 179–196.

Woody, E. Z., & Szechtman, H. (2003). How can brain activity and hypnosis inform each other? *International Journal of Clinical and Experimental Hypnosis, 51*(3), 232–255.

Wylie, M.S. (2004). The limits of talk. *Psychotherapy Networker, 28*(1), 30–41.

Yapko, M. (2001). *Treating depression with hypnosis: Integrating cognitive-behavioral and strategic approaches.* New York: Brunner/Routledge.

Yapko, M. D. (2003). *Trancework: An introduction to the practice of clinical hypnosis.* New York: Brunner/Routledge.

Zeig, J. K. (1980). *A teaching seminar with Milton H. Erickson.* New York: Brunner/Mazel.

Zeig, J. K. (1985b). *Experiencing Erickson.* New York: Brunner/Mazel.

Zeig, J. K. (Ed.) (1985a). *Ericksonian psychotherapy: Vol. I: Structures.* New York: Brunner/Mazel.

Zeig, J. K. (1990a). Seeding. In J. K. Zeig & S. J. Gilligan (Eds.), *Brief therapy: Myths and metaphors* (pp. 221–246). New York: Brunner/Mazel.

Zeig, J. K. (1990b). *The personal growth and development of the therapist* [Audiotape]. Phoenix, AZ: Milton H. Erickson Foundation.

Zeig, J. K, & Geary, B. B. (Eds.) (2000). *The letters of Milton H. Erickson.* Phoenix, AZ: Zeig, Tucker & Theisen.

Zimmerman, J. (2003). Cleaning up the river: A metaphor for functional digestive disorders. *American Journal of Clinical Hypnosis, 45* (4), 353–359.

Zwinger, A., & Teale, E. W. (1982). *A conscious stillness.* New York: Dodd, Meade & Co.

Index

285